Harry Norris is Professor Emeritus of Arabic and Islamic Studies at the University of London. Before this he was Professor of Middle Eastern Studies at SOAS and an associate Fellow at the School of Slavonic and East European Studies, University of London.

'A piece of fascinating scholarship ... essential reading for area studies scholars working on Eastern Europe and researchers working on Islam and nationalism, as well as useful reading for academics, students and the wider public interested in ethno-religious minorities in Europe.'
European History Quarterly

'An intriguing and fascinating book'
Journal of the Royal Asiatic Society

'With his usual thoroughness and wealth of knowledge, the author deals with the history of Tartar settlements, their culture and beliefs, their relationship with the native Christian population, and their contacts with the Crimea and Turkey. '
Father Alexander Nadson, The Francyska Skaryny Byelorussian Library, London

ISLAM IN THE BALTIC

Europe's Early Muslim Community

Harry Norris

LONDON · NEW YORK

New paperback edition published in 2017 by
I.B.Tauris & Co. Ltd
London • New York
www.ibtauris.com

First published in hardback in 2009 by I.B.Tauris & Co. Ltd

Copyright © 2009 Harry Norris

The right of Harry Norris to be identified as the author of this work has been asserted by the author in accordance with the Copyright, Designs and Patents Act 1988.

All rights reserved. Except for brief quotations in a review, this book, or any part thereof, may not be reproduced, stored in or introduced into a retrieval system, or transmitted, in any form or by any means, electronic, mechanical, photocopying, recording or otherwise, without the prior written permission of the publisher.

Every attempt has been made to gain permission for the use of the images in this book. Any omissions will be rectified in future editions.

ISBN: 978 1 78831 046 8
eISBN: 978 1 78672 973 6
ePDF: 978 0 85771 379 7

A full CIP record for this book is available from the British Library
A full CIP record is available from the Library of Congress

Library of Congress Catalog Card Number: available

Typeset by Swales & Willis Ltd, Exeter, Devon
Printed and bound by CPI Group (UK) Ltd, Croydon, CR0 4YY

To Duke Gediminas and Duke Vytautus (Witold) the Great, a hero of the Lithuanian Tatars until today.

'Iron would turn to wax, and water to steel sooner than we revoked our solemn word.' (Gediminas)

Contents

List of Illustrations — viii
Acknowledgements — ix

Introduction — 1

1 Waranğ of the Arabs — 4

2 The expanding Eastern Empire of the Grand Duchy of Lithuania — 18

3 The settlement of the Qipchāq Tatars and the Karaims in Belarus, Lithuania and Poland — 31

4 Islam and the 'Lithuanian Tatars' — 54

5 Islam and the contemporary religious scene in Belarus, Estonia, Latvia, Lithuania and Poland — 75

Conclusion — 131

Appendix — 140
Notes and references — 147
Bibliography — 175
Glossary — 182
Index — 215

List of Illustrations

Figure 1 'The Island of Men' and the 'Island of the Amazon Women' in the map of al-Idrīsī.   8

Figure 2 The Lithuanian Vytis.   30

Figure 3 This document is from the collection of the Lithuanian National Museum in Vilnius. It is a nineteenth-century *muhir* with talismanic drawings and prayers and praise of the Prophet.   74

Figure 4 Map showing mosques in Belarus.   89

Figure 5 A Tatar manuscript from Rīga, no 28, A 222S (no 28 Austrumtautu/Oriental), pages 171 and 172   141

Figure 6 A reproduced map that is to be found in the Tatar collection in the Białystok Museum. It shows the distribution of Muslim settlements in the region in the early twentieth century as well as the wooden mosques and major non-wooden mosques that were located there. It was drawn by Ali Smajkiewicz of Gdańsk about 1960. Many of these mosques have been destroyed.   198

Acknowledgements

It was over thirty years ago that my colleague at the School of Oriental and African Studies (SOAS) Professor Bogdan Andrzejewski, a great authority on the Somali language and the culture of its peoples, drew my attention to the small Tatar community in Poland, which, together with their brothers in Belarus and Lithuania, offered to Western scholars a relatively new field of Islamic studies to the east of the Iron Curtain. However, it was my visit to Kazan and Tatarstan, which was generously supported by the British Academy in London, which first introduced me to the Tatars and to Tatar culture. The meetings which I had with Professor Zakiev and his colleagues in the Academy of Sciences in Kazan and with Professor Halikov Alfred Hasanovich, then Professor of Russian History in the Faculty of History in the State University of Kazan, archaeologist and a respected authority on the great pre-Tatar culture of Bulghār and its peoples, which greatly strengthened my fascination for the Tatars and for their unusual contribution to the Islamic culture of north-eastern Europe.

I would like to acknowledge the very great help and kindness that I have received during the years that I have been collecting material for my research in order to complete this book. First, I wish to express my deep gratitude to the British Academy, especially to the Department of International Exchange visits, for their help in enabling me to visit Academies of Science, universities, libraries and scholars in Latvia, Lithuania and Poland, during the course of visits to these countries over a number of years.

The Tatar peoples of the Soviet Union had already been very well studied by many Western scholars. These visits, together with my visits to Lithuania, as a guest lecturer with Ace Study Tours, through the kindness of the Barnes family, considerably widened my contacts with these Tatars and also with the Turkic-speaking Karaims. It was also with Ace Study tours that I visited the Crimean peninsula where the indigenous Tatars have been resettling. I have been able to visit all the surviving ancient 'Tatar mosques' in Lithuania and in Poland, togther with Iwie, which is one of the most ancient mosques in Belarus. This took place during the course of a private visit to Minsk. In Poland, the generous help of Dr Jerzy Zdanowski, in the Polish Academy of Sciences has given me a unique opportunity to meet many Tatar and non-Tatar scholars who are engaged in Tatar studies in Poland's principal universities. Here, Arabic and Islamic studies have an important part to play in Tatar studies in particular. The list of scholars in Poland to whom I owe a great debt of hospitality would be a very long one. However, I would like to mention Mr Ali Kozakiewicz, former Imām and Custodian of the Muslim cemetery in Warsaw, also the scholar and poet Dr Selim Chazbijewicz, Professor Dr Tryjarski, Bogusław R. Zagórski, the Chairman of the Instytut Ibn Khalduna in Warsaw, Professor C. Łapicz of Toruń University, Dr Andrzej Drozd of Poznań, Professor D. Andrzej Zaborski, President of the Committee of Oriental Studies of the Polish Academy of Sciences, Cracow, Imām Mahmud Taha Żuk, Professor A. Dziekan, Warsaw University, and the late Turcologist Dr A. Dubiński. Likewise, I also owe a debt to the Tatars and the Karaims in Gdańsk, especially Dr Dzemila Smaykiewicz-Murman and her family, and in Białystok district. Here I would like to mention Mrs Maria Janov and her late husband Mike, whose house was my first base for the exploration of a number of the Tatar villages and communities in Podlasie district near to the border with Belarus. I also wish to thank the former *Imām* who extended an invitation to me to attend a Tatar funeral, both the 'wake' and the interment afterwards in the Muslim cemetery (*mizar*) in Kryszyniany, and the current Imām, Tomasz Miskiewicz, the first post-Second World War Mufti of Poland (formerly the previous chairman of the Council of Imāms in Poland and who was elected later to this high office, on 19 March 2004. He kindly invited me to attend an inter-faith gathering in Kruszyniany mosque, held on 18 May 2003, entitled 'Prayer for Peace and Justice all over the World' (Modlitwo o Pokój i Sprawiedlowość na Świece)). I shall also mention Mrs Eva Krebs and her sister Maria Bukin of Białystok University, as well as 'Abd al-Qādir, a Chechen teacher of Prophetic Ḥadīth in Białystok. The Curator of the Town Museum kindly gave me photos of rare objects in the Tatar collection there.

I am also grateful to my late colleague Professor Frank Carter, of the School of Slavonic and East European Studies (SSEES) in the University of London. He was an expert on Poland, and he helped me to integrate these Tatar interests into the life of the School of Slavonic and East

European Studies, in the University of London, where I was a visiting fellow after my retirement from SOAS. In matters of source materials, I am in debt to Dr Shirin Akiner at SOAS, and also to a former student, Mrs Barbara Cwiczewicz, a friend of Professor F. Carter and his wife, and who helped me to deliver an illustrated lecture at SSEES on the Polish Tatars at that time.

In later years I have regularly visited Lithuania where I have been given most valuable help by long-standing friends in the Institute of Lithuanian History, Lithuanian Academy of Sciences, in Vilnius, and more recently, in the Centre for Stateless Cultures, in Vilnius University. In the former, I should particularly like to mention Professor Tamara Bairašauskaité, Dr Vilma Žaltauskaité, Dr Agnius Urbanavičius and Dr Žylvitis Šaknys and also the librarians of the Seraya Szapszal Collection in the Library of the Museum of Lithuanian History. The Tatars and the Karaims figure prominently, together with the country's Jewish, Roma and Old Believer cultural heritage, amidst the scholarly and academic research activities of this newly established and rapidly developing University Centre in Lithuania. Several Tatar and Karaite friends, worldwide, have been of great help to me, including Dr Leonid M Lavrin, who is resident in Australia and who is a respected fighter for the preservation of the cultural and religious identity of the Crimean Karaims. We have kept in touch by the miracle of the Internet.

Yet more recently, the British Academy kindly supported my visit to Latvia. Here, I would like to thank Dr Anita Draveniece and Miss Diana Vucāne, in the Latvian Academy of Sciences, in Rīga, for their hospitality during an exchange visit, supported by the British Academy, in the autumn of 2006, as well as to thank Uldis Bērziņš, Latvia's leading poet and who is now translating the *Qur'ān* into Latvian for the first time, likewise Valters Ščerbinskis, Ināra Klekere of the Manuscript Department of the Latvian National Library, and to Rūfiya Shevyreva, Chairwoman of the Rīga Muslim Association. All have, in various ways, contributed to the information gathered and they have expressed valuable opinions that I acknowledge within this book.

Other Baltic visits have been of a private nature. In Tallinn, I wish to thank both Timur Seifullin (Seifullen), the Honorary President of the Bureau of the Estonian Union of National Minorities (EESTIMAA), and the Mufti, Mr Ildar Muhhamedshin, for giving me some of their valuable time in answering a number of my questions. I must also mention the kindness of Mr Karel Zova in taking me to our meeting place and for his help in translating where this was needed. The questions that I asked, and which were answered, were principally based upon the paper delivered by

Juri Viikberg (dated 20 September 1998) at the conference 'Multicultural Estonia', held in Helsinki on 26 December 1998. This took place on the subject of 'Ethnic minorities in Estonia: past and present'.

In Belarus, I would like to express my thanks to the former Mufti, Ḥājjī Ismael (Ismāʿīl) Alexandrovich, whom I first met during a Tatar conference that was held in Białystok. I am grateful to him, in particular, for his supplying me with so much information regarding his community, in Belarus, today, and especially for that which relates to the rebuilding of the Minsk mosque, now unfortunately postponed until some date in the future. He also gave me help in arranging for a guide so that I could visit – on a very snowy and freezing, yet sunny day – the famous Tatar village of Ivye, where, in the old wooden mosque, the *Imām* invited me to attend noon prayers in the building. The villagers were most hospitable after the *Ṣalāt*. The information gleaned is published in this book and further photographs may be found in my article, 'Islam and Qur'anic Studies in the Baltic Region: The Contribution of the Baltic Tatars amid the Growing Inter-ethnic Muslim Communities of Belarus, Estonia, Latvia, Lithuania, and Poland', *Journal of Qur'anic Studies*, Vol VII, Issue 1, 2005, pp 113–121.

I also wish to express my deep appreciation to my late friend Dr Ibragim Kanapatski from Minsk, whom I met first at a Tatar and Karaite conference held in Vilnius. It was he who took me on a tour of the future site of the Minsk mosque, a mosque that will be almost a replica of the mosque that was destroyed in Stalinist times. However, due to the current funding problems, the existing Cuma building has been closed by the Minsk municipal authorities and its use for mosque purposes very restricted. It is hoped that this situation will not be permanent. Dr Kanapatski has been buried in the cemetery of the mosque at Smilovichi. His daughter, Dr Zorina Kanapatskaya, of the Belarusian State Pedagogical University, in Minsk, has continued the work of her distinguished father on the preservation and study of Tatar literature for her community. She has received generous help from the British Academy to do this. She has attended conferences held in Cambridge University that were designed to celebrate the foundation of The International Association for Islamic Manuscripts. The Association was sponsored by the Thesaurus Islamic Foundation and The Centre of Middle Eastern and Islamic Studies in the University of Cambridge. Collections of Tatar manuscripts in both Tatarstan and Belarus have been discussed in the proceedings of past conferences, thus underlining the fact that, today, the Islam to be found amongst the Tatar peoples is now a growing field of interest for Orientalists and Islamists throughout the world.

Acknowledgements xiii

I have visited Scandinavia on many occasions, especially Denmark where I first met Danish Muslims in Copenhagen. Recently I visited Gothenburg, in Sweden, where I am grateful to Professor Åke Sander for allowing me to discuss matters relating to the history of Islam and the ethnic communities in Sweden, with him. I am also grateful to Dr Jonas Otterbeck, Assistant Professor at the Institute for Migration and Ethnic Relations, the University of Malmö, who has done pioneer research on the crucial influence of Finnish Tatars, and other Tatars, and non-Tatar Muslims, in the region of Stockholm, in the foundation of the parish of the Muslim communities in Sweden today. His generous gift of source materials was greatly appreciated.

In Denmark, I am grateful to Professor Marianne C. Qvortrup Fibiger, and her colleagues, in the Teologiske Fakultet in Århus University. It was kind of her to agree to meet me at very short notice during my visit to the city. It was an opportune moment since this took place only a short time before the crisis over the publication of the cartoons that depicted the Prophet Muhammad in *Jyllands Posten*.

In the United Kingdom I am grateful to the late Professor Charles Beckingham, to Professor George Hewitt, to Professor M.A.S. Abdel Haleem, and Dr Helen Blatherwick, assistant editor of the *Journal of Qur'anic Studies*, at the School of Oriental and African Studies, University of London, for supporting my applications to the British Academy in order to undertake research in the Baltic region, and assistance over the publication of its findings, likewise to Dr Andrew Peacock, then in the Oriental Faculty, the University of Cambridge.

As mentioned above, I first made the acquaintance of the Tatars far outside the Baltic region. Due to an outbreak of violence in the region of Dagestan, the Russian Academy of Sciences in Moscow sent me to Kazan, Tatarstan. It was there that I made the acquaintance of the Tatar scholars in Kazan and from Siberia. One of these scholars is Dr Nuriya Garayeva who is an authority on the major works of the great Tatar historian and Orientalist, Shihāb al-Dīn Marjānī (1818–89). In the summer of 2006, I had the happy opportunity to meet her again, together with Dr Zorina Kanapatskaya, at the second conference held in order to celebrate the foundation of The International Association for Islamic Manuscripts.

I would also like to thank Ms Katherine Holmes for her magnificent work in preparing the text of this book. I cannot praise her too highly.

Harry Norris
Newport, Essex
2008

Introduction

It is to be hoped that the expanding borders of the European Community will not sever the links between the Tatars of Lithuania and Poland, with the Tatars in Belarus. The ethnic and religious minorities in the region are facing a distinct undermining of their identity. This threat was brought to light in an article published in the *Financial Times* on 27 August 2002, by Stefan Wagstyl. Its introductory paragraph was very encouraging yet it was also distinctly ominous:

> In the small north eastern Polish town of Sejny, in one of the country's few surviving synagogue buildings, hangs an exhibition of theatre posters from neighbouring Lithuania. Behind a screen are stored instruments played by the town's kletzmer music band. In a corner is a bookstand selling works in English, German and Russian as well as Polish. This outpost of multiculturalism flourishes in rather unlikely surroundings. Sejny is poor and remote, with an unemployment rate of over 25 per cent.
>
> The town is home to Borderland, a cultural centre established in 1990 to promote interethnic contacts among Poles, Lithuanians, Belarusians, Ukrainians and others, including Jews interested in exploring the region's Jewish past. Its founder and president is 44 year old Krzysztof Czyzewski, a former theatre director who moved to Sejny from the busy western city of Poznan to promote cultural life in the border region.
>
> In just over a decade Mr Czyzewski has won an international reputation, helping to set up about a dozen similar centres as far afield as Mostar in Bosnia, Uzhgorod in Ukraine and Arad in Romania. It has secured support from sponsers including the European Union.

However, this article continues on a far less optimistic note:

> Mr Czyzewski warns that anything which deepens the practical and symbolic divide between central European states such as Poland and countries further east could undermine the cultural development of the whole region. He says cross-border ties are particularly important because today the region's countries are mono-ethnic. Before the Second World War, the territory from the Baltic to the Black Sea was ethnically diverse with a score of languages and half a dozen religions.

In fact, in the late Middle Ages, this entire region formed the geographical heartland and the ethnic core, of the remarkable 'Duchy of Lithuania'. The Tatars of Lehistan (Poland, Lithuania and Belarus), and, to a lesser extent, the Karaims, are living heirs to this remarkable medieval heritage as well as being heirs to the cultural heritage of the cultures in the Crimean peninsula. It was from thence they first came, or else from the Dašt-i Qipchāq, the steppes to the north and east of the Crimea, the Black Sea and the Caspian Sea. Divided by political frontiers, new political affiliations and cultural minority status, their Islamic traditions, centuries old, and marked by the ancient cultures of those Qipchāq steppes, are threatened by the new Middle Eastern Islamic movements of the twenty-first century. The aim of this book is to introduce and to appraise their Muslim and Qipchāq heritage and to demonstrate its roots in a 'pagan' past, their centuries old survival amidst Catholicism and Orthodox Christian communities, and also amidst a Judaism, both Karaite and Rabbinical. They live in a 'borderland' that has stamped their culture. This, I maintain, is a unique and almost totally neglected corner of the World of Islam.

H.T. Norris

Note on transcription

In the spelling of Arabic and in the spelling of Muslim Tatar names of Arabic, Persian, Turkish and Qipchāq origin and in the spelling of Islamic technical terms and expressions, I have followed the system employed in my *Islam in the Balkans* (Christopher Hurst, 1993). However, apart from specific instances, particularly in my Glossary, in order to avoid confusion, or in rare passages of translation from Arabic texts, I have rarely indicated all diacritical points or macrons. In the spelling of Lithuanian, Polish and Russian words, I have adopted the system used in *The Peoples in the Grand Duchy of Lithuania*, edited by Grigorijus Potasenko (2002), a publication sponsored by the Ministry of Culture of the Republic of Lithuania. In a number of respects, this little book is the best introduction for English readers to many of the subjects which relate to ethnic and religious identity in my own book. It has six contributors and the content includes the Ruthenians, the Jews, The Roma, the Russian Old Believers, the case study of the town of Kédainiai, the Tatars and the Karaims. My book is solely concerned with the two latter communities and principally the Tatars. I am particularly grateful to Dr Vilma Zaltauskaité for bringing this excellent little book to my notice as well as much other help in order to enable me to complete this study.

1. Warang of the Arabs[1]

The Baltic region of the sea of darkness (Baḥr al-Ẓulumāt), and its coastal peoples, according to the earliest Arabic and Islamic sources

> Then did Lemminkainen's mother answer in the words which follow:
> 'Take the boat your father left you, and betake yourself to hiding.
> Traverse nine lakes in succession, half the tenth one must thou traverse,
> To an island on its surface, where the cliffs arise from water.
> There in former times your father hid, and kept himself in safety,
> In the furious fights of summer, in the hardest years of battle.
> There you'll find a pleasant dwelling, and a charming place to linger'.[2]
>
> The *Kalevala*

Fate brought the Balts, the Poles, the Ruthenians and the Muslim Tatars together in the closing years of the fourteenth century AD. During the centuries that followed the peoples of Dār al-Islām, often through the Tatars, became better acquainted with the peoples of the Baltic region and especially with the Poles. The Tatars in Poland and in Lithuania often forsook their adopted countries on account of religious persecution, or to accomplish the pilgrimage, or to join their relatives in Ottoman lands.

However, in far earlier medieval times, the 'Dark Ages' and the obscure ages that followed in north-eastern Europe, one might well have asked 'what were the sights, the stories of the merchants and the missionaries of the Church and the fabulous reports that were told by those rare Orientals who dared to travel to the North and who had set foot upon the soil of the Baltic countries? What did they have to report about the strange and often offensive folk who dwelt near the 'Sea of Darkness'?[3]

When Arab and Persian geographers and travellers wrote about the Baltic and the northerly regions of Russia, and their peoples, during the tenth, eleventh and twelfth centuries, sundry interests and impressions preoccupied their minds. Those interests included a desire to please the curiosity of their patrons. It bore a scanty resemblance to the 'forests of Poland' that were still to be a poetic inspiration to the Egyptian poet Ahmad Shawqī (d. 1932). In his verses one senses an intense longing and, at the same time, an intense rejection:[4]

> *You sway not, from side to side, amidst the savagery of nature, nor in a dizzy spin.*
> *O frozen and inanimate world, how cruel and how harsh art thou. Will thy denial and thy rejection for ever be my bane?*[5]

The Baltic had varied names. Mustawfī Hamd Allāh of Qazwīn called it the 'Sea of the Warang̃ (Varang)' or the 'Sea of the Ğālātīqūn' (possibly a corruption of the name of the tribe, the Veletians, or possibly the Latgallians).

One of the earliest reported examples of Islamic mythological and magical thought among peoples of the 'Land of Darkness' is to be found in the record of a voyage that took place during AD 921 and 922. That voyager was Ahmad b. Fadlān. He was on his way, to the south-east of the Baltic region to visit the Volga Bulgars. It has been suggested that it was the sight of the aurora borealis that inspired his account and his narrative, though it may also be noted that the King of the Bulgars, who was a Muslim, was, in part, the source of his description. It was an Islamic interpretation, and the king's predecessors had been perfectly capable of telling this very same Islamic story.

The following quotation from Ibn Fadlān's account is translated from a slightly rephrased passage of the text made by the nineteenth-century Tatar historian, Muhammad Murād Ramzī.[6] It is included within his work, *Talfīq al-Akhbār wa-Talqīh al-Āthār* ('The shaping – even "fabrication" – of reports, and a reflection on the consequences of human traces'), a work which will be quoted extensively elsewhere in this book:

> On the first night during which we slept in his town, an hour before the sunset (al-maghrib), I gazed skywards towards the horizon. It had turned a deep red in colour. In the air, I heard high-pitched voices, a whispering sound and murmurings. I raised my head and, behold, I saw a cloud that was red like the colour of fire. It came close to me. Verily, the murmuring and those sounds issued forth from its heart, and, lo, within it, there appeared the shapes of men and of beasts. Those ghostly figures in the clouds held bows, spears and swords in their hands. They were clearly visible to my sight. I was able to picture them. Another cloudy fragment similar was also to be seen. Gazing

within it, I beheld more men, more weapons and more beasts. That latter cloud advanced against the former. It was though one squadron launched an attack upon another. We were terrified. We began to beseech the Almighty and to pray fervently, while the people of the town merely mocked us. They were amazed at the way we were behaving. We stared with fixed gaze at the turmoil and at the intermingling over the course of an entire part of the night. Then all of it vanished from our sight.

I asked the king about this matter. He alleged that his forefathers used to say that these beings took the form of believing and unbelieving 'jinn', who strove, one against the other, during the course of each evening. They never failed to do so. This happening took place every single night!

The basic monotheistic sentiments of the Turkic nomads and the settled Bulgārs, some of them ancestors of the Tatars of later centuries, in the Volga region, were nowhere to be doubted by Ibn Fadlān.

However, he seemed to harbour some doubts as to whether their seemingly Islamic and their formulaic expressions of their belief in the Divinity – Allāh and Tengri – whom he too worshipped, were the expression of a sound and orthodox spiritual vision of the Ultimate Reality amongst these folk. He questioned whether the common utterance of such formulae was little more than a mannerism or an attempt to impress Muslim travellers from the Caliphate. Bulgar was the cultural heart of Islam in north-eastern Europe at that time.

At a later date in the Middle Ages, something akin to the these same northerly and uninhabited landscapes on the rim of the world were to inspire Shamsī Tabrīzī with a Sufi reflection upon the Ultimate Reality within the border of the 'Sea of Darkness' (Baḥr al-Ẓulumāt):

> *I was born not in China afar, not in Saqsīn, and not in Bulghār;*
> *Not in India, where five rivers are, nor 'Iraq, nor Khorāsān I grew.*
> *Not in this world nor that world I dwell, not in Paradise, neither in Hell;*
> *Not from Eden and Rizwān I fell, not from Adam my lineage I drew.*
> *In a place beyond uttermost Place, in a tract without shadow of trace,*
> *Soul and body transcending, I live in the soul of my Loved One anew!*[7]

The Muslims first conceived the Baltic World as such a place beyond the uttermost place.

In the thirteenth century, in the text of the Icelandic Eddic poem of Håvamål, the *High Song of of Völuspa*, an even bleaker terrain was described to the peoples of the North;

In the beginning of Time
There was nothing,
Neither sand nor sea,
Nor cooling surf.
There was no earth,
Nor upper heaven, –
No blade of grass –
Only the Great Void.

Islamic trade with the Baltic

Trade between the North and the World of Islam was to change the landscape forever. On the map of the geographer al-Idrīsī (writing AH 548/AD 1154), the Baltic coastline, including Latvia and Estonia, distorted and disfigured, speculative and weird, is depicted almost like a vision seen in a 'lava-lamp', a table ornament that was once popular. Central to his scene is 'the Ocean of Darkness', 'the Surrounding Ocean', and, facing it, the land of Tabast, this name corresponding to Tavastia (Tavastland), the inland districts of Finland on the northern shore of the Baltic coast. In the twelfth century, the Christian influences from Sweden and beyond, especially the Cistercian Order of monks and nuns, were beginning to penetrate the pagan fastnesses of that remote region. As Carolus Lindberg has noted:

> Later than their neighbours, the heathen Finns turned from their old idols. The Christian belief, established before the close of the Xth century in Scandinavia, first sought its way over to Finland, according to the testimony of ancient documents, towards the middle of the XIIth century. But even this first mission, led by Saint Eric, King of Sweden, and the British missionary, Henrik, raised later to be patron saint of Finland, could not procure a safe foothold in the land for the new religion, and not until a century later, after a new crusade under Birger Jarl (1249) to the inner provinces, was the foundation laid for a firm Christian organization of which the church is the visible symbol.[8]

On al-Idrīsī's map, one sees two small rivers branching out from a far longer river. This major river is undoubtedly the Daugava valley, located

8   Islam in the Baltic

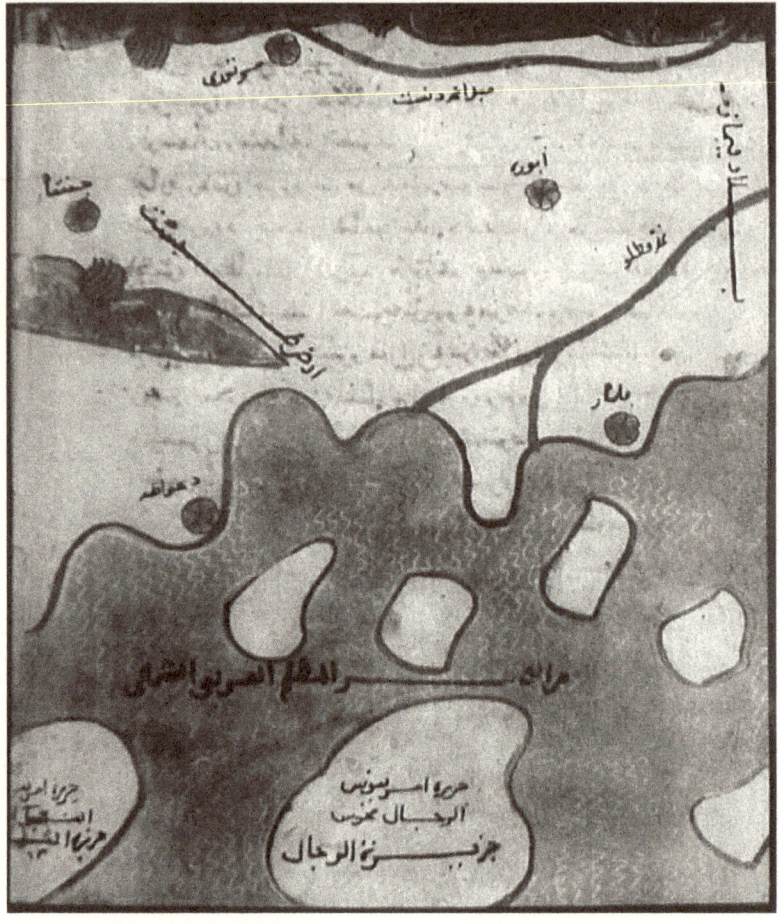

Figure 1 'The Island of Men' and the 'Island of the Amazon Women' in the map of al-Idrīsī.

in Latvia's heart, around which the Baltic states are to be found on the map today. More prominently shown are two large mythical islands, way out in the Baltic Sea, the (Amazonian)[9] 'Island of Men', and another, far more commonly known in medieval legend and literature, in both East and West,[10] the (Amazonian) 'Island of Women' (Jazīrat al-Nisā', Insula Feminarum, or Terra Feminarum). This name stems from those fabulous accounts and maps that are manifested in the Alexander Romance of

Pseudo-Callisthenes, or in the Hereford Map, and in numerous medieval and Oriental sources, not only in al-Idrīsī's book, *Nuzhat al-Mushtāq* (the Book of King Roger), but, likewise, in the writings of other Arab geographers, before and after him, writers such as al-Marwazī, who died after AH 514/AD 1120, and in al-Qazwīnī's *'Ajā'ib al-Makhlūqāt wa-Āthār al-Bilād*, written in AH 674/AD 1275. The 'Island of Men' and the 'Island of Women' differ in both size and resources. In the *Ḥudūd al-'Ālam, a Persian Geography*, which dates from AH 372/AD 982, where, on the former island the inhabitants were all men, and on the latter, women, each year for four nights they joined together for the purpose of procreation and when the boys reached the age of three years they sent them to the 'Island of Men'. On the 'Island of Men' there were thirty-six big rivers that arose there and emptied into the sea, while on the 'Island of Women' there were three rivers.[11] In view of the number of rivers one might question that the Arabic for 'island' (jazīra) had its other meaning of a 'peninsula', or a promontory. It was this word that was used to describe Denmark and Norway on al-Idrīsī's map. One might also note that in the Finnish epic, the *Kalevala*, the island is in the midst of ten lakes with little indication of a nearby coast.

Denmark, specifically Jutland and Schleswig, was by no means unknown to the Arabs, though visitors from al-Andalus were very rare. Ibrāhīm b. Ya'qūb al-Isrā'īlī al-Turtūshī, a Muslim from Córdoba, visited Hedeby, in Schleswig, around AD 950 and he has left quite a detailed account of what he saw.[12] According to O. Klindt Jensen:[13]

> Money circulated, and the people of Hedeby even began to mint silver coins thus imitating Dorstadt in Friesland. Commoner than these, however, were the coins of the rest of Western Europe and of Arabia. The latter came in a steady glittering stream by the trade routes of the Swedes along the Russian rivers. A few Arabs, dark types of perhaps the most cultured people of the time, walked down the streets of Hedeby among the tall, fair Northmen. We have some notes written by one of them. He did not feel so comfortable up here as at home. The singing reminded him of the howling of dogs, and the exposure of small children who could not be reared was alien to him.

We are told more:

> The women were free to divorce their husbands. Noise and filth was the overwhelming impression. The population subsisted on fish and its pagan inhabitants hung animal sacrifices on poles in front of their

homes. Throughout the North, and especially in the East, the Swedish traders in furs and amber brought back with them hoards of Islamic dirhams. In Sweden, a discovery in Uppland brought to light coins which had been minted in Baghdad, in Cairo, in Damascus, in Isfahan and Tashkent (al-Shāsh).

In Latvia, there are splendid examples of such coins dating from between the ninth and the eleventh centuries. Examples are on display in the History Museum (Latvijas Vēsturis Musejs) in Riga Castle. Up to 2,343 dīnārs and dirhams, dating between AD 699 and AD 1013 have been unearthed, principally in the Talsi region, a mixture of Bulgar, Būyid, 'Abbāsid and Sāmānid coinage. Elsewhere, Kūfic coins have been discovered in Kurzeme at Grobiņas, where the Gotlanders once had a colony.

In the writings of al-Idrīsī, centuries later, identifiable locations in Denmark appear. Towns appear to lie to the east and to the west of the main highroad, the Haervejen, which ran northward in Jutland from the Elbe region. These toponyms, going from south to north, include: al-Sīlah (Slien or Sly, Sliesthorpe, or Sylt), Tardhīra (Tyraborg), Khūw fortress (possibly Hobro with its eleventh-century Viking ramparts), Wandaslgādah (Vendelsgade at the northern tip of Jutland, the point of departure for Jazīrat Narfāgha (Norway)). Turning south, the route passed through 'Hursh Hunt' (possibly Horsens, a place of abbeys and fortresses) and then, leaving Jutland, it arrived at Sīsabūlī, which was almost certainly located near to Seebüll in the Schleswig region of Germany.

Beyond Denmark and Germany, eastwards into the regions of Poland, the Baltic States and North Russia the map is less precise and identifications are a hazardous pastime, especially as all of them are located within the mythological geography of the 'Island, or Peninsula, or City or Land of Women' and the 'Island, or Peninsula, of Men'. The duality and disparate size of this legendary pair of islands, or peninsulas, resembles, on the map, the shape of the two islands of Saaremaa and Muhu (the former far larger than the latter) both of which lie beyond the coastal regions of Estonia and Latvia, though one should not overlook the twinned Œland and Gotland islands which lie in the Baltic to the east of Kalmar in south-eastern Sweden. Al-Idrīsī mentions Kalmar (Qalmar) and Pērnu and Qulūwnī (Koluvaniga, the old name for Tallinn). Between the tenth and the thirteenth centuries, Saaremaa was the most populated part of Estonia. There are countless pairs of islands, within, and without, the Baltic region. Only Naissaar Island, outside Tallinn, with its two small settlements of Pohjäkulla bears the meaning of 'women's island', although, as mentioned, the *Kalevala* places Lemminkainen's island nowhere out to sea.

A duality of islands, or peninsulas, seems to bear a relationship to other dualites in these Baltic lands, dualities to which reference is made in G.J. Tallgren-Tuulio and A.M. Tallgren's exhaustive study of al-Idrīsī's description of Finland and the lands of the eastern Baltic Sea:[14]

> The name of Estlanda probably designates not only actual Estonia, but also Livonia and perhaps even the entire eastern littoral of the Baltic (the Baltic provinces). It is known that the word, 'Estland', originally denoted the country which was situated to the east of the Germans; the first time that it appears it denotes the territory of amber, somewhere near to the mouth of the Niemen.[15] Again, at the commencement of the Middle Ages, the extension of the expression, 'Estland', was uncertain. Often one attached the whole of Livonia to it. Al-Idrīsī makes no mention of Prussia, nor does he mention Curland. However, it is possible that the 'Estland' known to him, only signified actual Estonia, since Adam of Bremen (1070) speaks of the 'island of Estland', and the 'island of Curland',[16] which he differentiates, and in Henry's Chronicle, the 'Estonians' are indisputably only the Estonians besides whom are the Livonians, whilst the inhabitants of Curland and the various Lettish peoples appear separately. It is possible that the 'Estland' of al-Idrīsī did not include the large islands of Estonia, which the Scandinavians indicated by a special term, Eysyssela.[17]

The Baltic lands as described by Abū 'Ubayd 'Abdallāh b. 'Abd al-'Azīz al-Bakrī (d. AH 487/AD 1094)

Al-Bakrī's *Book of Routes and Countries* (*Kitāb al-Masālik wal-Mamālik*), parts of which cite the eye-witness, to whom we have referred, Ibrāhīm b. Ya'qūb al-Turtūshī, offers us a description of the Baltic peoples that far surpasses the meagre geographical information, the names of towns and rivers, and the random observations, or informant's reports, which form the bulk of the text in al-Idrīsī's *Nuzhat al-Mushtāq*.

In al-Bakrī, it is possible to build some picture of the medieval peoples in the Baltic countries, be they in Poland or in north Germany, or within today's Baltic States. These peoples ruled themselves, they conquered their neighbours, traded, raided, worshipped their gods and lived lives that were very different from those within the Caliphate. Yet here, as with al-Idrīsī, the abundant legendary content reveals how remote this region was from the great centres of documentation within Islamic civilisation, especially in al-Andalus and in the major centres of the Middle East. A vigorous trade existed, and Islamic coins were legion in the Baltic region, but, as has already been noted, the Muslims who had ever set foot there were very few.

Ibrāhīm b. Ya'qūb al-Isrā'īlī al-Turtūshī had visited Hedeby in Denmark in the middle of the tenth century. There were other places in the North he knew. Al-Bakrī's text is prefaced by a number of quotations from his accounts, especially those about the Slavs, amongst whom the ruler of Poland, whose territories bordered the Baltic, Mieszko I (Mashāquh), was a figure of major importance:[18]

> As for Mieszko's (Mashāquh's) land, it is the most spacious of these countries. There are, within it, great quantities of wheat and corn, meat and honey and the earth is tilled. The tax which is collected is in 'mithqals'. These are, in their colour, speckled white and black. They are the means of subsistence, paid to his men on a monthly basis. Each man is paid a recognized number of them. Mashāquh has three thousand mail-clad men. They are soldiers who, in valour, outmatch other men by ten to one. Mashāquh gives the men clothes and horses and weaponry and everything that they may have need of. If a child is born to one of his men, he gives the order that a gift be sent to him at the hour of birth, be the child a male or female. When the child reaches puberty, if he is a male, he marries him to another and he pays the dowry required to the father of the maiden. If the offspring be a female, then he gives her as wife to another and he pays the dowry to her father. Such a dowry amongst the Slavs is very expensive. Their manner of acting in this respect recalls the Berber custom. If two, or three, daughters are born to a man of his, these girls are the cause for his wealth. If he has two sons, then this is the cause of his poverty.
>
> Mashāqu has, as his neighbours, the Rūs[19] in the east and the Prussians[20] to the north. The inhabitants of Prussia dwell on the coast of the Baltic Sea. They have their own peculiar language. They do not know the languages of their neighbours.[21] They are renowned for their courage in battle. When an army comes to them, not a single one of them is weak or will he flinch until his companion joins him and assists him. He advances and he goes forth, boldly. He does not pause nor turn aside to confront another. He smites him with his sword until he is dead. The Rūs[22] (the Varangs or Swedish Vikings) make raids upon them from the west in their vessels.[23] To the west of the Rūs is the

'Land (City) of Women'.²⁴ They have lands and realms in which there are sweet smelling plants. They become pregnant through intercourse with their male servants. If a woman gives birth to a male child, she kills him. They ride upon horses and hurry forth to do battle.

They are courageous and heroic. (I, al-Bakrī, report) Ibrāhīm b.Ya'qūb al-Isra'īlī said, 'The report in regard to this land (city) is true. I was told of it by Otto, the Holy Roman Emperor.'²⁵

To the west of this 'Land (City) of Women' is found a tribe of Slavs, called the nation of Waltāba.²⁶ This tribe is settled in thickets and marshy lands within the country of Mashāquh, specifically in that part of it which lies to the west and in some part of the north. They have a mighty town. It is situated on the Baltic coast. It possesses twelve gates. It has a harbour and anchorage and they employ a law of equal sharing in the working thereof, or, they use 'a half split tree trunks in the construction thereof'.²⁷ They wage war against Mashāquh and the vehemence of their prowess is very savage and intense. No king rules over them. They are subject to no other people. It is their elders who govern them.²⁸

The settlements of the Balts and Slavs on the shores of the southern Baltic

Both al-Bakrī and, to a degree, al-Idrīsī are principally concerned with towns, with islands, with ports and with tribes, all of which were located along the Baltic coast or deep within its hinterland.²⁹ Information as to their whereabouts had been acquired by hearsay, or heard from the mouths of travellers and merchants whose tales circulated far away in Sicily or in the Islamic Mediterranean regions. The contrast with Ibn Fadlān's account, and, to a lesser degree, that of Ibrāhīm b. Ya'qūb, is striking. Even so, what is unusual in their joint accounts of the Baltic tribes is not that they give us colourful contemporary 'snapshots' of life, as they believed to be lived, but, rather, that they provide, in fact, an uncanny panorama of life as it was lived over a span of thousands of years in the remotest past of human history, a glimpse of that which recent archaeological research in the Baltic States and Poland has brought to light and shown to be a reality. One might question how al-Bakrī and al-Idrīsī could possibly have known this? 'Islands or Lands of Men and of Women', in fact, seem to mirror the sequence of events when the Balts and their predecessors and their contemporaries first settled in this northerly corner of mainland Europe.

The first settlers were chiefly reindeer hunters. They migrated from the south-western shores of Denmark, Germany and Poland. These people

14 Islam in the Baltic

lived in the pre-Neolithic and Neolithic ages, between 3,500 and 2,500 BC. In these societies, the family system was either matrilineal, or family rôles were divided between men and women. Horses and weaponry were unknown to these people. They worshipped a pantheon of goddesses and they were peaceful and sedentary. They were hunter fishers. They had trading links with Central Europe to where amber objects were exported from the shores of the Baltic Sea.

At some date before 2500 BC Indo-European tribes, known as the Boat axe culture, invaded the territories now occupied by the Lithuanians, the Latvians and the Prussians. Their culture and social structure was patrilineal and with a patriarchal three-tiered social structure. They brought with them animal husbandry and male deities. Perkūunas, god of thunder and lightning, came to overshadow Dievas, the god of the sky.

The original inhabitants of this corner of Europe, over a period of time, became assimilated into this new Indo-European culture. Hence, they adopted a new language, religion and way of life. A group of Indo-European nations and tribes who spoke kindred tongues began to form.[30] They inhabited the forested lands between the Wisla and the Volga, they settled along the Daugava river valley, in the heart of Latvia[31] and within the central section of the Dnieper. Scholars have named these peoples the 'Balts'. Later historical sources concurred with the report that the Balts formed clearly distinguishable tribes.

By the fifth and sixth centuries AD these tribes had become consolidated into their final forms. The Lithuanian and Aukštaičia people coalesced in the face of Slavic invasions from the East, so consolidating the Lithuanian and Latvian peoples. Animal husbandry and agriculture marked the region. They began to smelt native iron ore and began the manufacture of weaponry. Amber was brought along a route which reached its destination in the hands of Roman craftsmen. The Balts became wealthy. They constructed fortified mounds. The farmers lived in villages at the foot of these mounds. In time, the villages became towns and a few grew in size to become cities. This period was the Late Iron Age in Latvian history.

The name of 'Lithuania' was a latecomer to history, first receiving a mention in the early eleventh century (The Quedlinburg Chronicles, AD 1009).[32] It became divided into local duchies during the eleventh and the following centuries, but, due to pressure from the Teutonic religious order from the West and the Slavs and Mongol Tatars from the East it brought about the birth of the Grand Duchy of Lithuania, which, at its height in the fourteenth and fifteenth centuries, extended from the Baltic to the Black Sea.

When al-Bakrī and al-Idrīsī wrote for their world of Islam and the Normans their descriptions of this other strange world, the historical process in the Baltic region had not reached that remarkable dénouement. Their age was an age of 'Sturm und Drang', an age of Warangs̆, Rūs, Northmen, Vikings and Balts, an age that has been well summarised by Stasys Samalavicius:[33]

> Up to the eleventh century, regional rulers initiated Viking attacks on the Baltic territories. Such interventions were of a local character, but starting with the eleventh century they assumed a new, much wider, scope. At that time, Denmark and Sweden became the most powerful states in Scandinavia, and the rulers of those states themselves began organizing invasions into the lands inhabited by Baltic tribes. As Lithuanian and other Baltic tribes were pagan at that time, attacks on them were also launched under the pretext of spreading Christianity. In the eleventh and twelfth centuries, Danish Kings sought to conquer entire regions inhabited by Prussian tribes. Very successful and well organized were the assaults which were carried out during the rule of King Canute the Great.[34] ... The defence of the Lithuanians proved to be successful. The Vikings, and later the Scandinavian states of Denmark and Sweden, failed to conquer and settle down in the lands inhabited by the Baltic tribes. But soon a new and much stronger wave of expansion came, which had much graver consequences for the Lithuanians.[35]

The threat of the Teutonic Knights, and their 'Crusade', was a menace of a different order from that which the Balts had hitherto faced. As the growing and expanding Duchy of Lithuania reached and extended further and further in the direction of the Black Sea, the world of Islam, the world of the converted pagan Tatars there, was both a challenge and a source of fresh manpower to confront the Germans. By then, the northern lands had long forgotten the rare Muslim Arab or Persian visitor or the merchant who was to put his thoughts and his distorted impressions into his writings for the Muslim 'umma' to read. Islam, in that age, has only its treasure of coinage to remind one of its presence.

Instead, the captive, or recruited, Tatar refugees of Khān Toqtamish were to take their place. They were to stay for centuries in these marches, in Lithuania and Belarus. They were to establish homes of families and settlements and to grow in their number. They were to construct mosques and to proclaim the message of the Qur'ān. With them came the Qipchāq speaking Karaims. The Qipchāq world of the steppes, an offshoot of the Central Asian world, and the World of Islam, was henceforth to play a role within Baltic history and in Baltic culture. Its legacy remains with us until today.

Note

My colleague Professor Edward Tryjarski has kindly drawn my attention to an article which has been published recently in the Polish Orientalist Journal, *Rocznik Orientalistyczny*, Tom, L1V, zeszyt 2, Warsaw, 2002, pp. 171–82. It is by Jean Charles Ducène and is entitled, 'L'Ile des Amazones dans la Mer Baltique chez les géographes arabes: confluence du Roman d'Alexandre et d'une tradition germanique'. In this article, which is rich in sources and new ideas, Ducène describes the legend of the 'Island of Women' and he lists the Arab geographers who touch on this theme dating from al-Khwārizmī (dating from the first half of the third century, AH, the ninth-century AD), with a mention of Ya'qūb al-Turtūshī (dating from the second half of the fourth century AH, the tenth century AD), citing al-Idrīsī (circa AH 560/1165 AD). His survey is continued to include Ibn Sa'īd al-Maghribī (AH 610/AD 1218–AH 685/AD 1286), who mentions that the distances between the islands of women and men are very great, and also, al-Watwāt (AH 632/AD 1235–AH 718/AD 1318). Ducène also discusses the mention of this legend in the Shāhnāmeh of Firdawsī and, extensively, in the Alexander Romance itself. He then turns his attention to other historical and legendary sources. They include Tacitus and especially Paul Diacre's *Histoire des Lombardes*. The latter, and also Adam of Bremen (eleventh century AD) associate the Goths with the Amazons. Not only are the Amazons associated in particular with the Baltic region, in their migrations, but also elsewhere including the land of the Scythians (the Crimea). Their womenfolk, when widowed, banded together as warriors. The Goths are associated with the island of Gotland, 'in Scandia' and it is precisely reported by al-Bakrī (see above) that one of the nearest entries to the 'Island of Women' was via Kalmar, the part of the Swedish coast that lies due west of the island of Gotland (where numbers of Arabic coins have been found). It is the discovery of this article that, the Arabic, as well as other sources, have been integrated with those which speak of the history of the early history and the wanderings of the Goths. In his conclusion, Ducène speculates as to whether there was a cause that pushed Diodore of Sicily into believing that the Amazons were especially associated with the Baltic. Ducène wonders whether he had some notion that women warriors were to be found on the northerly borders of Germany. One can speculate whether the sundry traditions meet in some common source. The case for this should be given very serious consideration. My own interpretation has suggested a wide variety of mythical strands that made the southern Baltic and its adjacent islands a haven for almost supernatural warriors, both men and women. To many, the Vikings, the ancient Balts, the ancient Prussians and the Teutonic Knights all filled this rôle. To all these must be added 'the Tatars' who arrived on this northern scene long after these wandering peoples had left their historical relics and mythical sagas around the Baltic coasts and islands. The homeland of the Goths was also located in the Crimean peninsula and its surrounding regions of the northern Caucasus and the southern Ukraine. The Scythians and the Sarmatians, the Alans, and others, once inhabited these regions. Here, however, archaeology furnishes the evidence which has turned mythology into history. The treasures of the Scythians, on display in the Kyiv Historical Treasures Museum, housed within the Caves Monastery (Pechersk Lavra) complex, contains scabbards of gold for both male and female Scythian warriors. The 'Amazons' were therefore a part of history. The Tatars may be reckoned amongst the Scythians' successors.

2. The Expanding Eastern Empire of the Grand Duchy of Lithuania

Duke Mindaugas (1236–63), Duke Gediminas (1316–41), King Jogaila (1377–92) and Duke Vytautas (Witold) (1392–1430), the Hero of the Lithuanian Tatars and the Karaims

> Iron would turn to wax, and water to steel sooner than we would go back on our word
> *(pirmiauu gelezis vasku taps ir vanduo i pliens pavirs, nego mes savu zodi atshauksime)*

> I do not forbid the Christians to worship God according to the manner of their faith, the Russians according to theirs, the Poles according to theirs, whilst we ourselves will worship God according to our customs.
> Sayings attributed to Duke Gediminas of Lithuania (1316–41)

Mindaugas (1236–63)

Lithuania became organised into a united state in the thirteenth century. It was an agreement between the Dukes of the Dukedoms of Aukštaitija[1] who held fortresses in Kernavė, Trakai and Vilnius. In 1219, Mindaugas and his brother, Dausprungas, and other Lithuanian Dukes, signed a treaty with Volynia. This gave Mindaugas the power of leadership amongst equals. In 1240, Mindaugas united Aukštaitija with Žemaitija (eastern Samogitia) and with parts of southern Lithuania. Beyond this district several Slavic territories were also incorporated. They included Slonim and Volkovysk and the major fortress of Naugardukas (Novogrudok), which is now within Belarus. He expanded to the east to include Polotsk (Polatsk), Vitebsk and Smolensk (now in Russia). His task aroused opposition and this included the dissatisfied Samogitians and, even more important, the invading and aggressive Crusaders of the Knights of the Sword (the Teutonic Knights) who were established in Prussia and in Livonia (Latvia and Estonia). Mindaugas succeeded in stemming the advance of the latter though he found his position to be ultimately untenable. He negotiated for peace with the Knights of the Sword, offering to accept Christianity. By about 1245 Mindaugas was called 'Supreme King', it being understood that all the Lithuanian lands and neighbours which included southern Selonia, Black Rus', and possibly the Rus'ian castles of Breslav and Minsk (Mensk) were in the hands of a sole sovereign.[2] It is believed that a ceremony took place in 1251, during which Mindaugas was baptised, together with his wife, two sons and members of his court. In 1253 he was officially crowned king. Lithuania became a nominally Christian kingdom. He was acknowledged to be an equal among the other Christian kings. His task as ruler was far from easy. His efforts to subdue the pagan Baltic peoples were unsuccessful. They included the Yotvingians (Sudovians), who were at war against the Poles and against the Knights of the Sword, and his attempts to bribe them with silver gifts into loyalty were not reciprocated. The Samogitians (Žemaičiai) resisted the Livonian Order (Knights of the Sword) while Mindaugus was secretly supporting the Prussians who were also in full revolt. Frustrated, he turned towards the Russian lands of the East. He fought thirty-three major campaigns. Twenty of these were in the East. These plans had opponents and amongst them Treniota of the Samogitians, who was the leader of the pagan opposition to Mindaugas in Lithuania. In alliance with Daumantas, the Duke of Nalšia, Mindaugas was attacked in his castle and in 1263 he was killed, together with his two sons, Ruklys and Rupeikis. Lithuania returned to paganism. After a period of confusion, Traidenis mounted the throne of Lithuania in 1269. He turned from expansion and, instead, he encouraged the growth and the strengthening of his forces to defend Lithuania's territory and identity.

In the East, the policies of Mindaugas had important consequences. They were of significance in averting Tatar penetration into those territories that lay to the south of the Baltic region. The Tatars of the Golden Horde were regarded as a major threat. As a result of the campaigns of Mindaugas, he reached as far as lands that were subject to the Golden Horde. The Tatars, under Burunday, launched a raiding expedition against Lithuania in 1258–59. The Lithuanians thwarted this attack despite the ravaging of those eastern territories that they had occupied. In 1274–75, the Tatars plundered the Upper Nemunas and burnt the settlement of Nagurdukas. The swampy territory in southern Lithuania at least afforded an extra protection against Tatar raids.

Zigmantas Kiaupa has summarised the legacy of Mindaugas as follows:[3]

> The lands united and ruled for approximately 20 years by Mindaugas comprised the first Lithuanian state. Lithuania's geopolitical situation meant that it had to repel the deadly advances of the Orders, and Crusades from north and west, and to assume the initiative in the Rus'ian lands, expanding its territories in that direction. Three worlds collided in Lithuania under Mindaugas: a pagan Lithuania, Catholic Europe and Orthodox Rus' – each with its own ideology, concept of statehood, and other differences. Mindaugas tried to unite them all, but failed because of the Western world's dismissal of the interests of Lithuania and the other Balts; his failure became a warning for later generations of Lithuanian peoples and their rulers. It also determined the long-term isolation of pagan Lithuania from the cultural processes of Europe, and made it the object of enforced Christianisation and Western military aggression.

The world of the East, the world of the Tatars, was to figure increasingly in importance during the lifetime of his great successor, Gediminas.

Gediminas (1316–41)

The reign of Gediminas, which began in 1316, was to influence the life of the Lithuanians for some 250 years. He was to successfully withstand the German Orders that had subdued Prussia and Livonia. His success in the battles of the Nemunas river region against the Knights meant that the attacks from their direction were checked, so enabling him to turn his attention to the South and East towards the Russian lands and the Tatars and, thereby, expanding Lithuania's borders to an extent undreamt of by his predecessors. Indeed, many Russian towns and principalities sought allegiance to Lithuania in order to escape the tribute paid to their Tatar overlords. Gediminas opened up Lithuania to Western commercial, cultural and religious contacts, exchanges and missionary activities. These included tradesmen, craftsmen, artisans and priests, monks and bishops. The Church of St Nicholas, in Vilnius, dates from around 1320, if not earlier, and was founded by German merchants. Thereby, Gediminas sought to weaken the position of the German Orders and to raise cultural standards within his Lithuanian realm. The foundation of Vilnius, as his capital, notwithstanding its existence before his days and the dubious legend of the prophesy of its foundation by an iron wolf which howled with the voices of 100 wolves, and the prophesy of its future prosperity by the high pagan priest Lizdeika are lost in time. Vilnius, as we still see it today, was the achievement of Gediminas who centralised his control within his castle. Nearby, on the site of a temple to Perkūnas, the construction of a wooden church predated the Classical cathedral that we see today.

Over the centuries, Vilnius was to become an outstanding cultural centre for both West and East, not only for the huge Jewish community that was centred there and the small Tatar population, but also other peoples from the East, both Muslim and non-Muslim. Agnius Urbanavičius has mentioned[4] that during the latter half of the seventeenth and eighteenth centuries among the new citizens of Vilnius were to be found people who had come from many parts of western and southern Europe and also from certain Muslim or Muslim dominated countries in the Near and Middle East, each totalling some 0.02 per cent of the population. They included Armenians, Balkan peoples, especially Turks, and even Persians.

The policy of Gediminas in the East was linked to his parallel campaign against the Order. Lithuania advanced to the upper reaches of the Dvina and the Dnieper rivers. Kiev had been occupied by Gediminas' brother, Fedor, before 1331. Prior to the death of Gediminas, in 1341, he had invited Franciscan friars from Bohemia in order to baptise him. This baptism never took place since these friars were assassinated on their way to Lithuania. Gediminas had partitioned the state between his seven sons. Vilnius and its district was held by Jaunutis (1341–45). His brothers were active in the East, in particular, Algirdas (1345–77). In 1362, Algirdas organised an expedition to the Dnieper steppes and he defeated the Tatars. On the other hand he was not their implacable foe. Tatar help was sometimes sought by the Lithuanians This happened in 1349, against the growing power of Muscovy. Algirdas even sent his brother Karijotas to Janibeg Khān with a proposal to form a Lithuanian–Tatar alliance. The Khān declined. Algirdas defeated the Tatars in the battle of the 'Blue Waters' (Sinie Vody) in 1362. This success gave the Lithuanians the control of the southern Russian territories. During his campaigns in 1368, 1370 and 1372, Algirdas marched against Moscow though he was never able to capture the Kremlin itself. Algirdas died in May 1377, and, in accordance with pagan custom, he was cremated in Vilnius, despite the fact that his two wives and his offspring were Orthodox Christians in their faith.[5]

Jogaila (1377–92)

Jogaila is probably best known in the West for his Christianisation of the Lithuanians. Such was the outcome of his marriage to Hedwig, the daughter of the King of Poland and Hungary, Louis d'Anjou. This event took place in 1385 and the act of agreement was signed in Kreva castle in Lithuania. Jogaila was baptised in Cracow, on 14 February 1386, and, by the Act of Kreva, led to an agreement which lasted for four hundred years. A cathedral was built in Vilnius. After the establishment of Catholic institutions in Lithuania, Jogaila returned to Cracow, now titled King Władysław II, and much that was to follow took place within the series of special crises and opportunities that were to mark the changing pattern of Jogaila's relationship with Vytautas. Externally, this involved the continuing threat from the Orders, despite the conversion of Jogaila, and, on the other hand the Eastern Question, the threatening wars between the Tatars in the East and the rising power of Tīmūr in Central Asia.

In August 1392, Jogaila and Vytautas met at Astravas. Vytautas recognised the suzerainty of Jogaila, claimed possession of Trakai, obtained the right to rule Lithuania and to claim the title of its Duke. In 1395, Vytautas annexed Smolensk and took miltant action against the Order in Livonia, backed by a coalition of the Emperor Wenceslas of Bohemia, Pope Boniface IX, the bishops of Livonia and the Dukes of Mecklenburg. Between 1395 and 1397, unlike Jogaila, he granted concessions to the Order in return for an agreement to keep a long-term truce. It was during a respite between 1397 and 1398 that Vytautas campaigned in the region of the Black Sea where the Lithuanians had established castles in the approach routes to the Crimea. During this expedition the ancestors of the Lithuanian Tatars and the Karaims were brought to the North and were to be established in what is now Belarus, Lithuania and Poland. They were the first Muslim community of significance in the countries that lay close to the Baltic Sea. This success was to herald increasingly cool, even resentful, feelings amongst the Lithuanians over the Polish expansionist, domineering and unifying aims.[6]

Tatar affairs concerned both Jogaila and Vytautas. They were to be centred upon the increasingly desperate situation that faced the authority of Khān Toqtamish within the Golden Horde. Jogaila had for some time become involved in Tatar affairs. He had been in negotiation with Khān Mamay for a joint invasion of Muscovy. This was to prove to be impossible on account of the defeat of Mamay by the Russians in the battle of Kulikova Field (Kulikowe Polje) on 19 July 1380. The army of Russian princes was led by Dymitr Donskoy. Two hundred thousand men reputedly perished in battle on both sides and Mamay was forced to submit. The correspondence between Jogaila and Toqtamish has survived. One of these is a letter, written in Uyghur script, dated 1392–93 which was sent by Toqtamish. It was written five years before the campaign of Vytautas in the Crimean region. This letter, sent in the name of the Khān of the Golden Horde, 'Yarlik Khāna Zolotoi Ordy Tokhtamysh k Pol'skom Korolyo Yagailu' was published by the noted Dagestani Orientalist Muhammad 'Alī Kāzem Beg.[7] Other related correspondence and edicts of Toqtamish have been published by Gyorgy Kara.[8] These are earlier, dating from around 1381 when the headquarters of Toqtamish were located at the middle course of the River Don.

The end of the fourteenth century was an important juncture for relations between Lithuania–Poland and the Tatars. Certain events stand out as particularly significant. The first of these was the defeat of Mamay in 1380. It was to be of a special importance in the relations between Lithuania and Moscow. Following the policy of his father, Jogaila had allied himself with Mamay and it was his original intention to meet him on the bank of the Oka river. It was said that the Grand Duke moved to the East with 'all the forces of Lithuania' and if Dimitri Ivanovich had been defeated it is conjectured that the influence of Lithuania could have been extended into the basin of the Volga. The security of Lithuania's eastern border would have been assured well into the future.

Jogaila had advanced close to his destination when he learnt of Mamay's defeat. One might ask, had he loitered deliberately, or had Dimitri advanced so rapidly that the Tatars were unable to join forces with their Lithuanian allies? Jogaila appears to have rapidly retreated. In the event the victory of Dimitri was to prove to be short-lived. Two years later, the Khān, Toqtamish, avenged the Tatar defeat.[9] Dimitri abandoned Moscow and Tatar devastation was to follow. Control of the routes that led to the Black Sea was of a vital concern for both Jogaila and Vytautas. Trade with Byzantium was particularly prized though trade with the Tatar territories and Islamic lands beyond was also important. The greatest threat to Lithuanian interests was that route which linked Kyiv to the Black Sea. This threat was particularly acute during the days of Vytautas. Lithuania possessed a coastal strip of some 150 kilometres between the mouth of the Dnieper and the River Dniester on the Black Sea. Odesa today is the site of its principal seaport.

However, one victorious battle was yet to bring the Tatars, Vytautas and Jogaila together. This is best described in our introduction to the greatest Lithuanian hero of both Tatars and Lithuanians, Vytautas the Great.

Vytautas (Witold) the Great (1392–1430)

Vytautas the Great, who in Belarus is known as Вялікі Князь Bitaŭt, is the supreme hero, side by side with Khān Toqtamish, among the Tatars of the Baltic region. His unsuccessful exploits are overlooked and his achievements are crystallised in two major acts: the first of these being the resettlement of their ancestors between Vilnius, Białystok and Minsk, and the second, that battle which was known in Western Europe as the Battle of Tannenberg, and in Eastern Europe as the Battle of Grunwald. Amongst the Tatars this battle represents the first occasion in history when Muslim units participated in a major battle fought in Northern Europe.

The battle between the villages of Tannenberg (Grunwald) and Ludwigsdorf was a decisive moment for the Lithuanians and the Poles in their war against the Knights. It followed the revolt of the Žemaitijans in 1409. The Lithuanians were supported by Jogaila, whose kingdom had been invaded by the Knights, in 1409. Many so-called 'Crusading Knights' from Western Europe had joined with the Germans. The latter had expected an attack from two directions. In order to defeat them the joint Lithuanian and Polish forces advanced through Prussia and on 3 June 1410 the army of Vytautas (Witold), or as Muhammad Murād al-Ramzī has mentioned him, 'Wītūft Kināz Līlwā, the Grand Duke of Lithuania', marched to Grodno (Hrodno, now in Belarus) where the allies were joined by units of Tatars, Russians and Czechs. They numbered around 20,000–30,000 soldiers. The army marched deep into Prussia. Their final goal was to reach Marienburg (Malbork), the great fortress and capital of the Knights. The Order assembled some 20,000 soldiers. Each assembled side joined in battle before dawn on 15 July. At one point the Lithuanians tactically withdrew. The battlefield was ever afterwards known as Tannenberg or Grunwald. Jogaila gave the signal to commence battle. Vytautas was at the forefront and mounted upon his steed. The fighting continued for ten hours. At the close of that day the Knights had been routed, having suffered grievous losses including the death of Ulrich von Jungingen, the Grand Master. After burying the dead, the alliance continued their march to Marienburg, but the giant fortress was semingly impregnable and disease had begun to spread amongst the allies. Vytautas withdrew and Jogaila, who was the formal commander-in-chief, followed him. Following the peace treaty, signed in Toruń on 1 February 1411, Vytautas became the master of Žemaitija (Samogitja) and Sūdva and the Orders were no longer a threat to the Lithuanians.

Tatar participation in the engagement was significant. They were led by Jalāl al-Dīn, son of Toqtamish Khān, whom Muhammad Murād al-Ramzī refers to, in his *Talfīq al-Akhbār*, as 'daring, bold and hot-tempered'. Four years after his participation in the battle the Tatar warrior was killed by an arrow that was lodged between his ribs. His slayer was a Tatar, one of the fellow Tatars who were at that time fighting among themselves.

Vytautas and the Tatars as they appear in the works of Ghillebert de Lannoy (1386–1462)

Some insight into the life in Lithuania in the days of Vytautas (Witold) and his relations with the Tatars, both in Lithuania and in the Black Sea region, may be read in the writings of Ghillebert de Lannoy (1386–1462), traveller, diplomat and moralist, who visited Lithuania and who met the allies of Vytautas amongst the Tatars near the approaches to the Crimea, and, later, at Salkhat within the peninsula itself.[10] Attracted by the thought of participating in a new Crusade, the journeys that he undertook led him into the lands of the Northern Crusade, lands which had suffered exceedingly from pillages, burning of villages and rustling of livestock. Ghillebert came to the area only four years after the Battle of Tannenberg (Grunwald). In 1414 he visited Vilnius. On route, between Dunaburg (Dimmebourg) and the Lithuanian capital he stopped at Svenzjany, which he referred to as 'Court-le-roy'.[11] Following this and after a journey of seven leagues, he entered deeper into Lithuania. He described it as an empty country of villages, great lakes and forests. Upon his arrival in Vilnius (Wilne), he described it as dominated by a lofty castle on a mountain in which, both externally and internally, wooden structures and fittings were prominent. His is clearly a description of the 'Castle of Gediminas'. He also describes the walled fortifications beneath it and the river that wound its way through a narrow town of meagre wooden houses. Only a few visible churches were built of brick.[12] Ecclesiastical clergy were few in contrast to the fine towns and the lordly realm of the German Order in Prussia and in Livonia. The Lithuanians spoke their own tongue. They let their hair hang loose over their shoulders whilst the womenfolk wore a simple dress recalling that worn by the women in Picardy.[13] Two sisters of the wife of Vytautas (Witold) resided in Vilnius.

On his way back to Prussia, Ghillebert de Lannoy passed through Trakai (Trancquenne).[14] It was a wooden built, a cottage filled and an unwalled town. One of its castles was built of wood and clay near to the lake. The other castle was situated on an island in the middle of a second lake. It had been recently constructed and it was built in brick 'à la manière de France'. Ghillebert was struck by the number of the

Tatars who lived in villages just outside Trakai. They paid tribute and were 'Sarassins, sans avoir rien de la loy de Jhésucrist'. They spoke the Tatar language.[15] Other nationalities lived in Trakai, including Germans, Lithuanians, Russians and a great number of Jews, each one speaking his language.[16] It was the principal seat of Vytautas (Witold) himself. The latter undertook to offer hospitality to his guests and he ensured their safe conduct throughout his realm at his own expense. Ghillebert praised his might having subdued twelve or thirteen kingdoms by his sword. Vytautas had ten thousand men within his cavalry unit. Trakai had other peculiar sights to see. These included an enclosed park for wild beasts, the meat of which was sold, also asses and horses, elks and moose-deer.

Vytautas and the Tatars were to appear later within the narrative of Ghillebert de Lannoy. It was in the part of the journey of Ghillebert that took him through parts of Russia, through districts which he passed, and, in particular with the town of Salkhat (Starjyi Krym), the Tatar centre within the Crimean peninsula. Stasys Samalavičius has referred to the interests of Vytautus in these regions:

> Lithuania had trade relations with the territories ruled by the Tatars too. As the trade route between the Black Sea and Kiev was dangerous, many military posts were established to guard it. Due to these measures trade became much safer in Vytautas' times. Some fords across the rivers were known by the name of Vytautas. Those names were still used in the seventeenth century. A peninsula in the Crimea is called to this day the Lithuanian Peninsula (Litovski Poluostrov) in Russian.[17]

On his way, in 1421, Ghillebert stopped in a locality called Kamenich (Kamenich), 'en Russie', and Volynie. He met a gathering of women who were accompanied by a Tatar Duke and a large number of 'dukes', 'ducesses' and knights. Fulfilling his mission of peace to Vytautas as the representative of two Christian kings, he presented words of peace from the King of France and a gift of jewels from the King of England. On three occasions, Ghillebert was seated at the high table. He was placed next to the Duchess (Juliana, the second wife of Jogaila) and the Saracen Duke of Tartary[18] with a beard that extended to his knees. He also wore a headscarf. Two ambassadors were ushered into his presence: one from Novgorod, the other from Pskov. Rich presents were presented by servants with their heads bowed to the floor before the Duke. The latter gave to Ghillebert letters to present to the Turks, on his way, letters that were written in Tatar script and in the Tatar tongue, also in Russian and in Latin. Ghillebert was to be accompanied by two Tatars, as well as by Russians and Vlachs. He was informed that he could not pass over the Danube due to the current warfare there. The Duke himself was to join the King of Poland and the King of the Turks against the King of Hungary. Upon his departure, Ghillebert was presented with two silk robes, called soubes. These were sable fur-lined cloaks (pelisses), other silk raiments, four horses, three or four cylindrical peaked military hats, each with a plume, and ten head scarves, four pairs of Russian tasses, namely stuffs used as cover for folds in suits of armour, bows, arrows and Tatar quivers, three scarlet embroidered tasses, a hundred old ducats and twenty-five silver units that totalled one hundred ducats. Ghillebert refused to accept all these gifts with the plea that his faith was being attacked by the Hussites who had already received the support of Vytautas and who were seeking the support of Jogaila who was shortly to despatch an emperor to oppose Sigismund of Luxemburg. The Duchess, the wife of his host, sent Ghillebert a golden fillet and a Tatar florin to wear around his neck for his livery. Other gifts of a similar kind are listed including gifts for his clerk to be conveyed to the King of England. Silk cloth was also presented to five gentlemen who had accompanied him.[19]

Ghillebert's journeyings within the realm of Vytautas was to take him into the Crimea. He sent gifts by sea ahead of him to Kaffa (Theodosia), while he, and his company, travelled overland from Romania, through the 'Desert of Tartary' for eighteen days, crossing the Dniester and Dnieper on his way. Near the banks of the latter he met a young Tatar Duke who was a friend and vassal of Vytautus, 'amy et serviteur au duc Witholt'.[20] Here was a large village. It was Tatar inhabited, subject to Vytautas, an assemblage of men, women and children who had no proper dwellings to shelter them. The Duke was called Jambo. Ghillebert was fed on sturgeon and a sauce made from berries and olive oil or wine. After this sojourn, Ghillebert and his companions were transported by boat over the river.[21] Misfortunes lay in their path. Ghillebert lost all his horses, his men, his interpreters, Tatars and guides, up to a total of twenty-two men, all lost, during a single day and a night. This was due to savage and hungry wolves. They devoured his horses overnight as he was resting in the desolate forests. They pursued his men for a distance of three leagues. On the following day, on account of God's grace, 'miraculous pilgrimages' and searches undertaken by his men who were left with him, he was able to find all the interpreters and guides, and a loyal Tatar, who went in pursuit of his horses. As if by a miracle, he came across them due to a sole horse that had been in the company of a mare whom he found to be quietly pasturing together. The Tatar mounted in order to find the others. The name of that Tatar was Gzooyloos. He was a loyal guide whom Ghillebert praised for the way that he carried out his duties, and who, after having found his horses, felt responsible for snatching them and gathering them together and bringing them back to him. They had nigh lost faith in their survival in these forests and desert stretches since they had reckoned the nearest town to be seven days journey away from their location.

Only a short while after their departure Ghillebert was faced with another adventure. It happened while he was on his way to an 'Emperor of Tartary', who also was a friend of Vytautas (Witold). He was resident in the Crimean town of Kaffa and was titled 'Emperor of Salkhat (Salhat)', today Stary Krym. Ghillebert was acting as an ambassador and he was carrying gifts from Vytautas himelf. At two days distance from Kaffa he was ambushed by sixty-four mounted Tatars. They had been hiding in the reeds.[22] They intended to take him prisoner. This had been caused by the quite recent decease of the 'Emperor of Salkhat' and now there was a mighty issue of succession facing the Tatars of that part of Tartary and the Great Khān of the Golden Horde. It was the appointment of a new emperor, each party having his own client, and had taken up arms in that country. Ghillebert found himself in great danger. The worst outcome did not happen on that day to him nor to his men who were wearing the hats and liveries of Vytautas (Witold). The Tatars who had ambushed them were men who had been subjects of the deceased Emperor of Salkhat. He had been a great friend of Vytautas (Witold). They liberated Ghillebert and his companions after the latter had given them gold and silver, bread, wine and sable. They guided them on their way by another route from Salkhat to Samiette. They travelled without any rest or break until they reached Kaffa (Theodosia). Now they had reached Genoese territory. The Genoese received the party with pomp and with great bounty and hospitality. Ghillebert was placed aboard a ship and he arrived safely in Constantinople.[23]

The above abridged account of the narrative gives us much insight into the realm of Vytautas, the level of culture in Vilnius, his capital, the individuality of his seat of power in Trakai and the presence of the Tatars in Lithuania. The account also reveals the span of the fame, military control, and diplomatic alliances of Vytautas within Eastern Europe, and especially amongst the Tatars on the routes and along the banks of the rivers leading to the Crimea. The account explains why the Tatars settled in Belarus, Lithuania and Poland have over the centuries raised Vytautas into the status of a national hero and thus linked forever with their ancestors, Toqtamish and Jalāl al-Dīn. In the same way, the Qipchāq

Karaims of Trakai have joined with the Tatars in honouring Vytautas the Great.

Jurgita Šiaučiūnaitė-Verbickienė has analysed the question of the Tatars who were both foes and allies within the Grand Duchy of Lithuania.[24] They were a unique paradox, both as Tatars and as Muslims, within the communities of the Duchy. Their rôle had diametrically opposed stereotypes within Lithuanian society. On the one hand, they were settled, free to practise their faith and to serve in a military capacity or as landowners. They were also increasingly tradesmen and even bureaucrats and high-ranking military officers, with their own heraldry and coats of arms. But, as has also been seen, they were formidable enemies, who at times raided Lithuania and Poland, and, at other times served as allies.

On a larger scale, Lithuania was confronted by the Golden Horde. The raid by Algirdas was an outcome of this. Hence, control of the lands of Russia, of Kiev in particular, was a necessity for the Lithuanian Dukes and for their successors. The commercial route to the East that led to the world of Byzantium and later to the Ottoman territories, in the Near and Middle East, was of a major importance. Mention has been made of the battle of Sinie Vody, in 1363, and the unhappy engagement at Vorskala in 1399. Harassment of southern Lithuania, of Kiev, of Podlia and Volynia was a danger. Vytautas at times had to obey the Pope's demands for a crusade against the Tatars. Between 1505 and 1522 extra fortifications were built around Vilnius to ward off Tatar attacks. Yet, paradoxically, the Tatar gate in the city was probably given that name because Tatars were its defenders. As time passed, diplomacy superseded military raids and major battles. Diplomatic relations with the Crimean Khānate were established and Tatar scribes and clerks were employed in the ducal chancery and in the diplomatic service. Tatar missives were sent to the Crimea at a time when the Tatars in residence were forgetting their Qipchāq language which was to survive amongst the Karaims.

Jurgita Šiaučiūnaitė-Verbickienė has mentioned that Ibrahim Timirchin, Marshal and man of letters, who was an active participant in diplomatic exchanges between the Grand Duchy and the Golden Horde frequently resided in the Crimea. It was also customary to send officials of Tatar descent on diplomatic exchanges to the Crimean Khānate. An example of one who took part in these diplomatic missions was the princely family of the Glinskis, who were shown respect in the Duchy and among the Tatars. They traced their descent to a Tatar nobleman named Aleksa, or Alexander, who was the owner of the manor of Glinsk. He had been converted to Christianity. Tatar clerks who were later called 'Arab clerks' were employed in the affairs of the dual chancery into the eighteenth century.[25]

Figure 2 The Lithuanian Vytis.

3. The settlement of the Qipchāq Tatars and the Karaims in Belarus, Lithuania and Poland

Their life and co-existence with Paganism, Catholicism and Orthodoxy during the age of the Grand Duchy of Lithuania and in later centuries

'It is no small person with whom you propose to deal.'

'But it is over a small matter', remarked Nicholas of Longwood prudently. 'For whether Tochtamysz or some Kutluk rules over the sons of Belial far away in the tenth kingdom, what is that to us?'

'Tochtamysz would receive the Christian faith', answered Macko.

'He might receive it, or he might not. Can we believe these "dogs" brothers who don't acknowledge Christ?'

The Teutonic Knights[1]

This memory of Vytautas (Witold) is highly revered amongst us. He did not order us to forget the Prophet, whose name we honour, together with those of our Caliphs, as we turn in the direction of the Holy Places. We swore an oath upon our swords to love the Lithuanians when the fate and destiny of war brought us to their homeland, and they said to us upon entering into this treaty, 'This land, these waters, this sand and these forests will be shared between us. Our children do not neglect the memory of Vytautas. Near the salt lakes (that is to say, in the Crimea and in the Qipchāq steppes) they know that we are not strangers in your country'.

The Tatar petition addressed to Sigismund I (1519)

The name of this monarch, who was like a pillar of Islam in the land of the unbelievers, is Vytautas, and the memory of him has been preserved to this day, for every year we celebrate a day dedicated exclusively to the memory of that king.

Risāla-i Tatar-i Leh (1558)

The Story of the Lithuanian and Polish Tatars

The story of the Lithuanian and Polish Tatars (the Tatars of Lehistan, or the Lipqa Tatars)[2] began in the days of the Golden Horde, when Khān Batu established his capital at Saray on the Volga. This city was an important centre for Muslim culture and Islamic life. Saray was a city of scholars, Sufis and poets. It has been made familiar to us in medieval English literature through the verses of Geoffrey Chaucer's 'The Squire's Tale':[3]

> At Tsarev in the land of Tartary
> There dwelt a king at war with Muscovy
> Which brought the death of many a doughty man
> This noble king was known as Cambuskan.

The latter half of the fourteenth century also brought about the formation of the Grand Duchy of Lithuania. It included what is today a large part of southern Lithuania, much of Belarus and eastern Poland. It expanded widely. For a while it dominated all the territories that extended from the Baltic Sea to Wallachia in Romania, it advanced into the Ukraine and, for a while, extended as far as the Crimean peninsula. It also extended to the East to the Dvina River and, at times, to the east of Smolensk and even to Moscow, itself.

The Lithuanians were recent converts to Latin Christianity. In 1386, Duke Jogaila embraced Catholicism, in Kraków. He married Queen Jadwiga, and, in 1387, Lithuania also officially embraced the faith.[4] However, alliances with the Golden Horde Tatars had preceded this event, at a time when the Lithuanians were either converting to Christianity, by the sword of the Teutonic Knights, or, peacefully, in the urban and trading centres on account of the settlement of German and other merchants and through the preaching of monks and missionaries. Yet, despite this, many Lithuanians remained stubborn in their paganism that had shaped their cultural identity for many centuries. They had few doctrinal reasons for displaying any special hostility, nor a special empathy, either, towards Muslims, nor for that matter towards Judaism, and especially towards the Mosaic Karaite sect.[5]

The interfaith dialogue between Tatar Islam and Karaism[6] had lasted for a long a period of time – al-Qirqisānī, the Karaite, in the tenth century, had stated in his book, the *Book of Lights and Watch Towers* (*Kitāb al-Anwār wa'l-Marāqib*), that Jesus was a righteous man (*kāna rajulan ṣāliḥan*) and that the Prophet of the Arabs, Muhammad, had been sent by

God to rescue his people from the love of riches. Both Karaites and Tatars in their origin were Qipchāq – speakers from the Eastern steppes. There were cultural influences that had brought them very close together.

The Muslim Tatars found the Lithuanians to be polytheists (*mushrikūn*, or, *kuffār*) or kinsmen of the *Majūs*, that is to say, they classified them as 'Vikings', or, as 'fire worshippers', adopting the vocabulary of religious terms that had been accepted by Muslim scholars and by writers in the Muslim lands of the Middle East over many centuries.[7]

In 1220, the Bishop of Paderborn wrote, 'They honour nymphs, mountain spirits, werewolves and they worship virgin forests.' In a land without mountains this makes curious reading, however, in many other respects it captures the character of much ancient Lithuanian religion. The centre of devotion was the cosmological tree (the roofed pole is its sole survivor). This tree was associated with a sacred hill (*alkakanlis*) and with holy rivers (*alkupis*). Many of the religious beliefs were common to their pagan Latvian and Prussian neighbours and also to some of the Slavs.

Reincarnation was commonly believed. Souls (*veles*) might ride to the Milky Way or might sail in heavenly boats. The soul, or psyche, was the etherealisation of the deceased. There was some variation in regard to the disposal of the body. It was either cremated, or buried, or it was frozen. Duke Algirdas was cremated with his weapons and with eighteen horses, in 1377. Duke Kestutis was burned in a like manner, in 1382. Even as late as 1413 – when Muslim Tatars were already settled in the land – there was a cremation of a body in full dress. In 1336, bodies were cremated after the decapitation of an entire tribe when they were confronted by the onslaught of the Teutonic Knights who had threatened them with a forced conversion. Fire was sacred. It was adored, and it was only extinguished on the eve of the midsummer festival. Then it was rekindled. Bloody human sacrifices took place on occasions, and house burials were to be found alongside common cremation.

Perkūnas was Lithuania's High God. He was the enemy of evil and the god of thunder. He was similar to the Scandinavian Thor, and he was armed with lightning bolts. Stone axes were the missiles of Perkūnas. His portrait was conceived of as a copper-bearded man who was armed with an axe. He rode in a drawn chariot. He lived in a castle in the sky.

In addition to other gods and goddesses, the Lithuanians believed in many dievas (*dievaitis*, indicating 'god', 'idol' or 'image') some of whom demanded human sacrifices or offerings which were placed at *alkas* (shrines in groves and especially under oak trees). Shamans (*krivis*) were important members of society. Krive was named as a high priest, or 'pope', in Prussia, in 1326. These Shamans also fulfilled the role of priests. They carried elk-headed staves. There were also priestesses who tended the sacred fire, the Vaidilutes. Archeological excavations have revealed astronomically orientated shrines. There was much use of oak wood in the construction of religious edifices. Duke Mindaugas nominally embraced Christianity, for cultural and for political reasons. In 1251, he built a stone cathedral, in Vilnius. Later, he forsook Christianity altogether and the cathedral was converted into a pagan shrine. In 1387, Lithuania was officially 'baptised'. This shrine was replaced by a Gothic cathedral that was built on top of its former pagan site.

Elements of Lithuanian paganism survived into the seventeenth century. There are some traces of it even today. In considering what we mean by 'paganism' (*pagonybe*) one has to bear in mind that:

a   There were degrees and shades of superstition and there were customs that varied in time and in place. These co-existed with Christianity, with Judaism and, later, with Islam. For example, the north-western Samogitians, who lived in the region of the Baltic Sea, were particularly stubborn in their paganism. Whilst the southern and eastern Lithuanians believed in 'higher' deities of a varied power and function, the pagan culture of Samogitia centred on beliefs about the Underworld and about the life of the dead who were there. Even after their very late adoption of Christianity, they continued the rituals of pagan days, the adoration of fire, of grass snakes and the woods.
b   As in other countries, the monkish writers have given us a distorted picture of 'paganism', as they saw it,
c   There is frequently some confusion between 'belief', folk tale, custom and ritual. Identity was intertwined with local factors and a local situation. In the larger towns, such as Vilnius and Kaunas, where German and other merchants resided, or, in areas which were occupied and were forcibly converted by the Teutonic Order, or, where Eastern Orthodoxy prevailed, living side by side, with 'pagan' peasants, there was some shading within beliefs. There is no evidence to suggest that sophisticated rulers, such as Mindaugas, or Gediminas, were unacquainted with the so-called 'higher religions'. Some assimilation of Perkūnas into God, into Jehovah, Tenrai, and Allāh is more than likely in medieval Lithuania.

Paganism of a similar type also prevailed in what is, today, Belarus. That too was to form a part of the Grand Duchy of Lithuania. It had its capital at Novogrudok (Novogrodek). In the tenth century, the ancestors of the Belarusians were among a number of tribes from the eastern Slavs. Branches of the Kryvichi intermarried with several of the tribes of the Balts, including the Yatviangians. A number of their gods were nearly identical in their functions. The river Niamunas, or Neman, flowed through their territories and it gave its name to the goddess of war. Kupala was an ancient water goddess. The mixed tribes acknowledged Yaryla as the god of the sun, who was celebrated in the season of spring. Kupala survived in the name of the summer solstice, Kupalle, 'She who bathes'. At a later date, this festival was Christianised. Many of the celebrations were remarkably similar to those that were observed and celebrated by the Lithuanian Balts. The feast of Dzyady took place in April, or at the end of October. It honoured the dead. Food and drink were placed upon their graves. Christianity adopted a celebration, called Kaliady, which was observed during the Christmas season. Certain locations, particularly where giant rocks had been deposited during the ice age, came to be recognised as holy places. Some of these boulders provided altars for human sacrifice.

Similarities between pagan Slav practice and those of the Lithuanian Balts may also be observed in the rituals in honour of Piarun, the Slav god of thunder who was clearly the same deity as Perkūnas amongst the Lithuanians. Portrayed as a tall man with black hair on his head, though with a long and golden beard, he held arrows in one hand and a rainbow in the other. The stones that fell to earth as chipped boulders from his mill littered the ground. Some were very large. In Belarus these are known as 'Piarun stones' and, in pagan times they were frequently used for sacrifice.

Another stone was attributed to the god Volas, god of prosperity and cattle herders. Such stones are to be found in small clearings in the woods. In pagan times the stones were encircled by the skulls of cattle that were hung up from adjacent trees. The pagan priest, who participated in a fire ritual, cured sundry ailments and predicted the future. These beliefs long survived the arrival of Christianity. Other gods had their sacred stones: Dazhdzhbog, the god of the warmth of the sun, as opposed to the sun's disk, Yaryla (Yur'ya). Stones that were dedicated to Dazhdzhbog were sacral grain mills for making sacrificial bread. Stone idols were common in the Baltic lands and in Belarus and Poland. Known as 'babas' they took the form of a rounded cross. Symbols frequently adorned sacred stones. Often they were stars, or boats and stylised people. Such stones conceivably influenced popular beliefs among the Muslim Tatars. Large stones in honour of Vytautas are to be found in the yard adjoining

Keturiasdešimt mosque, in Lithuania. Ancient gravestones in Tatar cemeteries, in all the countries mentioned, take the shape of, and in certain instances actually once were, ancient ritual stones and boulders.

The Tatar settlement

The éntente which was concluded between the Tatars of the Golden Horde and Gediminas, Duke of Lithuania (Didysis Kunigaikstis), a little while after he came to power in 1315, was to mark the beginning of the settlement of Muslims within the heart of Lithuania. The contrast with the forced conversions of the Teutonic Order could hardly have been greater. The Lithuanians may then have totalled no more than one quarter of a million souls. In 1319, they formed an alliance with the Golden Horde. The major Tatar settlement took place later. According to the noted authority on this period of Lithuanian history, S.C. Rowell:

> Under Khan Uzbek (1313–42), the Golden Horde reached its zenith, transferred its central administration to Sarai Berke on the banks of the Volga and converted to Mohammedanism. In Lithuania, however, there were no Tatar settlements. The first reliable evidence we have of Tatars settling in Lithuania is the case of Tokhtamysh's allies who sought asylum with Vytautas in 1398. The legend of Tatar settlement in Lithuania in 1324 is false.[8]

In 1398, Qipchāq-speaking Tatars and Karaims from the Crimea, from the Qipchāq steppe (Dašt-i Qipchāq) and from the Volga region were brought, sometimes as captives, in small numbers into lands in specific regions in order to stiffen the strength of the Duchy of Lithuania, which was under severe threat. This situation prevailed between 1380 and 1412.

Parallels can be found to this situation in other regions of the medieval world. David IV, the builder of Caucasian Georgia during the twelfth century, recruited a standing army of mercenaries from amongst the Ossetians and the Qipchāqs. His wife was a Qipchāq princess. Fortresses were built in the Daryal which gave David direct access to his allies in the north. About the year 1118, David formed a special guard of 5,000 Qipchāq slaves, who were converts to Christianity, and he introduced through the Daryal pass a very great number of Qipchāq families whom he settled in depopulated districts of Georgia and Armenia which he had reconquered. These Qipchāq settlers provided him with 40,000 trained warriors. He had problems with them from time to time, but they furnished him with a force that enabled him to master the Seljuk Turks and his own baronage.⁹ The Qipchāqs, in Georgia, had been converted to Christianity, whereas the Tatars in pagan and Catholic Lithuania were resolutely loyal to their Muslim faith.

From the earliest period of their settlement the Tatars were to be established in villages and towns in the border regions, bounded by Kaunas, in Lithuania, as it is today, Białystok in Poland, and Grodno and Minsk, in Belarus.[10] In the fourteenth century, however, they were particularly concentrated around Trakai and Vilnius, where three hundred Karaite Qipchāqs were allowed to settle in the residence of Vytautas in Trakai castle. Later, Tatars settled in, or near, Asmena, Aukstadvaris, Semeliskes, Butrimonys and Alytus. The Tatar princes were housed close to the seat of the Duchy. They were obliged to perform military service for twelve weeks, armed with swords at their own cost. In return for this service, they were exempted from taxation. Over the centuries, the Tatar nobility was to become an integral part of the Lithuanian and Polish aristocratic social structure. Tatar agricultural and artisan settlements were generally to be found in towns and villages, each with its commune (*Djemat*) and its mosque. The Tatar nobility had its own serfs. They were able to marry non-Muslims and they brought up their offspring in the Muslim faith. Duke Vytautas (Witold), now converted to Christianity, assumed the 'patronage' of the Tatars between 1392 and 1430 and he gave refuge to the exiled Toqtamish Khān and his family and followers. They effectively served him with the Polish–Lithuanian forces most notably, as we have seen, in the battle of Grunwald, or Stebark-Tannenburg (15 July 1410), where the Teutonic Knights were decisively defeated and the myth of the invincibility of the Teutonic Order came to an abrupt end.

The relations with the Tatars of the Golden Horde in the East and towards the South, in part because of this alliance between Vytautas and Toqtamish, were to be far less happy and successful. At times they were potentially disastrous for the unity of Lithuania and Poland. Toqtamish proved to be an unpredictable ally. He was to suffer an ignominious defeat at the hand of Idige (Edigey or Idigu), the ally of Tīmūr. Vytautas backed the cause of Toqtamish, however he was to be defeated by the Eastern Tatars on the Workala on 12 August 1399. Toqtamish, after these events, was condemned to live the life of an adventurer. If we exclude the participation of his son, Jalāal al-Dīn at Grunwald, this long established steppe-orientated alliance drew to its close and the Tatars of the Baltic region were to become ever more isolated from their co-religionists in the greater Tatar world. In 1414, as we have seen, the Bourgogne knight Ghillebert (Guillembert) de Lannoy records that they still spoke the Qipchāq Tatar language. However, it was not destined to survive amongst them, unlike their neighbours, the Karaims, who still speak Qipchāq, today.[11]

The Muslims became integrated. More and more Tatars became burghers and took up civilian careers in Lithuania and in Poland. This policy was to be followed, in general, by the Jagellonian kings of Poland. Centred in Kraków, their aim was to bring the rights of the Tatar nobility into conformity with those of the Catholic Polish nobility. At times, the process bore the marks of the earlier personal agreement made between Toqtamish and Jogaila.[12] It is not surprising that the Polish Tatars of today, with their long record of military service to Poland, throughout the centuries that followed, still take a pride in their genealogies and in their heraldry. Some of this can be traced back to the fifteenth century, if not earlier. Their blood ties, through Hajji Giray of the Crimean Tatars, the descendant of Toqtamish, also made them relations of the rulers of the Crimean Khānate. In 1443, the Tatars of Perekop, Barin and Sirin, whose Khān had died without an heir, sent to Casimir, the grand prince of Lithuania, and requested him to give them Hajji Giray as their Khan. Hajji Giray had been born in Lithuania. In 1428, he had tried to gain the supremacy of the Golden Horde. Having failed in the attempt, he returned to Lithuania. Later he went to the Crimea and from that time, onwards, as an independent ruler, he vacillated between a friendship and an alliance with Lithuania–Poland, on the one hand, and with Muscovite Russia, on the other. The Lithuanian, Polish and Belarusian Tatars have always maintained, as far as they have been able to do so, very close cultural and religious ties with the Crimean Tatars. For some time it was the seat of their Muftiate prior to its establishment in Vilnius in 1925.

Rivalries between the Lehistan Tatars and Russian Kazan Muhammad Murād Ramzī, a Russian Tatar historian's view of the Lithuanian Tatars, their history and their religion[13]

This major Arabic work, the masterpiece of the Russian Tatar Orientalist Muhammad Murād Ramzī, is in Arabic and is entitled, *Talfīq al-akhbār wa-talqīḥ al-āthār fī waqā'i' Qāzān wa-Bulghār wa-Mulūk al-Tatār*.[14] It has received only limited attention despite its massive volume of facts, its broad scope in its original research and its individuality. It is by no means a mere appendix to its better known encyclopaedic predecessor, the work of Shihāb al-Dīn al-Marjānī (1818–89) of Kazan, entitled *Mustafād al-akhbār fī ahwāl Qāzān wa-Bulghār*.[15]

In many pages of Ramzī's work there are nuggets of original and little known historical data, even if much else has been gleaned from others. From his book, one may obtain a comprehensive picture of the cultural roots of the Muslim Tatars, extending from Siberia to the Polish border, and from the Arctic regions to the Black Sea. In Marjānī's master study (both works draw upon Arabic geographical and historical scholarship), the city of Bulghār (to be followed by Kazan) is considered to be the bedrock of Tatar identity. Ramzī's reading of past events is less formalised, less logical, or theoretical. His content may ramble at times, yet it is rich in its diversity. Russian sources and statistics are juxtaposed amid the records of Greek historians. There are many Arabic, Persian and Turkish quotations, wherever these would seem to shed some light, in Ramzī's view, on the ancient and medieval history of all the Tatars. Ramzī explored archaeological sources that were lacking in Marjānī's age. Ramzī was well travelled and his approach was influenced by fashions, in vogue, at the 'fin de siècle'.

The Tatars of Lehistan are mentioned only twice in Ramzī's text. In both instances there is almost nothing to show that the author had any personal acquaintance with Lithuanian or Polish Tatars. Yet, it seems hardly likely that he had never met any of them at all during the course of his lengthy sojourn in the Muslim Holy Places, or in some of the Russian or Middle Eastern centres where he had carried out his research, whether this be in Moscow, or Kazan, or possibly in Istanbul. One page is devoted to Lithuania. At times, Ramzī quotes the historian, Ibn 'Arab Shāh. Referring to the invitation which was given by Duke Vytautas (Witold) to Toqtamish to find a refuge in his Dukedom, he penned:

> The Muslims who are now present in Lehistan are the descendants of the remnants of the soldiery of Toqtamish Khān and the offspring of the Tatars whom Vytautas (Witold) settled there, as has been reported. They chose to settle there when confusion and anarchy had befallen the kingdom of Juchi Khān. Then it came to pass that the 'spiders of forgetfulness' spread their webs over their customs and their tongues with the passing of the ages. Yet, despite that, they have never lost their faith in al-Islām though they have no scholarly knowledge of that faith. They have become submerged in the sea of ignorance amongst an accursed infidelity (*kufr*). They sought the permission of the Sublime Porte to emigrate (*muhājara*) to the Muslim kingdoms. That took place during the reign of Sultan Muhammad IV, mercy and pardon be his, through Selim Giray Khān of the Crimea, in the year 1082/1671. The Khān sent this person to the Sublime Porte. However,

due to the baleful endeavour of some of the vizirs who surrounded his most mighty presence and observing the loss of some personal advantage in accepting the same, there was issued a decree whereby His Excellence announced his rejection and his refusal of that request submitted by them.[16]

Ramzī remarked, elsewhere:

Toqtamish Khān, when he had heard of the dislodgement of Tīmūr from those provinces, assembled his scattered soldiery and his dispersed followers. Now that the Tatars had settled down in the Khānate, he entered the city of Saray without hindrance. He seated himself in the seat of authority and the buttress of the Khānate was exclusively his own. He was without a rival, or an opponent. He sent word to the governors on every side and to those who were in the remote marches, so as to notify them that he had become the Khān, that he now held the supreme power over the kingdom of Batu and that he was an independent ruler as had been the case, hitherto. Nonetheless, he only tarried a short while before Tīmūr Qutlugh [Tīmūr-Kurtluka] went forth to face him. The latter suddenly launched an attack upon Saray. Toqtamish fled from it with his wife and his two sons and with his personal treasury as well as with the people who were of the households of his closest companions.

He set out in order to reach the city of Lwow [Lviv], in the Duchy of Lithuania, and he sought refuge with the governor, Duke (Kināz Litwa) Wītufat (Vytautas). He sought his help against Tīmūr Qutlugh. The aforementioned Vytautas received him gracefully and he honoured his supporters. He was pleased to do so since he was flattered because of the might of the Tatar Khāns who had so astonished Europe, indeed the entire world. He, the most famous amongst them, the most courageous and the toughest in strength, namely, Toqtamish Khān, had fled to him in order to seek for refuge and had sought his help. Vytautas promised him succour and his reinstatement in the Khānate. In his heart, he, Vytautas, had concealed such conceits because of the 'intoxicating vapour' of it all having clouded his brain. He would meet Tīmūr, in battle, through Toqtamish Khān and his followers, Batu's offspring. With that intent, he assembled some of the Tatar tribes, who were hesitant and were perplexed, upon the shore of the Sea of Azov, where Tīmūr had scattered them, having devastated their territory.

Vytautas had settled them in the district of Vilnius. Their descendants are those who remain there to this day, that is to say, the Muslims in the land of Lithuania and Poland, they who are called 'The Tatars', though they have completely forgotten the ethics of the Tatars, their customs and their language. That is on account of the long period of time during which they have sojourned amongst the Lithuanians, the dire fate of protected confessional minorities (*dhimmīs*) who are few in number and who live amidst a people great in number. All that remains of their identity is the name of al-Islām, may God be praised for that.

After this idea had become firmly fixed in the mind of Vytautas, and after vanity had confused his senses, he began to assemble his soldiers and to prepare the wherewithal to wage war and to strike a hard blow. While he was preoccupied so, behold, an ambassador came to him from Tīmūr Qutlugh Khān. He addressed him, acting as the spokesman for Tīmūr, saying, 'Hand over our enemy to us. In times past, he was the greatest of the Khāns and he has now become the greatest of fugitives. Such has always come to pass when times have changed'. Vytautas said to him, 'I shall go to meet Tīmūr Qutlugh Khān and I shall give him my answer in the flesh'.

So he went forth in the direction of the southerly realm of the Tatars. He acted speedily, in the manner of Vladimir Monomakh (1113–25), when he raided the Polovici (Qipchāqs and Cumans). He encountered the Mongol soldiery, who were under the command of Tīmūr Qutlug Khān. That was beyond the rivers Suli and Khur Walim, and he joined battle with them in a place that is called Bur Saqla (Vorskla). It was there that the Mongols were manifestly in favour of making peace. They showed flexibility and they showed an affability towards Vytautas.

Tīmūr Qutlugh Khān said to him, 'What reasons bring you here with your soldiery? I have never entered your country with soldiers'. Vytautas said to him, 'God has given me a readiness and might in order to possess all the land, so pay me the tax (*kharāj*). Become like a son to me, do not become my slave'. Tīmūr Qutlugh Khān sued for peace. He acknowledged the might of Duke Vytautas and his followers until the latter was satisfied by the payment of the sum that had been fixed as an annual tax. This is proved from our historical documents.

But when Vytautas thought of the idea of opening up the route to the East by fighting the Tatars, because of the happenings of past times, he increased the conditions that he had imposed and which have been mentioned. The Tatars placed his emblem, or his private and personal seal, upon their coinage. Vytautas proclaimed that he would no longer protect Toqtamish Khān. This was on the pretext that they had accepted the aforementioned conditions. Tīmūr Qutlugh Khan asked for a delay for three days in order to ponder the matter and to seek for the advice of his companions. He sent gifts and he expressed amiable thoughts to Vytautas and his companions in regard to all this.

Toqtamish was to end his days in exile, probably in Siberia, where he was said to have died at Tumen in 1406. Ramzī's account of events may be compared with those described by George Vernadsky:[17]

The bulk of Vitovt's forces in his steppe campaign of 1399 consisted of the Lithuanian and West Russian army and Toqtamish's Tatars. The Lithuanian–Russian army was well organised and equipped with cannon. The rulers of the Golden Horde were also well prepared for the contest. Instead of waiting for the enemy deep in the steppes, as Subudey had done in 1223, Timur Qutlugh Khan and Edigey decided to advance toward the middle course of the Dnieper in the general direction of Kiev. Early in August 1399 the two armies faced each other on the banks of the Vorskla (a tributary of the Dnieper) probably not far from where the city of Poltava was one day to be built and where Peter the Great would defeat the Swedes in 1709. According to the Nikon Chronicle, Khān Timur-Qutlugh proposed an agreement to Vitovt instead of fighting. Vitovt demanded that the Khān acknowledge himself his vassal and that Vitovt's name appear on the coins of the Golden Horde. Edigey rejected Vitovt's demands on behalf of Timur Qutlugh and, in turn, demanded that his 'tamga' (his clan emblem) be stamped on the Lithuanian coins. There was now no way out but war. A fierce battle raged for several hours. Vitovt's troops seemed on the verge of victory over the main Mongol army commanded by Edigey when Timur Qutlugh Khan's reserve squadrons attacked the Lithuanians from the rear. Toqtamish's Tatars were the first to take to flight, and soon Vitovt's whole army was in confusion. While Vitovt himself succeeded in escaping with a few followers, a great number of Lithuanian–Russian princes perished in the battle, among them Andrew of Polatsk, Dimitri of Briansk, and 'Dimitri Korlatovich' (Bobrok-Volynsky). 'And who could count all the Lithuanians, and the Russians, the Poles, and the Germans slain on that day?' commented the chronicler bitterly.

It is hardly surprising that the Tatars of Lithuania and Poland, who claim their descent from the supporters of Toqtamish, should have exalted Vytautas to the rank of a national 'godfather' for their exiled ancestor. This balanced the sponsorship of Edigey, by Tīmūr Qutlugh Khān. Edigey was to become the great rival of Toqtamish in Tatar heroic literature. Edigey enjoyed a high esteem in the oral literature of Tatarstan after the fifteenth century.

The predecessors of Shihāb al-Dīn al-Marjānī saw most Tatars in Eurasia as being heirs to the sophisticated culture of Bulghār, Saray and the Zolotaya Orda (Golden Horde) who had been greatly influenced by the Islamic culture of the Mamlūks, of Iran and also from the peoples of Central Asia. The Nogais and the Qipchāq were amongst these Tatars. This pan-Tatar point of view is also to the fore in Ramzī's book. However a pan-Islamic argument is often preferred.[18]

When Ramzī wrote his history, it was in an age that had been preceded by one of violent Russian suppression of Muslim communities in the Caucasus and in Central Asia. Wahhābī influences were also in vogue. In 1829, the Avar Daghistani, Ghāzi Mulla, had declared, 'A Muslim may obey the Sharī'a , but all his giving of alms (*zakāt*), all his daily prayers (*ṣalāt*) and his ablutions, all his pilgrimages to Mecca, are as nothing if a Russian casts his eye upon them. Your marriages are not lawful, your children are bastards, while one single Russian is left to live in your lands.'

Marjānī, the Jadīdist reformer, stressed high Tatar culture whereas Ramzī tended to stress Muslim fidelity and Christian infidelity (*kufr*). The Tatars of Lehistan were still 'believers' – 'God be praised' – to quote him, however, he lamented the loss of Islamic culture, their knowledge of Arabic, or of Turkish, and he clearly saw that that their long-term assimilation into Catholic and Orthodox Europe would be a sad compensation and end in disaster. In his view it would debarr them forever from a place in the future World of Islam. Happily, their re-acceptance within the bosoms of the faithful would be a marked turn of fortune in their history and in their leadership during the course of the twentieth century. Ramzī also saw the history of Toqtamish's alliance with Vytautas as but one ephemeral stage in the timeless saga of Tatar heroism. This saga was centred upon a saga of winner and loser. It pitted Vytautas and Toqtamish against Edigey (Idigu) and Tīmūr-Qutlig Khān. Toqtamish and Edigey were both warriors. Savage tyrants at times, yet they were receptive to many kinds of Islamic influences – part Mujāhid, part Sufi. This Tatar folk memory still extends from Lehistan to western Siberia.

Edigey, according to the historian, Ibn 'Arab Shāh, became a Muslim hero in his lifetime. Strange tales and reports of super-human exploits were coined about him (*wa-lahu hikāyāt 'ajība wa-nawādir gharība*), as they were about Sari Saltuq, an earlier charismatic figure of the steppes. Edigey's piety was greatly praised, 'he made the Book (Qur'ān) his *Sunna* and the words of the scholars (*'ulamā'*) were a medium of access (*dharī'a*) between him and his God'.

However, Ibn 'Arab Shāh was equally forceful in expressing his opinion that the protracted and seasonal skirmishes and raids between Toqtamish and Edigey were the prime cause for the desertification of the steppe to the north and to the east of the Crimean peninsula. The tidal war of attrition brought disaster to the Tatar princes, 'the eyes of tranquillity were like the sleepy eye-lids of the age which was blind to such peace-making'. In summer, the steppe was a dust bowl of the wind that carried sand. It obscured the routes of travellers who quickly lost their way. In winter, great drifts of snow hid the landmarks that they knew. The defeated nomads dispersed and became refugees. Some sought refuge with the Byzantines or with the Russians. They fell into the clutches of 'infidels', both Christian and Muslim. It was a ragged band of exiles and captives who sought asylum in pagan and Christian Lithuania and Poland. Some fugitives had fled from the militant Islamic policy of Khān Uzbek. They were a small wave that was to precede a larger wave that brought Toqtamish, his family and his followers into the Baltic regions.[19]

Like Marjānī's mammoth study, Ramzī's work also has a list of eminent Tatar scholars and aspiring *imāms*, of humble origins, who travelled abroad from Russia. Not all of them came from Tatarstan. They went to Central Asia, the Caucasus and the Middle East and a few came to today's Belarus and to Lithuania. Many of them were to return as *Qāḍīs*, teachers and founders of madrasas in poorly served localities. Disciplines, such as Qur'ān reading in accordance with established rules and intonation (*tajwīd*), jurisprudence (*fiqh*), poetry (*shi'r*) – many of the Tatar *imāms* and scholars were poets and skilled in figurative speech, metaphor and trope (*majāz*), Qur'anic recitation (*qirā'a*), canonic law (*Sharī'a*), epistolatory art and style (*rasā'il*), double hemistiched verse (*mathnawī*), mathematics, astronomy, Prophetic tradition (*ḥadīth*) and even Sufi liturgical practices, in assemblies (*samā'*), such were amongst the many arts, skills and vocations which were to be learnt in such major Islamic centres as Mecca and Medina, Cairo, Beirut, Damascus, Baghdad, Istanbul, Kabul and in India (especially in Lahore and Delhi).

Other centres were under Russian influence, or direct control, such as Daghestan, Bukhara, Samarqand, Tashkent and Khwarazim and to a lesser degree Astrakhan and Aqqerman (Aq Kirman), near Odesa. The latter was to be a centre for the Baltic Tatars from Lehistan. Ramzī mentions that novices and scholars of mature years came from localities as far afield as Kazan, Bashqurd, Ufa and Siberian towns. When they had returned, these men founded their own centres in today's Tatarstan, and beyond, and they wrote works that applied Islamic principles and instructions which were based upon their studies.[20]

Ramzi wrote his book at the turn of the century. Early in the twentieth century the learning that had been acquired by the scholars whom he mentioned was being published abroad. The Kazan Missionary Committee of Lithuania and Poland was a part of that mission.

Between 1905 and 1910, Lithuania and Poland were a mission field for Tatar 'proselytism' which sought to awaken the faith and it was inspired by the Islamic revival movement in Tatar society in the East. It was spearheaded by devout Mullas and Beys (rich merchants and land owners) in Kazan and the Volga region in particular. The goal of the Kazan Tatar Missionary Committee was to encourage the revival of Tatar Muslim identity in the two Baltic countries, notwithstanding the fact that the seeds of a renaissance were already beginning to flower afresh in the literary, religious and scholarly circles in the communities of the north-western Tatars. The Kazan Missionary Committee had two chief programmes: to enrol Tatars in local madrasas and to despatch teachers from the Volga region to the Baltic area. This interest of the Kazan Tatars in the religious life of the Tatars of Lehistan was to continue until the First World War. Tatar refugees from the Baltic area, who had sought asylum in Kazan, were also given help. Ramzī draws attention to the great number of Tatar scholars who were affiliated to Sufi brotherhoods during their sojourn in the Islamic East, especially the Naqshabandiyya and the Qādiriyya.

Mme Olga de Lébédeff, in her *Abrégé de l'Histoire de Kazan*, offered to the participants at the XIIth Congress of Orientalists, in Rome, 1899 (pp. 85–9) an insight into the training of *imāms* in *madrasas*, five in Orenburg, two in Ufa, two in Kergaly, several in the Crimea and in the Caucasus and three in Kazan. 'The Tatars are very pious and even fanatic. There are some "Nakchabendy" dervishes in Kazan but they have no convent.'

The end of her remark, 'they have no convent', they have no *tekke* nor *zāwiya* is significant. It should be stressed that in assessing the character of Islam in the Baltic region one should be wary of the assumption that because al-Islām – both popular and scholarly – in a Muslim community (*umma*) is without:

46   Islam in the Baltic

a   Brotherhoods, orders, sub-orders (*turuq* and *ṭawā'if*)
b   Lodges (*tekkes*, or *zāwiyas*)
c   Communal gatherings for worship and prayer (*zikr*, *dhikr*, *ḥaḍra*, etc)
d   A long established chain of initiation and spiritual induction by a master to form a chain of initiates (*silsila*),

that, as its consequence, Sufism is conspicuous by its absence from the Islamic life and practice of that community. This is particularly relevant in a Sunnite congregation (as in Bosnia, Lithuania and Poland) where, as always, especially under strong Ottoman influences, remote though they may be, any heterodox elements disguised as Sufism, which one would expect to permeate and corrupt the popular beliefs, could be severely checked by a higher authority in order to enforce orthodoxy and conformity.

The debt owed to Sufism in the Islamic traditions and in the religious life of the Lehistan Tatars has not been thoroughly explored, though some positive opinions have been published by Selim Chazbijewicz. These have attracted some attention in Poland. An assessment of the degree of the Sufi contribution to Tatar life in Belarus, Lithuania and Poland will be one of the subjects in the next chapter.

Before closing those pages of Ramzī's great book where he comments on the poverty of Islamic practices amongst the Baltic Tatars of his age, one point needs to be made. He came from the Tatar community for whom Edigey embodied both Islamic and Tatar standards of idealism. Toqtamish hardly lived up to such standards and the portrait of him in his masterpiece would, for the Baltic Tatars, seem to be close to a caricature and an injustice. Vytautas is mocked, his vanity is said to have been the cause of his defeats. For the Tatars of Lehistan and for the Karaites he was once, and still is, a folk hero. He had paved the way, and so had others, for the integration of the Qipchāqs into societies that looked towards the West, towards a dialogue with Christendom, and it has eventually assured them a place within the peoples of the new Europe. In this respect, Ramzī had a contemporary, and, indeed, shared with him much of his thought and his critical views in regard to the Baltic Tatars. That contemporary of his was Hāfiz Jahānshāh b. 'Abd al-Jabbār al-Nīzghārūtī al-Hājjītārkhānī, the author of *Tārīkh-i Astārkhān* (The History of Astrakhan) which was published in that city in 1907. Amidst the text, admirably analysed by Allen J. Frank, there are two chapters which are concerned with the contrast between the faith of Islam among the Qazaqs and among the Polish Tatars. Jahānshāh argued that the presence of Russian missionaries in their midst in fact enhanced their Islamic consciousness, compelling the nomad parents to give a proper Islamic education to their children, including the demands of the *Sharī'a*, in contrast to Poland, where, in his opinion, piety was weak. The Polish Tatars were forced to use the Polish and Russian languages, having forgotten their Turkic tongue. He also noted that they shared a Russian prejudice against the Muslims of Kazan. In spite of this, he praised the cultured qualities of the Polish Muslims though he feared for their ultimate assimilation and with it the de-islamisation of their culture, especially as the urbanised Polish Muslim élite were isolated from the rural Muslims. Frank has summarised his critique as: 'regardless of the emotional or historical attachment of Polish Muslims to Islam, Jahānshāh decries their assimilation into Russian and Polish culture, an assimilation that manifests itself in Polish Muslims' ignorance of Islamic traditions and Turkic languages, and in their adoption of the Russians' stereotypes of the Volga Tatars; and he especially faults the Polish Muslim élite for working primarily as "bureaucrats" (*chīnovnīkī*)'.[21]

Polish and Lithuanian views on Tatar assimilation

Andrzej B. Zakrzewski, in an article about the assimilation of Tatars within the Polish Commonwealth between the sixteenth and eighteenth centuries, has explained, in detail, several of the issues that have been raised by Jahānshāh.[22] He has drawn attention to the constant migration of Tatars within the entire region. Up to the eighteenth century they were arriving in the Polish Commonwealth, yet, at the same time, they were emigrating from it, principally into Ottoman territories. Most Tatars reached the Baltic region between the end of the fourteenth up to the middle of the sixteenth century. However, two mass flights occurred during the seventeenth century. The first, was on account of the so-called Lipkowie Tatars who were living in Volhynia and Podolia (Białystok region). Its cause was the arrears of payment for the Lipka military company. Some two to three thousand fled to Turkey, in 1672. The second flight occurred at the close of that century and after that due to political unrest and economic distress. Assimilation at this time was hindered or helped on account of the manner of Tatar settlement. Some Tatars settled in well-established communities, others in new settlements, or they were settled on *hospodar* or boyar estates.

The Tatars were socially divided into three social layers: Ducal Tatars (*hospodar*), Cossack Tatars and the commoners. The first were eligible for military service, they shared the same rights, save for political rights, with the Lithuanian boyars. The Cossack Tatars had less land. The third group dwelt in villages and towns and were employed as waggoners or as traders.

The number of the Tatar population at that time is difficult to assess. According to Olgierd Górka, 7,000 Tatars lived in Lithuania alone, during the sixteenth century, and, in the following century some 9,000, of whom over half that number were *hospodar* Tatars. It was the Muslim religion that identified them, not their varied ethnic origins.

During this period, the Tatars adopted first the Ruthenian language and then, gradually, Polish. According to Zakrzewski, up to 1,650 signatures from surviving documents reveal half of them in Cyrillic and half in Arabic script, but from the middle of the century and to its close some 75 per cent were in Roman script and the remainder mostly in Arabic. This feature is also to be found in other documents that survive. Many Tatars were not even familiar with the Arabic alphabet. Arabic survived on gravestones from the sixteenth century onwards. However, Tatar literature preserved the Arabic script, and more will be said about this in a following chapter. At this time they had developed a religious literature of their own, Islamic in character, but highly individual. At the heart of it was the sacred text of the Qur'ān. According to Zakrzewski,[23] quoting the Karaite scholar and Turcologist Seraja Szapszal, and the seventeenth-century Turkish chronicler Pečewi 'They copy the Koran in Arabic characters, but to interpret and explain it they use the language of the unbelievers.' As will be seen, the *Kitāb* was to become one of the symbols of Muslim Tatar identity, despite, or because of, its employment of Polish and Byelorussian (Ruthenian). One, dated 1792, is written in Arabic, Cyrillic and Roman. Creativity abounds in an Old Polish Apocrypha that has been analysed and quoted by Andrzej Drozd. Five manuscripts which date from the eighteenth and nineteenth centuries quote an Old Polish religious romance of 1543, Krzystof Pussman's *Historyja barzo cudna o stworzeniu nieba i ziemie* – the romance itself being an adaptation of the apocryphal *Vita Adam et Evae* of a Jewish origin and widely known in Europe. The core of the Tatar work, written in the adapted version of the Arabic script, describes the ages that had passed following the creation of the World and up to that age when Abraham commenced his Prophetic mission. The entire work is an unusual blend of sources: Pussman, the Qur'ān, the Old Testament and the hagiographical Muslim work *The Tales of the Prophets* (*Qiṣaṣ al-Anbiyā'*), apart from Polish religious works and the author's own personal observations.

This fusion of sources is a pointer to religious assimilation with the faiths of the eastern European peoples who lived near the Baltic. The key religious guides to the Tatar communities were the need to have *mullahs* and *imāms*. To do so, a reasonable number of Muslim believers needed to be located within the vicinity. Zakrzewski quotes a request which was sent by the Tatars of Slobodka to Radziwiłł in the Principality of Slutsk,[24] 'We humbly entreat Your Highness to grant some land for our mullah and for our Tatar mosque, which would be free of all burdens and obligations.'

Conversions to Christianity took place, principally to Catholicism, in the fifteenth century and to Calvinism during the second half of the sixteenth century. Contact between Muslim Tatars and Unitarians was not uncommon. Mixed marriage was the cause of some conversions particularly as the offspring were brought up in the Christian religion. Converted Tatars were known to have asked for the protection of the King. In the seventeenth century, attacks on Tatar religious buildings may have brought about conversion in order to secure protection. All in all, conversion was rare and an estimate made for the year 1791 would seem to indicate that only 25 per cent of the Tatar population were Christians. The gentry raised no objection to Muslims. On the other hand there is some evidence to suggest that the Tatars made converts among the Ruthenians. Sir T.W. Arnold, in his *The Preaching of Islam* (1935),[25] noted that

> These Muslim immigrants, dwelling in the midst of a Christian population, have preserved their old faith, but (probably for political reasons) do not appear to have attempted to proselytise. But they have been in the habit of marrying Lithuanian and Polish women, whose children were always brought up as Muslims, whereas no Muhammadan girl was permitted to marry a Christian. The grand Dukes of Lithuania in the fifteenth century encouraged the marriage of Christian women with their Tatar troops on whom they bestowed grants of land and other privileges.

Zakrzewski noted that Islam as it was practised in the Polish Commonwealth was very different from that in Arabia and Turkey. He noted that the pilgrimage was a rare occurrence and that alcohol was widely consumed. Discrimination against women was not observed and the will made by Fatma Kalwolska stated that:

> Also my body when in accordance with the Divine Will it shall be separated from my soul is to be returned as dust to dust and buried by my above-named spouse Sir Roman Sienkiewicz at the Sienkiewicze mosque with all our rights according to the Muslim faith.[26]

In the sermon (*khuṭba*) on Friday, when the health and well-being of the Caliph was within the prayer proclaimed in the mosque, the Lithuanian Tatars substituted the name of the Grand Duke for that of the Caliph. Pečewi, according to Szapszal, wrote 'They say that they recite the Chutbe to the name of the Polish King.' In 1519, the Tatars when petitioning Sigismund I, the King of Poland and the Grand Duke of Lithuania, declared to him that they repeated the name of his ancestor Witold (Vytautas) in their prayers.

Professor Tamara Bairašauskaité has analysed this situation as it appeared during the nineteenth century amongst the Baltic Tatars in general.[27] In the first half of the nineteenth century there was a marked development of administrative system and judicature in the regions of Russia. Courts were reformed in 1831, assemblies in that same year and the district police in 1837. The local Tatars were involved. The 'minor group', those who had been all but eliminated from the political life of the Grand Duchy of Lithuania, saw before them an opportunity to obtain advantages from the situation which had been created in annexed territories. Those who wished to do so expressed a willingness to participate in the nobility assemblies. During the second decade of the century it was quite common to find a Tatar participating in the district assemblies. Furthermore, the nineteenth century was the crucial turning point in the military service of the Tatars. The traditional military service as a part of an ethnic formation was replaced by a personal career opportunity in the military. In 1819 a separate Lithuanian corps was formed which included the Lithuanian Cavalry Regiment and the Tatar Cavalry Regiment, known since 1807 as the Tatar Uhlan Regiment.

Tatars became civil servants, serving in the bodies of the provincial administration and they sought posts in the police system. A few Tatars held judicial positions in the criminal or the civil courts. The Tatar religious community remained conservative during the century. Russian policy was favourable to this and was based on their assumption that the Tatars, as a group, although of a different faith, presented no threat to the interests of the authorities. The religious community itself retained its organisation, namely the traditional structure of mosque and '*jamiat*', or parish.

During the nineteenth century, the Tatar communities were able to expand the network of mosques that was their legacy from the days of the Grand Duchy. Restrictions were placed on their activities by Russian laws. The number of the faithful determined the case in favour of mosque construction. Ten new mosques were built and these supplemented seventeen that had survived. The mosques were in towns such as Mir,

Slonim, Smilaviči, today all of them in Belarus, and older mosques were repaired or reconstructed. The Tatar drift to towns and cities, however, hampered the '*vakuf*'[28] institution, relating to the bestowal of land, or donations to mosques, for their upkeep, or the maintenance of cemeteries within those towns themselves. In the middle of this century, the Lithuanian Tatars obtained permission to elect their clergy from the local Tatar communities.

It was during this period that a publication took place which had a profound effect upon the Tatar's knowledge of their sacred scriptures. Curiously, the urgent desire to publish a Polish translation of the Qur'ān was not a strong sentiment within the Tatar communities. They had their manuscript copies that they had inherited from past generations or from copies of the text printed in Kazan or beyond, copies that had their own commentaries in Byelorussian or in Polish. In the nineteenth century these manuscript copies, elegantly written, functioned, but problems arose when more and more were unable to read the texts of the scriptures that they had cherished. Only today in Belarus, Latvia and Lithuania are there steps afoot to publish translations in their languages to replace the Russian translations which were formerly available. The Polish initiative was the brainchild of individuals and an exercise for priests. Such a translation did not circulate within the Muslim Tatar community itself. It began as fragmentary *sūras*, published in Poznań, under the eye of J. Sobolewski, in 1828 and 1848. The Polish text of the integral *Qur'ān*, 'J. Buczacki's *Qur'ān*', was first published in Warsaw in 1858. Tatars from Podlasie were actively involved in its checking and completion. It heralded a series of translations and the latter are a controversial issue amongst the Muslim community in Poland at the present time.

Within the Soviet Union, and after the devastations of the Second World War, displacement, imprisonment and redefining of boundaries, the Baltic Tatars suffered grievous losses. According to Dr Zorina Kanapatskaya, quoting from a survey that she made of the losses in Belarus, alone:

> During the Communist era (1917–90), the Tatar community suffered severely. Many mosques were closed and were used for other purposes. The teaching to Tatar children about language, culture and religion was strictly forbidden. Despite this, the Tatars practised their religion in the privacy of their homes. Prior to the Second World War the country possessed nineteen mosques and only one remained after the War. This last mosque, in Minsk, was destroyed in 1962.

During the period between the two World Wars there was an intellectual renaissance in the academic life of Belarus. Historians, ethnologists and philologists undertook research into the history and the culture of the Tatars. It was only at the beginning of the 1980s that scientists returned to their fields of research. The cultural history of the Tatars was one of these fields.

In 1990, the Tatars of Belarus launched their struggle to re-establish their identity and, today, they have the possibility of studying and of practising their religion, culture and language but they do not have the infrastructure, be it religious institutions, or finances, or premises, to undertake the task.

According to the Census in Belarus of 1999, the Ethnic Minority Tatars number 10,289. The largest community lives within the City of Minsk. Tatars number 3,841 in the Minsk Region (Oblast), 2,155 in Grodno Region, 1,258 in Vitebsk Region, 1,127 in Gomel Region, 933 in Brest region, and 775 in Mogilev Region. 8, 237 Tatars live in towns and 1,762 in villages. Minsk and its region is the home for 44 per cent of the Belarusian Tatars, today. In Grodno, the figure is 23%, In Vitebsk and Gomel Regions this figure is 9%. In Brest it is 8% and in Mogilev Region it is 7%. The Tatars include Lithuanian Tatars and the Kazan Tatars who came from the Volga region to Belarus during the era of the Soviets.

There is a continuous decrease in the number of the Ethnic Tatars. In 1938, in Vidzy (Vitebsk Region) there were once 760 Lithuanian Tatars whereas today the figure is below 50. In Slonim (Grodno Region) there were once 413 Tatars. The figure today is 96. Once the village of Dovbuchki had 480 Tatars. Today, only a few families live there. Its original mosque was built in 1557 and was therefore a monument of cultural interest and value in pre-War Poland. It suffered destruction and in 1991 it was dismantled. What woodwork remained there, on the site, was brought to a museum of wooden architecture located near to Minsk.

Between 1989 and 1999 the population of Qipchāq Tatars in Belarus decreased to 31%. This tiny figure is rapidly dwindling and there is a real possibility that they will disappear as a Muslim people in the Baltic Region (26).

In Poland the Tatars feel that there is a greater hope for their survival. The Tatars have lived through years when their identity was in even graver danger. Their will to survive exists and it is very strong.

Dr Dżemila Smajkiewicz-Murman, a much loved and highly regarded

Tatar lady today, lives in Gdańsk. She and her family take an active part in the life of their mosque. When that mosque was officially opened, and she was invited to speak, she recalled an earlier event which gave her joy, hope and optimism for the Tatars' future:

> Now after so many years reaching back to my childhood, I see a little girl wandering to the mosque with my grandfather, to the mosque in Vilnius which no longer exists. I see the Vilnius *Imām*, my grandfather, Ibrahim Smajkiewicz explaining to me the principles of Islam, and every morning I hear his voice commencing the prayer. And I pray together with my grandpa, who explains that the 'rug for prayer' (*namaziyk*) must be highly esteemed, because, within it, is sewn one piece of the cloth covering the Ka'ba and brought by Mufti Szynkiewicz. Now, this little piece of cloth, still present in my mind, seems to lead me to Mecca where I shall see it whole. All my life I have kept that Ka'ba in mind. I keep in my mind my grandfather, and my father, and the principles of the faith engraved forever after by them; the feeling of the honour of my descent and my religion.
>
> I have a distant recollection of an afternoon when grandpa and I were praying on that rug. Suddenly, someone closed the shutter. It was my father who had returned from the NKVD prison at Lukiazki. I still believe that our prayers had brought this about.[29]

4. Islam and the 'Lithuanian Tatars'

How the faith took root in the North

> If one of them is the victim of an injustice wherein he experiences a personal misfortune, he raises his head, looks upwards into the heavens, and he says, 'Bir Tengri', which means in the Turkish tongue, 'By the Sole God'. This is because 'Bir', in Turkish, means 'One' and 'Tengri' means 'God', in the language of the Turks.
>
> Aḥmad b. Faḍlān b. al-'Abbās b. Rāshid b. Ḥammād,
> AD 921–22

Tatar beliefs, their Islamic literature and the influence of Sufism upon their culture

The Islam of the Tatars of Lehistan is 'Orthodox'. They are stalwart and traditional Sunnīs, and they stand shoulder to shoulder with the Tatars of Kazan, with those in the Dobrogea in Romania, with the Crimean Tatars, and with kindred peoples such as the Tatars of western Siberia and the Kazakhs of Central Asia. Throughout their history, Islam in the Crimea, though most of all in Ottoman Turkey, has deeply influenced and inspired their culture and the daily practice of their faith. Yet, at the same time, they are Europeans. They have lived, and still today live, amongst Catholics, amongst Uniates (Greek Catholics) and amongst Orthodox Christians, Calvinists and other contemporary Protestants, Karaites, Jews and atheists. Many people around them are the offspring of forebears schooled in the former Marxist system of non-belief, or a way of life where the spiritual world was accepted as being the myths of the pre-scientific age, a world wherein man had groped, in vain, to discover any spirituality whatsoever in a Godless universe. In everyday life, the Tatars have been influenced by the Kazan Tatars and also, from their long association with the peoples of the Balkans and Asia Minor, by the spiritual life that existed during the Ottoman age. Kazan, Turkey and the Crimea were for centuries major centres of Sufism, particularly the Qādiriyya, the Khalwatiyya the Naqshabandiyya and, to a lesser degree, the Rifā'iyya and the Bektāshiyya brotherhoods. Unlike Kazan, and some of the Tatars in western Siberia, the Muslims of those countries that we know today, in Belarus, Lithuania and Poland, were never known for having established such Sufi brotherhoods. Sufis, therein, were individuals who had entered a brotherhood while they were abroad in the Ottoman Empire. This was the case until recent times. Sufism, today, has become a 'way' of a very limited interest to Muslims in these countries, as also in Latvia, Finland, and in the other Nordic countries. Popular books on 'Sufism' are on sale in the bookshops. Yet, despite this reality, it cannot be denied that at least some features of Sufism have had a tangible influence upon the culture of the Tatars of Lehistan in the past. These features have left their mark upon their beliefs, their rituals and their everyday habits even though many of them throughout their lives may have been totally unaware of the very meaning of Sufism.

The past presence of Sufis amongst the Tatars of Belarus, Lithuania and Poland is a topic that has been seriously aired and debated recently amongst specialists in Tatar life and religion and within the Tatar communities themselves. Although not wholly unmentioned in articles and books of an earlier date, this revival of interest has largely been due to the enthusiastic researches of the Tatar scholar, and *imām*, Selim Chazbiejewicz (himself a Sufi and a poet).[1]

His views have been published and debated, and frequently rejected, in articles and at conferences where Tatar life has been a topic of reflection. It has left his co-religionists with an awareness of Sufism, and the suspicion that it may have once played an important role in their religious history and their devotional life. Yet how significant was that role? One might pose the question whether Sufism was forgotten for some reason amongst them, or whether their religious practice was so framed and limited by the formal observances of Islam, its superstitions and its rituals, in rural communities, or, so overtaken by the need to resist 'Christian mission' through the spiritual message of the Qur'ān, and the Prophet, alone, or by an ethical code, shaped by the Sharī'a,[2] that the mystical life of Islam has been eschewed and all but vanished over the course of time.

It seems certain that amongst these tiny Muslim communities (tiny, that is, in more recent times, since, in the late medieval age, the Duchy of Lithuania housed a Tatar population which numbered scores of thousands),[3] the continued presence of family-centred brotherhoods (*ṭuruq*) has never been mentioned, or officially recorded, or recognised.

In resolving this dilemma, then, how may one define 'Sufism' amongst the Muslim Lehs of yesterday and today?

One is faced by several alternatives. Three of them are listed below:

a   If well established Sufi brotherhoods were absent in the past, despite the affiliation of numbers of Tatar individuals, beyond that community's borders, does this exclude the presence of a popular, possibly ill-defined, Sufism, within the daily religious life of the Tatars, whether they lived in small villages or whether they resided in towns such as Vilnius, Trakai, Minsk or Warsaw?
b   Is a redefinition as to who is deemed to be a Sufi demanded in the light of our current knowledge of Tatar Islam?
c   To what extent had the seeds of Sufism been planted in these communities and countries, then nurtured and have flowered amongst the Tatar *jamā'a*? Were this to have been true, then, where is one likely to find the evidence and proof in the beliefs, rituals, literature, astrology, magic, music, art and architecture amongst the Tatars who lived in past centuries and who do so amidst these communities today?

Chazbijewicz has provided several sources of evidence to show that in the sixteenth century, if not earlier, Sufi activities were sufficiently common in the Duchy of Lithuania that, in some localities, the *jamā'a* might have supported a brotherhood structure, or, at least, groups of Sufis who might have exerted an influence amongst the Tatar communities. At that time they would have been in regular contact with the religious centres of the Ottoman East. The relationship was especially close with the Crimean peninsula and with the Sufi centres that had been long established there. They also regularly made the pilgrimage to Mecca. These contacts were the lifeline of individual Sufis, who, in the Baltic region, were otherwise bereft of any contact whatsoever, except with the subdued, oppressed and outlawed Sufi brotherhoods that existed within the borders of the Russian Empire. Chazbijewicz writes:

> According to the discoveries of researchers, there were attempts to organize a uniform religious structure for Muslims in the territory of Greater Poland. However, the sporadic nature of those attempts and formal difficulties meant that there were no positive results until the twentieth century. According to a document of 1594, however, it is possible to affirm that at that time an institution called 'Kadim' existed amongst the Polish Muslims. A 'Kadim' (*muqaddam*) was a

Tatar dervish, also titled 'Hadzy' and 'Chelebi'. 'Murzich' – a title of a 'Chelebi' – belonged to those who supervised the *tekkes*, the lodges or religious buildings used by local sects of dervishes, buildings that are sometimes incorrectly compared to 'monasteries'.

The title of 'Hadzy' meant that a given 'Murzich' had completed his pilgrimage to Mecca. When such a title was given to a 'Murzich' it suggested the types of contacts and the possibilities of influence on Polish Muslims. Amongst the Tatars there was also the institution of the so-called 'Mutiviles' (*mutawallī*), namely, the honorary guardians of mosques. The mosques belonging to the Lithuanian–Polish Muslims, as a rule, were, and still are, small wooden structures built in the style of the Tatar mosques from Powolze (the Volga area of Tatarstan). They typified Tatar and Islamic craftsmanship in Poland. The interiors of these mosques were decorated with 'Muhirs', handwritten decorated verses from the Qur'ān. The mosques and the 'Muhirs' are rare examples of Islamo-Tatar folk art that still remains until today in Poland. The same may be said about manuscripts on parchment, written in saffron and bound in leather, manuscripts that are a valuable treasure written down in the Polish territories and are unique of their kind, world-wide.

An important part of this religious culture of the Lithuanian and Polish Tatars was connected with Sufism. Sufism was the current that firmly established itself amongst the Muslim peoples of the East and had an influence in Powolze (in Tatarstan), the Crimea and in the Polish territories. In Crimean Evpatoria (Gözlewe in Polish), near to the mosques, there existed places for communal living, dedicated to contemplation that were called 'dervish monasteries'. These were active up to the 1930s, when the last of the dervishes were transported to Siberia by the NKVD. Today, only ruins remain. Similar devastation affected the Sufi centres in Powolze, where this movement arose, emanating from Khurasan and Turkestan way back in the Middle Ages.

The Jancars (Janisseries) formed a sort of Muslim Knightly Order. On the whole, the chief influence upon the traditions of the Lithuanian and Polish Muslims were some traces of the culture of the Ottoman Turks, which, to this day, may be seen in their religious observances as well as in their melodic recitation of the Qur'ān, and in their linguistic features.[4] The Tatars who settled on the Polish territories brought their own culture with them together with the fundamental religious customs of Islam. The popular legends of the Polish Tatars about the Prophets, Ibrāhīm, Sulaymān, the Flood, the Prophet Muhammad and about the Caliph 'Alī, all belong to the treasure house of Islamic legends, fables and sayings. The form of those legends was perpetuated in Prophetic *ḥadīths*, as well as by popular 'eschatological' legends regarding the creation of the world, the Garden of Eden, the Devil, the Day of Judgment. All such existed among Arab, Persian and Turkish Muslims. They likewise exist in the manuscripts and in the oral traditions of the Polish Muslims.

The cult of honoring the graves of 'saintly men' (*zijaretami*)[5] by offerings of candles and of food, is opposed to the theological theory of monotheism (*tawḥīd*). In places such as Turkey, the Maghrib, Morocco, for example, such cults do not interfere with the official faith. In Istanbul, close to the Adam Mickiewicz Museum, there is such a shrine dedicated to a local saint.[6]

Whatever may have been the case in the distant past, it is certain that nowadays such Sufi brotherhoods have disappeared from Tatar life. The Sufi message had been preached in earlier days by individuals. These individuals may, or may not, have been 'dervishes or poor mendicants (Qalandars)', or amongst small groups of Tatars, who, in 'house churches', perpetuated half-forgotten Sufi-influenced rituals of a popular, medical or devotional kind. The presence of 'Qalandarism' (wandering dervishes) and the combination of the role of *imām* and dervish (*Szorc*) is attested to in the documents that furnish historical support to the thesis of Chazbijewicz, outlined above.

This Sufi influence that came into Polish and Lithuanian Tatar spiritual life was also a part of the legacy of the numerous *imāms*, who, over the centuries, came from abroad to pass on their knowledge. According to Piotr Borawski:[7]

> As early as the sixteenth century, Tatars willingly brought imāms from the Crimea and Turkey; for they themselves did not know liturgical Arabic. The anonymous author of the *Treatise on Polish Tatars*[8] wrote: 'We are not forbidden to bring priests for the posts of imām from the adjacent countries of Islam so we have imāms from the Crimea, or the Horde maintained by us and they teach our children. Some of them are being prepared to fulfill the call of faith.[9]

The Tatar population of the Republic was governed in communes by its own religious law. Clear traces of that autonomic religious jurisdiction date from the second half of the sixteenth century. The author of the Treatise mentioned that rules of the Qur'ān were regulating everyday life of his tribesmen and that only cases that exceeded a Muslim 'commune' belonged to land jurisdiction. *Imāms* probably functioned as judges. Sources confirm the existence of an office of 'Kaji' of all Tatars in the Grand Duchy of Lithuania. Three documents dating from the second half of the sixteenth century mention this office. The first one probably dates from 1586. It is a privilege given to 'Dervish' Czelebi, appointing him as 'Kaji' (Qāḍī) of all Tatars, that is to say, 'the highest authority among clergy and over all Tatars in the Grand Duchy of Lithuania'. In the register of the Dowbucizki estates, belonging to prince Alikiecz Begimowicz Ulan, we find the following reference to 'Dervish' Czelebi Hadji Murzicz. He is mentioned there as 'Kaji' and *imām* of Dowbucizki. The third document comes from the books of Vilna court in the first instance.

On 2 March 1594, 'Dervish Czelebi Hadji Murzicz, "Kaji" of all Tatars in the Grand Duchy of Lithuania stated to the court that he freed a prisoner, Iwazka Piotrowicz, who had been bought by him some years ago.'[10]

The above documents prove the existence of the office of 'Kaji' in sixteenth-century Lithuania. Those who bore the title were competent in religious matters for all 'Lithuanian Mohammedans'. Apart from his title of 'Kaji', his title of 'Dervish' would seem to indicate that as part of his religious office of *imām*, the teaching of some Sufi establishment, its name unknown, may also have had a part to play in his religious vocation.

Interrupted contacts between the Lithuanian and Polish Tatars and the Kazan Tatars brought them news of the Sufi movements in the Volga region. Through the Tatars of Kazan they were made aware of the Naqshabandī Shaikhs, and others in the Qādiriyya and the Khalwatiyya, in Istanbul, Bukhara, Kabul, Delhi, Daghestan, and in Russian cities with sizeable Muslim populations. They included towns such as Ufa, Orenburg, Samara, Saratov (where Tatars built its first mosque in 1843), St Petersburg and Helsinki. From all these cities they acquired written works that stimulated Islamic thought and spurred others to pursue the mystical quest. In some localities Tatars from the North-West were to be found. In the Black Sea area during the seventeenth century, the town of Ak-Kirman (now Bilhorod-Dnistrovsky) sheltered fifteen thousand Tatars from the Baltic region.

The pilgrimage to Mecca, Medina, Cairo and Damascus allowed for some personal contact with important Sufis. One might recall also that some Polish intellectuals were especially interested in Ottoman culture and religious thought, and that this included Sufism. The latter fascinated a number of Polish thinkers, writers, poets and artists. Jan Potocki

(b. 1761) was acquainted with local Tatars. In his literary works, such as *The Journey of Ḥāfiẓ* and *The Saragossa Manuscript* (1797), and in his other writings, many of which were inspired by his travels in Egypt, Morocco, the Caucasus and beyond, he displayed a lively curiosity about Sufism. It interested other Polish 'Orientalists' in the eighteenth and nineteenth centuries.[11] However, the authors of *The Cambridge History of Poland from the Origins to Sobieski (to 1696)*[12] encourage one to be cautious when they remark:

> Frequent wars with the unbelievers made the Poles acquainted with Oriental customs, their servants, even their music. But this Orientalization never went deeper; in spite of external influences, Poland remained Western at the core, a bulwark of Christianity, an outpost of Western culture against the Schismatic East or the Mohammedan Orient.

This did not prevent individual Poles from exploring the spiritual riches of the Islamic East.

An example of the influence of Sufism in a kindred community, the Tatars of western Siberia, may shed light on this question.

To what degree the Qipchāq Tatars, who settled in the Duchy of Lithuania in the fourteenth century, were influenced by Sufism and, if it were so, what was its nature, can only be conjectured through a comparison. One may do so by comparing them with Tatar communities of a kindred type elsewhere in Eurasia. It is of interest to take note of the part played by Sufism amongst the Siberian Tatars. Some insight into this phenomenon has been offered by Dr Alexander Seleznev.[13] Apart from other Central Asians, western Siberia is the homeland for 180,000 Siberian Tatars, and 60,000 Volga Ural Tatars. Two periods, it is alleged, were noteworthy for the diffusion of Sufism in this region. The first is clouded by legend. It tells of the arrival of horse riding *shaikhs*, their chiefly ally Sheibani Khān and one thousand soldiers on the banks of the Irtysh River. The event took place in AD 1394/5 (AH 797). A great battle was fought against the pagan Khotan, Kara-Qipchāq and Nogaj. The 366 missionaries were said to have been followers, or disciples, of Bahā' al-Dīn Naqshaband, the alleged founder of that major brotherhood in Central Asia and its most significant political force. Officially, Islam became established (in fact, a long drawn out process) in the Siberian Khānate in the sixteenth century.

Shamanism long survived the official conversion. The Baraba Tatars retained many of their Shamanistic beliefs and practices until the beginning of the eighteenth century. Pockets of pre-Islamic belief survive even to this day. Underpinning popular belief were the teachings of other faiths, principally Manicheaism, Buddhism and Christianity, either Nestorian or Eastern Orthodox. Such a faith recalls the description, by Professor Edward Tryjarski, of the religion of the medieval nomadic Pechenegs. He informed me, during a discussion, that in examining the history of the Pechenegs in their entire span of history one ought to take account of their connection with:

1 Their primitive belief systems.
2 The survival of Zoroastrianism.
3 Manicheaism which is revealed in the manner of instruction:

    a by the Denavaryya
    b by the Paulicians and the Bogomils.

4 Islam.
5 Christianity.[14]

However, Seleznev, in his article, concludes that Shamanism had left the deepest mark on Siberian Muslim culture. Certain of its features survive amongst the Qipchāq Tatars and even among the Karaims in Lithuania. He remarks:

> For example, the term *Tengre*,[15] (meaning God, deity) has been maintained amongst Kazakhs and almost all groups of Siberian Tatars. The same word meant 'supreme deity' in the Old Turkic epoch and in modern times it has spread among the followers of Shamanism in the Sajan-Altai region. Other deities and spirits known to Siberian Tartars and Kazakhs (*jer'-su*, Earth/water, *umaj*, *qut*, *natigaj*) were considered sacred by Medieval Shamanist-Turks and Mongolians as well. The traces of a fire cult, preserved among the Kazakhs and Tartars, can be explained by the influence of Middle Asian culture. The word Qudai (*Huudai*), signifying God, is Persian in origin, and is known to the Western Siberian Muslims and Sajan-Altai Shamanists. 'Animistic' beliefs are also connected with ancient Shamanistic beliefs. They are expressed in the form of hunting-fishing cults of the spirits (*ijasy ese*): the spirits of the water (*su ijasy*), the forest (*picin pichin urman-isasy*), houses (*oj ijasy*), fire (*ot ijasy*) and others.[16]

Many of the above practices were also characteristic of the pagan Balts, and they were practised until quite recently, this despite the measures adopted by the Catholic and Lutheran churches to eradicate them. It is inconceivable that the incoming Tatars (and possibly the Karaims) were not subject to their baneful influences. Despite this, their Baltic vision of the world of the Spirit left its mark in popular Sufism and upon the magical beliefs that they had brought with them from the Qipchāq steppes.[17]

Sufi teachers of Ghiyāth al-Dīn Toqtamish Khān

What were the forms of 'Sufism' which could have influenced the Muslim Tatars, back in the fourteenth century, at the time of their exile in the Duchy of Lithuania? Our most promising source of information is what is known from the documentary evidence about certain known Sufi teachers and their likely impact upon their leader in exile, Toqtamish Khān, who was the former ruler of Saray (AH 778–97/AD 1376–95). Sufi ideas were well known in the Saray court. They were also known in the steppe, and in Tīmūr's court in Samarqand where Toqtamish resided for some time. Toqtamish was not only the leading figure and the key ally of Vytautas within the new Tatar homeland where he was exiled, but he was also influential in keeping Tatar contacts open with the Crimea, with the Middle East, and with other eastern regions that were cultural centres for Muslim Tatar groups.

The first of the major Sufi figures who had a direct influence upon Toqtamish, as ruler of Saray, was Kamāl al-Dīn b. Mas'ūd, known as Kamāl al-Khujandī,[18] who died in Tabriz in AH 803/AD 1400. Renowned for his saintliness and miraculous powers (*karāmāt*), possibly more than his Sufism, and also famous for his Persian verse, it is apparent from the information furnished by Jāmī that his mystical experience was largely disassociated from the many monistic and heterodox tendencies in the Sufism of his age.

According to Browne,[19] citing Jāmī, his goal was 'To conceal the fullness of his saintly nature and spiritual attainments, to prevent the complete suppression of his exoteric by his esoteric life, and to maintain the position of "servitude" to God against an overmastering tendency "to be merged in the Deity".' As a novice, he was tutored by Khwāja 'Ubaydullāh of Shāsh (Tashkent). Khwāja Khujand left Central Asia and he journeyed westward to the Qipchāq steppe and to Saray where his miracles and his sanctity gained him a high reputation. He moved to Tabriz and he spent much of his life there. The Jalāyirī Sultān Husayn, son of Uways (AH 776–84/AD 1374–82), built a retreat (*khānaqāh*) for him in its locality. He was deeply attached to Tabriz and he composed many verses in praise of the city, its beauty, culture and religious activities.

In AH 787/AD 1385, the city was raided by Toqtamish and his Tatars. It was sacked with a very great savagery. Toqtamish forcibly took Kamāl al-Khujandi with him to Saray, and with him other scholars and men of piety whom he prized, men whose apparently supernatural powers were of use to him, and whose scholastic repute enhanced the reputation of Toqtamish and Saray in the Tīmūrid era.

According to Leonard Lewisohn, following Toqtamish's invasion the poet was forcibly transported to Saray, the Golden Horde capital on the Volga river, that same city where he had resided in his youth, after abandoning his father and wife in Khujand. It is unclear exactly how long Kamāl was detained there. Most historians follow the dictum of Dawlatshāh that the detention amounted to four years. Jāmī omits to mention the exile. Ibn Karbalā'ī affirms that the period was exactly eleven years, stating that 'according to the chronicles of history, when Toqtamish Khān pillaged Tabriz in the year AH 787/AD 1385, he took the master with him'. The latter remained there until the year AH 798/AD 1396. During this period he recalled, with longing, his former life in Tabriz and he longed to return to its countryside. In the end, Tīmūur attacked Toqtamish Khān and pillaged the city of Saray, bringing the revered master back to Tabriz.[20] In the poetry of Khwāja al-Khujandī, translated by Lewisohn, it would seem that there was little love lost between him and his captor, furthermore, the savagery of the Qipchāq Tatars, their acts of rape and pillage, suggest that many were barely Islamised, let alone influenced, to any degree, by any kind of Sufi teaching, save perhaps in its most Shamanistic aspects. But it is also clear that it was a matter of pride, prestige and fear that Toqtamish took Khwāja al-Khujandī to be with him in his court in Saray. Tatar scholars and divines had been drawn to Tabriz for generations.

This was not the first time that the Tatars of the Golden Horde had removed scholars by force. The Azerbaijanī scholar Khwāja Hasan had been taken captive by the Qipchāq Tatars when he was twenty-three years old. He lived for seven years amongst the Qipchāq. He gained a following amongst them but he decided to take the path of the Sufi wanderer and preacher (*al-siyāḥa*) and he was to meet many respected Shaykhs. He stayed in Bulghār for nine years and in Bukhara for three. He also visited Persia. He spent seven years in Kirmān and a year in Maragha Tabriz, where he died, aged ninety-three, in Rabī'l AH 692/AD 1292.

Mahmūd Ramzī[21] also makes a brief reference to Shaykh Kamāl al-Khujandī. He includes him amongst the famous scholars of Saray. His sojourn there and his relationship with Toqtamish differ, in his account, from the grim descriptions which have been presented by Lewisohn. Ramzī refers to the Shaykh as 'a great Sufi'. He was formerly a resident in Tashkent, a saintly man for whom Sufism was 'mainstream' and orthodox, and who was at the opposite pole to those who had embraced an extreme monism (*lā yakūnu'l-ẓāhiru maghlūb al-bāṭini*). His company had been sought by the father of Khwāja Ahrār, who died in AH 895 /AD 1490, and whose name is associated with the Naqshabandiyya Sufi brotherhood.[22] Ramzī confirms that when the soldiery of Toqtamish Khān captured Tabriz, the residence of Kamāl al-Dīn, they took him with them to Saray. The city's beauty and scholarship pleased the Shaykh. The length of his stay there was fourteen years (*sic*, possibly an error for four). During his residence his sanctity and his miraculous acts spared the city from a catastrophic flood. Ramzī further adds that the Shaykh died in Tabriz, where he had a retreat (*khalwa*), well secluded and furnished with the most basic of bedding and furnishings. It is unusual that Ramzī should have mentioned him so specifically. His fuller biographies of Sufis are almost entirely of a later date and, in the main, from Kazan, Ufa and Tatarstan.

Toqtamish Khān and Faḍlallāh al-Ḥurūfī

Kamāl al-Dīn was by no means the only major Sufi figure whose life coincided with that of the turbulent career and the marching seasons of Toqtamish Khān. Events coincided with the call which came to the self-claimed man-god, Mahdī, Ismā'īlī gnostic and Cabbalist, Faḍlallāh al-Ḥurūfī, who was living in the region of Baku and Shamākha, in Azerbaijan. He also had links with the Qipchāq steppes and the Crimea, on the one hand, and with Tabriz, on the other, and it is likely that he was known to the disciples of the Turkoman dervish Sārī Saltuq, who led a movement in the Dobrogea having strong links to the Qalandariyya and Rifā'iyya brotherhoods.[23] According to Lewisohn, the Ḥurūfis 'replaced Mecca with Tabriz as the holy city of his new religion'.[24] Contacts with Persia had marked Faḍlallāh's career in its early days, when, at the age, of thirty, he was initiated into an order of wandering dervishes of the Qalandariyya.[25] It was in his work, the *Jāvidān-i Kabīr*, 'the Great Eternal',[26] composed between AH 765/AD 1363/4 and AH 796/AD 1393/4, in an appendix, that the dreams and esoteric revelations of Faḍlallāh are disclosed, claims and pretensions of an Ismā'īlī character which inspired him and urged him to propagate amongst the leading secular and religious figures of the age. These included Tīmūr himself, Shaykh

Uways al-Jalayirī (AH 757–77/AD 1356–75), in Tabriz, Toqtamish, and several amongst the dervish fraternity, including the Ḥurūfī poet al-Nasīmī, who became the leading disciple of Faḍlallāh. Mention is also made of a certain Kamāl al-Dīn, who may possibly be Khwāja al-Khujandī himself. Tīmūr totally rejected Faḍlallāh's pretensions. This may have predisposed Toqtamish to draw closer to him, especially so as it is known that Faḍlallāh sought the hand of the daughter of Toqtamish. According to Hamid Algar:[27] 'It had long been Ḥurūfī policy to seek the conversion of rulers. Faḍlullāh seems to have come close to this goal when he visited the Jalayirid court in Tabriz in 775/1373–4: and it was no doubt for political purposes that he aspired to marry the daughter of Toqtamiš Khān, ruler of the Golden Horde.'

The course of events is undisclosed. Tīmūr routed Toqtamish and the latter, together with many of his men, sought, and found, refuge in the Duchy of Lithuania where he was housed in Lida castle. Faḍlallāh died, as a martyr, at the hands of Mīranshāh, the governor of Azerbaijan. Kamāl al-Khujandī returned to Tabriz and was admired and cultivated by Mīranshāh. Lewisohn, quoting Ehsan Yarshater, writes, 'besides his love of poetry, Mīranshāh was also interested in mysticism (*'irfān*) and history. According to the author of 'the *Ḥabīb al-Siyar*', Mīranshāh was utterly devoted to Kamāl Khujandī and his belief in him was overwhelming'.[28] Lewisohn adds 'Many of the Sufi poets of Tabriz vied among themselves in eulogizing the character of the Tīmūrid prince.'

The position of Toqtamish in his religious sympathies does not suggest that he personally pursued any interest in Sufis and Sufism, once he had forsaken the Dasht-i Qipchāq and while he was an exile in the region of Vilnius, though Lithuania may have been a refuge for a few Tatar Sufis who had fled with their leader. Some idea as to their background may emerge from the previous actions of their leader. That a few, possibly Ḥurūfī, traces may be detected in Tatar religious works (*Kitāby*, *Chamails* and talismanic (*dalawar*) texts) have been put forward by Selim Chazbijewicz, and also by Andrzej Drozd. But, as so many other influences penetrated the Tatar community in the Baltic region, from the Crimea and beyond, during the Ottoman age, it would appear that Sufism – even where Ḥurūfī features are discernable – was probably an influence of significance long after the age of Toqtamish.

The imprint of Ottoman Sufism

Tatars from the Duchy of Lithuania served in the Ottoman army and the *imāms* and religious leaders amongst them were the pupils of teachers in Istanbul and elsewhere in the Ottoman Empire, including in some instances its numerous *tekkes*. However, it is with the Crimean Peninsula that all aspects of the spiritual life of the Lithuanian and the Polish Tatars were the most closely associated, notwithstanding the cultural links that they acknowledged with Kazan and with the cities of Central Asia.

Popular Sufism amongst the Tatars has to be considered and to be judged against the background of pressures, at times discriminatory, to the point of persecution. Families were forced to leave in order to seek refuge in Ottoman domains or a life of exile elsewhere. Amongst the least tolerant of Polish and Lithuanian rulers was Sigismund (Zygmunt) III Vasa (1566–1632), who was also King of Sweden between 1592 and 1604. At that time it has been estimated that there were up to 100,000 Tatars in 'Lehistan'. In 1591, the Ottoman Sultan, Murad III, interceded with the king on behalf of the Tatars. The latter were described as 'Saracens'. In 1609, the mosque in Trakai was destroyed. Tatar women were accused of witchcraft and anti-Tatar tracts were published. One of these, *Alfurkan tatarski prawdzway* was printed in 1616, in 1640 and in 1643. It might also be mentioned that tracts were also printed against the Protestant reformers. This attack was countered by a sympathetic defense of the Tatars, entitled *Apologia Tatarów*, by Azulevicz, in 1620. Some Tatars fled to Turkey, in 1672. Others remained royalist in their sympathies. Some fought for John Sobieski, in 1673, some other Tatars were converted to Catholicism. In the eighteenth century Tatars emigrated to Moldova and to other areas around the Black Sea where sizeable Tatar communities already lived.

For the remnant who stayed behind, and clearly the size of that remnant is remarkable in itself, the sundry and sometimes subtle influences of Catholic and Orthodox Christianity and of Judaism and from a lingering 'paganism', brought about an effort to 'domicile' certain features that reflected popular Sufism. These were a bridge to Christianity and they were features of Islam elsewhere, under Russian rule. They were also to be found in districts which bordered *Dār al-Islām* but which were subject to the controlling strategies of non-Muslim empires and communities. These latter had strong and ever increasing national aspirations and a nationalist urge for uniformity. With no single Sufi brotherhood to take command and to guide, individual dervishes had to set an example and they provided a model.

The isolated situation is reflected in the legendary tale of the holy man, Kontus (Konteja).[29] This is by far the best-known and best documented of such personalities even if some have suspected that he was an 'Islamised'

Orthodox saint who once lived in a village which is today in Belarus. His role combined that of a saint, a dervish, a wonder-worker, a Shaman and a 'holy fool'. His legendary personality typified the Tatars' dilemma. His story dates from the age of unhappy times for the Muslims in the Polish domains. The holy man, Kontus (Kuntus as he is known amongst the Tatars of Belarus) is buried in a simple grave in the graveyard (*mizar*), at Lowczyce (Loucycy) in Belarus, near Novogrudok, which is situated to the west of Minsk.[30] He bore the title of 'Aulija' (*walī*), 'saint'. He had associations with other Tatar villages including, it is said, Bohoniki, now in Poland. His tomb has also been sited in other remote localities. The following version of the story is based upon that which was told by an *imām*, Aleksander Bajraszewski, to the Polish Turcologist Dr Alexander Dubinski in the summer of 1967.[31]

Stephan Batory (1576) gave land to his chief huntsman, a loyal Tatar, adjacent to the so-called 'silver stream', later renamed 'the royal stream'. This locality was also known as Lowczyce (Loucycy). The hunter married, but his daughter forsook the faith, and, persuaded by the Jesuits, embraced Christianity. That was the chief reason why this now rich, though deeply distressed, Tatar, ex-huntsman, undertook the pilgrimage to Mecca after he had sold much of his property. While in Mecca, he discovered that he had no money left to pay for his return journey. He prayed repeatedly for guidance as to how his problem might be resolved. He was in deep grief, when, as though by a miracle, he was met by another poor man whom he had not met hitherto during his sojourn in Mecca. The stranger drew the notice of the Tatar to a pilgrim who might be of help to him were he to wait patiently until that pilgrim had left the mosque. The pilgrim was none other than the shepherd Kontus (Kuntus),[32] who was in the service of the rich Tatar. He was already deemed locally to be a saint. Because of his spirituality, he had the power to circumvent the globe and to perform the *Hajj* to Mecca and Madina, aided alone by his magic whip (or crook) that guarded his herd during his absence. The rich Tatar and Kontus, the shepherd, entered into a spiritual bond, an '*ahret*'. This Polish Tatar word denoted one of two men who had joined themselves together by a friendship which not only lasted during their lifetimes on earth, but it would also continue in the world to come (*al-ākhira*). Kontus at first was unwilling to aid his former master, but at length he relented. Kontus told him to close his eyes, and, then, using the power of his magic whip, he transported him back to Lowczyce. The Tatar made no mention of these experiences. He praised Kontus and neglected his wife. The secret remained between them until Kontus died. Then, the Tatar's oath of silence was no longer binding.

He told the story to his wife and afterwards to his relatives. The local population were amazed to learn of the supernatural powers of Kontus. They deemed him to be a very important saint and they buried him with great honour close to the mosque. 'Two oaks grew over his tomb, one at his head, the other at his feet. Bushes, both spiraea and black alder, also grew there. Crowds of pilgrims flocked there in order to be cured. They included many Christians.'

Selim Chazbijewicz has seen signs of a Sufi hand at work in the details of this story.[33] It is impossible to date it with precision. Certain minor details recall hagiographies of the dervishes of Rūm. The Sufi who is a shepherd or a cow herder (as is the case here) occurs frequently in popular Sufism. In a Belarusian version, outlined by G.M. Meredith-Owens and A. Nadson,[34] the rich Tatar was assisted by a Shaikh 'who took him to the chief mosque at the time of the night prayer, and, showing him a man in a green coat sitting in the front row, told the Tartar to go and sit by him and take hold of his coat, so that the man might not go away after the prayer. The Tartar did as he was told and, to his surprise, discovered that the man in the green coat was none other than his cowhand, Kuntus. The latter told him to hold tight to his coat and to close his eyes, and in no time they were back at home'. This little detail of the green coat suggests a Sufi touch.

Yet another herder who became a Sufi, but who, in this instance, founded a brotherhood of historic importance, was Kunta Haji. Called Kishiev, a Kumyk of the northern Caucasus, he brought the Qādiriyya brotherhood to that region in the 1850s and it was to play an important role in the Islamisation of the Chechens and Ingush during the second part of the nineteenth century.[35]

It is possible that, amongst the Lehistan Tatars, narratives of this type date back to the days of much earlier 'epics' that they brought with them from the Crimea to the Duchy of Lithuania. It is not known whether the Lithuanian and Polish Tatars at any time, in the remoter past, possessed their own version of the so-called 'Epic of Toqtamish and Edigey'. According to Nora Chadwick and V. Zhirmusky,[36] that epic has been recorded amongst the Nogay Tatars in the Crimea and in the Black Sea region of the Romanian Dobrogea, as well as in Russia and Central Asia. It is not unreasonable to assume, therefore, that it was at least known to Tatars in Belarus, Lithuania and Poland prior to their loss of their Qipchāq tongue in the sixteenth century. It may even have been known by them at a far later date.

These authors make the important point that 'the epic of Edigei is an example of how historical events are integrated and reshaped into epic tales. Popular memory has retained nothing of the external policy of the reign of Edigei, for example his victory over Vithold (Vytautas), Grand Duke of Lithuania, on the Vorskla River in the year 1399, which is mentioned by the Polish historian Dlugosh and by Russian chroniclers, or his unsuccessful campaign against Moscow in 1408–9'.

The rivalry between Toqtamish and Edigey was a personal one. Astrakhan, the Crimea, and Kazan figure prominently in their adventures. The hero, Edigey, in this instance, was a noble figure and deeply sympathetic to Sufism, to the extent that he became an initiated Sufi himself. He had sprung from a herding background and, according to the Kazakh tradition, he was deemed to be a descendant of a popular saint, Bābā Tukles Shashli 'Azīz, 'The Hairy Saint'. This suggests that popular Sufism left its mark as the epic story evolved. In a very minor way, similar kinds of theme may be detected in the story of Kontus, the saintly herder, pilgrim and dervish.

Sufi influences in the religious literature, the medical lore and in the 'Songs of Praise' of the Tatars of Lehistan

It is the Semitic language of Arabic (albeit corrupted, and mixed with Byelorussian, Polish and Turkic loan words), the language of the Qur'ān, which is found at the very heart of Tatar religious expression and religious commitment. Sufism may have infiltrated the melodic themes that are to be heard in mosque worship and in devotional songs. Certain designs and pictures in Tatar manuscripts, in mosque ornamentation, in *Muhirs*, in astrological tables, star maps, calendars, the schematic representation of the Ka'ba, genealogies of the Prophets, numerology in talismans, letter Cabbalism, in the pointing of letters within the *Chamail*[37] and in Tatar charms and medical prescriptions, each and all, display the art of a popular Sufism, under the influence of Ottoman design, or from the Tatar art of Kazan. However, the higher flights of Monism, as it was expressed by Ibn al-'Arabī, al-Hallāj, or Jalāl al-Dīn al-Rūmī, are mystical experiences reserved for the very few who would say little about such personal beliefs. Suspicions of fanciful notions that wander far from the Qur'ānic text are so entrenched amongst the Baltic Tatars, especially amongst the *imāms*, that, in their view, they would seem to have been penned by an infidel's hand.

Tatar literature has various and numerous categories, *Kitābs*, *Chamails* (*Chamaiły*) and written medical texts and writings about omens and magical formulae. To these must be added calendars and astrological tables. The *Kitāb* is the most elegant and the most complete expression of Tatar belief and ethical ideals. Orthodox Islam prevails. The other documents draw upon styles and symbolism which, on occasions, are to be associated with Sufism of a more heterodox character. Amongst the latter are found Bektāshī, Ḥurūfī and Shī'ite symbols.

Kitābs (Kitaby/Kitabas)

The *Kitāb* (*Kitaby/Kitabas*) is the most comprehensive expression of Tatar Islamic thought. This genre of literature, preserved in manuscripts, contains rules and commands, the history of the Old Testament and of Qur'ānic Prophets, the biography (*sīra*) of Muhammad, parables and poetic verse, some of which is satirical. Elements of the Polish, Byelorussian, Arabic and Turkish languages are all present in the *Kitāb*. One of the finest examples is to be found in the British Library.[38] Some examples, which date from the eighteenth century, belie the impression that Tatar Islam was devoid of any scholarly expertise. These earliest *Kitābs* also contain genealogies, Qur'ānic *sūras* (*Sūrat Yā'sīn*, (No 36) is extremely popular), eschatology, prayers, religious duties (*farā'iḍ*), legal rulings, the prohibition of alcoholic beverages, legends, the nocturnal ascent of the Prophet (*al-Mi'rāj*),[39] the story of Jesus, the Prophet, in conjunction with the story of Ḥabīb al-Najjār,[40] converted by St John and St Stephen in Antioch (Yaḥyā and Sevbān). The martyrdom of Ḥabīb (*Sūrat Yā'sīn*, vv.11–26), the death of Mary, attributed to Wahb b. Munabbih (d. AD 728), and the miracles of 'Alī b. Abī Ṭālib. Despite the great respect shown to 'Alī, he is certainly not the semi-divine figure of the extreme Shī'ites nor does his presence display the adoration which is to be found amongst some Iranian Sufis. Where Cabbalistic borrowings are detectable they do not appear to be more than a popular system that is borrowed from Ottoman culture.

The *Kitāb* in the British Museum contains an anecdote about the two ninth-century Sufis, Abū'l-Ḥasan al-Nūrī and Abū Bakr al-Shiblī, both of them from Baghdad. The content is concerned with the Day of Judgment. Nurī was addressing a group of people, warning them about the questions that the Lord God would put to them on that fateful day. Shiblī, who was passing by the door of the mosque, heard what he was saying and he remarked to his brother Sufi, 'Do not frighten the people thus. God will not ask much, He will only utter two words, 'my servant, I have been with you, but with whom have you been?'[41]

Faw (Fortune Telling)

This has always been popular amongst the Tatars. The relationship of the Arabic letters to numbers of a magical or oracular importance and to astrological tables may be seen in the significance of such digits as 26, 12 and the seven planets. Each weekday was named after a planet. There are similarities here to the '*Ilm al-Sīmiyā*', described by Ibn Khaldūn and by others. Each planet had two spirits, one of them evil (*fierey*), whilst the helpful and benign counterpart was known as *spornik*. Such astrology is widespread in popular Sufi practices and superstitions, elsewhere, especially in such brotherhoods as the Rifā'iyya that, at one time, was established in the Crimean region.

Melodics (Lahis and Zikers/Zikiers)

Tatar ritual and worship is a mixture of ancient Turkic rituals from the steppes, though, overwhelmingly, is of mainstream Sunnite ritual prayers. Influences, sometimes subtle, which have come from the adjacent, or surrounding Christian, or secular, communities have left a distinct mark.

Prayer meetings, often held in private houses and flats, resemble the 'house churches' in countries where believers have had to meet regularly, often in secret. A ceremony, almost in the form of a communion service, may take place where those present partake of bread, water and salt. The latter ritual is also a regular habit on other occasions. Bread, water and salt are brought to the table with the Qur'ān during special celebrations such as the naming of the newly born, at weddings and during the prayers that are recited after a decease, or during the celebration of a child's recitation of the Qur'ān (*ḥāfiz/ḥifz*). The custom of lahi, the tying of the Qur'ān to the head is, according to Chazbiewicz, a ceremony that is possibly borrowed from the Bektāshis, although no proof has been offered by him to substantiate this claim. Influences from Catholicism, or Orthodoxy, have also been suggested. Whilst candles are used in *tekkes* of the Rifā'iyya in Macedonia, it is likely that the candles that are to be found in Tatar mosques in Poland have been inspired by Catholic and Orthodox practices that are common amongst their neighbours in their village churches.

A more important channel for Sufi influences within Tatar Islam is the melodics (*tilāwa*) of the Tatar prayers. These, at times, take the form of a kind of 'liturgy' in mosque worship. Such chants, called *tekbīrs*, with a regular refrain, 'God is great' (*Allāhu Akbeer/Ellahu Ekbier, Allāh bir*), a confession of faith, *szahadę*. Others, are repeated by the congregation, and are frequently given the name of *zikier* (*Ar,dhikr*). The latter may be translated as a 'laud', a term used for a hymn of praise in parts of medieval Europe. That word is derived from the Latin, '*laus/laudis*'. *Zikier/Zikierów* (*dhikr*) amongst Sufis indicates a communal séance. Sometimes accompanied by musical instruments, in certain brotherhoods it is accompanied by violent movement of the body, self-laceration and 'out of the body' experiences. Though the latter is rarely found in Sufi circles – though known among Albanian Muslim communities – in Belarus, in Lithuania and in Poland, among the Tatars, the *zikier* is, exclusively, a 'laud'. The melodies, it is believed, were those once found among the early Qipchāqs, brought to Belarus, Lithuania and Poland from the steppes centuries ago, though it is possible that they may have been modified by the choral traditions of Orthodox Christianity and Catholicism. Others have proposed that the influences of Catholic and Orthodox styles of chanting may be the predominant influence. The call to prayer (*azanu*) from a minaret is almost unknown amongst the Tatars. The small wooden mosques have stumpy and purely decorative minarets, although high and pillar-like minarets characterise some regions of Tatar Islam in Russia. These latter are to be found, in ruins or rebuilt, or are newly constructed, for example in Old Bulghār, and in Kasim-Khāna (both in Tatarstan), uniquely in Gdańsk, in Poland, and in the eccentric Ottoman 'folly' of General Von Todleben, at Kédainiai, in Lithuania. A minaret of modest height survives in Kaunas, but the minaret that once graced the mosque in Minsk has been destroyed together with the rest of the building. Slender height may have been a response of the Muslim Tatars to their location amidst vast stretches of plain, steppe, forest, heath and on river banks (compare them with the soaring church towers in Norfolk and Lincolnshire and with those which are to be seen on the Swedish island of Gotland). At times, worship, prayer and meditation have been an intimate affair. This has taken place in lowly wooden mosques, similar to nonconformist chapels, with only a small circle of worshippers. However, it has never been, as is the case within the Balkan Bektāshis, a 'congregational' service in which the participants face one another in a circle. Amongst the Tatars, prayer and worship are directed towards Mecca. The *qibla*, the *miḥrāb*, is central to their worship. The womenfolk are kept separate from the men, frequently in galleries.

Aside from the observations of Chazbijewicz, some traces of Sufism are to be observed in a Tatar *zikier*, the text of which has been published in the Belarus Tatar publication *Bayram Tatarina Zyamli Belarutsi*,[42] and in *Acta Orientalia*,[43] by Henryk Jankowski.

The *zikier* is divided into stanzas. It largely consists of a repeated proclamation of the Unity of God and the Prophethood of Muhammad. It is a refrain (the rhyming pattern is a.a.a.b). The Prophet is praised to the point of adoration. The *zikier* is not only a voiced expression of faith, but it may also be written down in a *Kitaby* for reading and for recitation. This *zikier* may not be a *dhikr* in the strictest sense, and as it is understood by initiated Sufis attached to long established brotherhoods. In the case of the Balkans, brotherhoods, such as the Khalwatiyya and the Rifā'iyya, or in the Caucasus and in Central Asia amongst the Naqshabandiyya and the Qādiriyya, more 'classical' Sufi *dhikrs* are the norm. Amongst the Tatars of Lehistan, as elsewhere, there are, however, some borrowed expressions from Sufi vocabulary. These echo the 'gnosticism' of *Taṣawwuf*. An example is offered in the following verses:

> *Muhammad, the smiling faced,*
> *His face is like Shams and Duhā*
> *Moon faced like Mustafa*
> *Allāh's thing, Muhammad.*
> *All dervishes are from Him*
> *From Mustafa's light*
> *From the ranks of dervishes*
> *Muhammad, who proclaimed the announcement,*
> *It is he who founded the Dervish order.*

The repeated references to the 'Divine Light' of Muhammad and to the creation of the dervishes as an important part of the divine plan is derived from some Sufi source. One detail seems to have a faint echo of Bektāshism.[44] This is a reference to the eyebrows of the Prophet (commonly 'Alī in Bektāshi verse). The brows are depicted in the form of the Arabic letter *nūn*, 'His eyebrows are written like (the letter *nūn*)'.[45] It can hardly be doubted that a *zikr/zikier* of this kind was known to the Lehistan Tatars in past centuries. What survives today is derived from forms that have been influenced by Ottoman Sufism, and possibly dervish inspired. These were exchanged into expressions, in local Tatar languages, of a popular piety.[46]

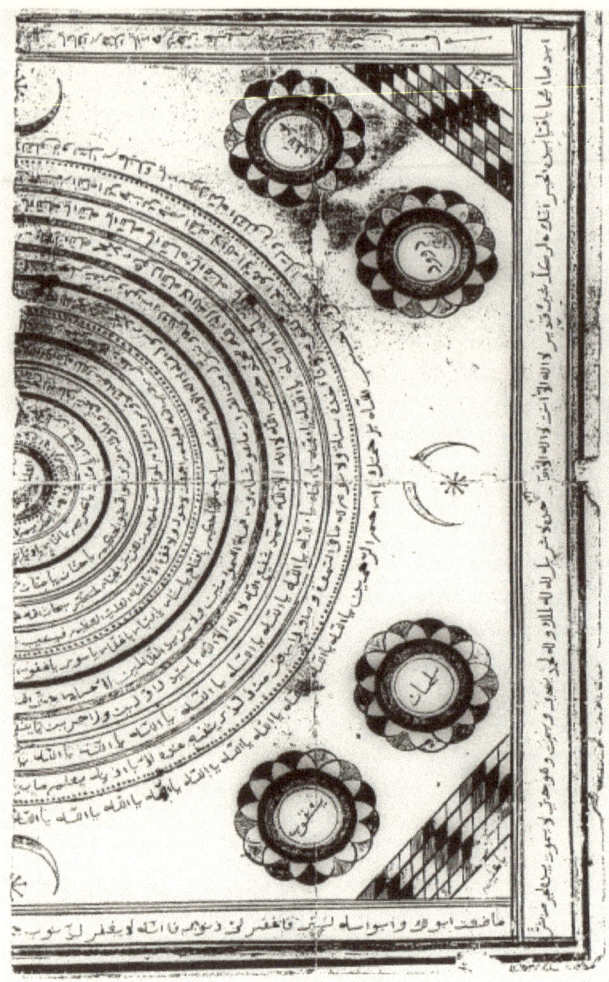

Figure 3 This document is from the collection of the Lithuanian National Museum in Vilnius. It is a nineteenth-century *muhir* with talismanic drawings and prayers and praise of the Prophet.

5. Islam and the contemporary religious scene in Belarus, Estonia, Latvia, Lithuania and Poland

> Our eloquent and resonant strings reverberate
> in resounding praise to King Berendy.
> Let us lower our sightless eyes. The gloom
> of a dawn free night has for ever sealed them
> Let our roving thoughts, with vision endowed,
> survey the nearby kingdoms of our neighbours.
>
> The song of the blind Psaltery players in Act 11 of Nikolai
> Andrievitch Rimsky Korsakov's (1844–1908) opera
> *The Snow Maiden*, 'a pillared court in King Berendy's palace'

The Islamic revival in the Baltic and the challenges of the new European nations

Polish Islam today and the practice of the faith in Belarus, Estonia and Latvia and Lithuania are little known topics that are discussed, or even mentioned, in this country. The true character of the Tatar and non-Tatar Muslim communities in this entire region of central and north-eastern Europe has been distorted by the bizarre image which life in Poland and the Baltic States appeared to many in the West over past centuries. This was, in part, on account of the writings of travellers. They were only superficially acquainted with the remarkable tolerance and the generous openness of heart and desire to assimilate that marked the Polish character since earliest times.

As Andrew Wheatcroft, in his book *Infidels, The Conflict between Christendom and Islam 638–2002*, has remarked, 'The Slav world was (largely) Christian and the Ottoman world was predominantly Muslim; yet Western travellers saw both of them as sunk in ignorance, lust and violence.'[1]

Wolff quotes the Comte de Segur's writing about Catholic Poland as a void, with its vast forests punctuated by open plains, and 'a poor population, enslaved; dirty villages; cottages little different from savage huts; everything makes one think that one has been translated back ten centuries and that one finds oneself amid hordes of Huns, Scythians, Veneti, Slavs and Sarmatians'.

An English visitor, William Coxe, travelling in Russia and Poland, also found the source of the 'Eastern barbarians' within the primitive peoples of the region, which could be subsumed under the broad heading of the people under the 'Tartar Yoke'.

The true picture was more complex, and it touched every class of Polish society. Amongst them a local 'Orientalism' was popular. It was often of a refined culture, and of a deeply spiritual character. As Beata Biedronska-Słotowa has explained:

> The application of stylistic forms of Islamic origin became so natural as to be acknowledged as a specific national characteristic. The extent of the problem was described most clearly by Cyprian Kamil Norwid in this letter of 1864 to General Wladyslaw Zamoyski: 'what is nationality – with us remains a mystery ... Nationality is not exclusiveness, but it is the force of appropriating all that is necessary for the progressive development of the nation's own elements ... it cannot be otherwise if the Homeland is not a sect – if patriotism is a creative power and not the power of becoming separated and withered away ... This is why those at the head of our nation, in Polish crowns, were heads from different nations, when we were not a sect but a – creative – power ... We even thought that nationality consists in the force of appropriation and not in that of puritanical exclusiveness, Therefore, while beating the Tatars, the Poles shaved their heads at the back in the Tatar fashion; they defeated the Tatars and at the same time followed the Tatar way of horse riding.[2]

Thus, while fighting against Turkey, carrying out negotiations with Persia behind the Porte's back, and at bottom considering the two nations as unworthy, nevertheless, the Poles adopted their enemy's outward features, this being manifested most spectacularly in the cut of Polish costume, equestrian style, love of horses, and construction of saddles and riding accessories.

The radiation of Oriental culture was the strongest amongst the burghers, though it also had an appeal among the intellectuals, who were sometimes especially drawn to Sūfism. This may be illustrated by the works of Jan Potocki (1761–1815), who revealed his sympathies in his literary works, such as *The Saragossa Manuscript* (*Rękopisie znalezionym w Saragossie*, 1805), and in his *The Journey of Hafiz*. His writings were especially influenced by his travels in Egypt, in Morocco, the Caucasus, Central Asia and the Far East. On the other hand, the dogmatisation of the Polish gentry's consciousness counter-balanced these trends, 'The most essential of these dogmas concerned the exceptional role of Poland as the bulwark of Christendom in its struggle with Islam.' This fact has been emphasised by the authors of *The Cambridge History of Poland, from the Origins to Sobieski (to 1696)*:

> It is interesting to observe how Poland seemed to turn towards the Orient in the seventeenth century, whilst Moscow at the same time became strongly Polonized. Oriental fashions became noticeable in the way the gentry dressed, in the way they wore their hair, in their weapons and horses. Frequent wars with the unbelievers made the Poles acquainted with Oriental customs, their servants, even their music. But this Orientalization never went deeper, in spite of external influences Poland remained Western at the core, a bulwark of Christianity, an outpost of Western culture against the Schismatic East or the Mohammedan Orient. It never swerved from this task.[3]

The phenomenon produced some eccentric 'follies'. According to Jan Reychman, 'the appeal of Ottoman and Oriental culture reached its heights during the sixteenth and nineteenth centuries'. In Eastern Europe, the introduction of elements of Turkish architecture found itself greatly facilitated by the presence of an important number of mosques, notably at Camenetz, Sawran, Kowaloka, and in Miedyboz, in the Ukraine. Near to the town of Olesno, in Silesia, a '*türbe*' (mausoleum) was raised, as a funereal monument over the tomb of a member of the Turkish delegation, who died in the Prussian court, in 1763. The minaret, often of a dizzy height (compare this with the existing minaret in the Gdańsk mosque or the Suyum Bike tower, or mosque minarets in Kazan), was a characteristic feature of this Ottoman taste. Prince Casimir Poniatowski, the brother of Stanislas-Augusta, the last king of Poland, erected a series of pavilions, dubbed "Turkish", in his residence at Soletz, close to Warsaw. In 1776, the architect, Bogumil Zug, had erected for this prince a very high minaret with a spiral staircase within. Prince Charles de Ligne, a great traveller, admired this minaret and he spoke of the bells that were supplied therein in order to call the faithful to prayer. Such a notion would have horrified Muslim viewers and visitors. We know that they horrified the Moroccan traveller, Ibn Battūta, in the Crimea during the fourteenth century.

In October 1942, L. Bohdanowicz published his lecture 'The Muslims in Poland. Their Origin, History and Cultural Life' in the *Journal of the Royal Asiatic Society*. It was one of the first articles to be published on the largely unknown 'Lithuanian Tatars' in this country. Amidst historical background and anthropological discoveries and theories of the time, he commented about the religious life of the Tatars, 'There are some reminders that in the sixteenth century the Tatars often brought imams from the Crimea and Turkey to fill the ranks of their clergy' (p. 167). He gave a brief description of the 'Hama'ils' (*Chamails*), which he described as 'breveries'. He mentioned *Tefsirs* and *Kitabs* which he described as collections of 'short stories and legends, generally on religious subjects'. He also wrote a section on 'The Polish Tatars in Modern Times' (pp. 172–8). Within it, he underlined the deep attachment of the Tatars to their faith and to the mission of a number of its leading religious figures to strengthen contacts with the wider Muslim world. On page 176, he remarked, 'A Tatar who changes his religion immediately ceases to belong socially to the Muslim community, Divorces, though quite simple under Muslim law are relatively rare'.

The mission to make the tiny Polish Muslim community better known in the World of Islam was to be remarkably successful. In the spring of 1925, Olgierd Najman Kryczyński (1884–1941) attended the International Geographical Congress in Cairo as a member of the Polish delegation. He was received by the members of the Egyptian government as well as by the Grand Sheikh of al-Azhar University, and he had the honour of being decorated by King Fu'ād with the Order of the Nile. The journey to Egypt had practical results: it was to some extent the prelude to diplomatic relations between Poland and Egypt. On his way back Kryczyński visited Syria, Palestine and Turkey, receiving everywhere a warm welcome. Mufti Szynkiewicz, too, had made many journeys to Muslim countries, not counting his attendance at Islamic congresses as the regular representative of the Polish Muslims. In 1930 he went to the Hijaz as a member of a diplomatic delegation led by Count Raczynski, the ambassador of Poland in London. In 1932 visited Cairo to present King Fu'ād with an address of thanks in the name of the Polish community. Bohdanowicz mentions other Polish Tatar missions. The journey of Arslan Kryczyński (to Morocco and his reception by its sultan, in 1934, is a notable example. He likewise mentions a publication on the Muslim Tatars of Poland by the students of the al-Azhar University in Cairo.

Many articles on the Tatars were to appear regularly in foreign journals and in other publications. The lectures and articles written by Arslan Kryczyński were to be published and made known in Russia (especially in the Crimea and in Azerbaijan), Poland, Lithuania, and in the Arab World, as the lists of publications which are furnished by Leon Najman Mirza Kryczyński (1887–1939), widely travelled in Morocco and the East, in the *Bibliografja do Historiji Tatarow Polskich*, published in 1935 make abundantly clear. In the Arab world itself, Middle Eastern readers were to become increasingly aware of the culture and the identity of these Tatars. In Algeria, a report was published by Aḥmad b. al-Ḥājj 'Abd al-Qādirī on 12 August 1931 about the Polish Tatars. In the 1920s and 1930s articles and statements by Najman Mirza Kryczyński appeared in Tbilisi, in Georgia, and also in Azerbaijan. On 13 May 1926, an article on the Muslim Poles was published in *al-Muqattam*, in Cairo. Articles and reports on the Tatars were published in the Hijāz, in Idel-Ural, in India and in Jugoslavia. Kryczyński described the Polish Muftiate in the publication *Vrijeme*, in Sarajevo, on 6 December 1930. His visit to Morocco received wide publicity in the 1930s in that country.

The *Lehistan Turk'leri* were widely welcomed in Turkey in the 1930s. Their existence and their reputation reached as far as Afghanistan and China. The Polish Tatars played an important role in the nationalist movements of the Russian Muslims. This was particularly noticeable in the Azerbaijan region of the Caucasus, and in the Crimea, which had for centuries enjoyed a special place in the affections of the Polish Tatars. Crimea's regional government contained three Polish Tatars, who were led by General Sułkiewicz, the premier. Many others held posts in the administration and in the armed forces. When General Sułkiewicz's government was overthrown by the White Russian army, after they had occupied the Crimea, many of the Polish Tatars returned to their independent homeland, others joined General Sułkiewicz, who went to Azerbaijan where he had accepted the post of chief of staff in the army. He was later to be shot when the Azerbaijan republic collapsed.

Numbers of Tatars returned to Poland. It was here that the Polish government created a Muslim community under an autonomous Tatar Mufti. Mufti Jakub Synkiewicz (1884–1966) organised courses of instruction for the *imāms* who were appointed, as well as courses for Tatars in Cairo's al-Azhar University. There were seventeen mosques and three houses for prayer in Poland before the Second World War. Several of these were outside the post-war borders of present-day Poland.

The revival of Tatar life and the practice of Islam were greatly assisted in Poland on account of the new annuals and the journals that were to be regularly published. Indeed, Bohdanowicz saw this as perhaps the most interesting form of cultural activity that was to characterise the Polish Tatars at the commencement of the twentieth century. These journals survived all the turmoil of war, occupation and indoctrination in the Communist years that were to follow. They were *The Islamic Review*, which was founded in 1930 by W.G. Djabagui, who was a journalist of Caucasian origin. Its content reflected the religious issues that were of topical importance at that time. *Tatar Life* was a monthly journal, founded in 1934. It has been revived relatively recently due to the labours of Dr Selim Chazbijewicz and his editorial helpers. Originally founded as the organ of the Mufti, it covers a wide spectrum of articles about the culture and history of the Tatars, not only in Poland and Lithuania, but its content is extended to include Central Asia, the Caucasus and beyond. *The Tatar Year Book* was, and still is, a publication with scientific goals and standards. Founded in 1932, it was edited by Arslan Kryczyński. Amongst other publications that have remained classic studies of the Tatars, is Stanislaw Kryczyński's masterly work *Tatarzy Litewscy, A Monograph on the History and the Ethnography of the Tatars of Leh*. It was first published as *Rocznik Tatarski* (*Tatar Yili–Annuaire Tatare*, T.111, 1938). It was republished, separately, in Gdańsk (Wydanie 11), in 2000. Other publications have appeared in more recent times. For example, *The World of Islam* (*Świat Islamu*) is a cultural magazine which concentrates on current religious issues, especially those which relate to Qur'ānic studies and to major moral questions. Special attention is paid to political crisis points in the Muslim World. It is published in Sokółka, a partly Tatar town between Białystok and the Belarus border. It carries on the task of interpreting Islamic culture and history to Tatar readers worldwide, though at a more popular level than the *Rocznik Tatarów Polskich*.

The foundation of the Gdańsk mosque

Despite its size, up to the last century Poland had few mosques within its borders. The post-war frontiers of Lithuania and Belarus fractured and split the ancient complex of Tatar villages, with their wooden mosques and enclosed cemeteries. Within the entire frontier region to the north-east and to the east of Białystok – the district known as Podlasie – Tatars are now to be found within and without the borders of the European Union.

Plans to erect a mosque in Warsaw had long been planned. Plans and photographs of the model of this mosque survive. The design (*rasm al masjid al-muṣammam*) of a mosque, by S. Kolendo and T. Mizak, which dates from 1935, reveals an impressive edifice, Middle Eastern in its general style, with four slender minarets placed at each corner of the building and capped by a fine dome not unlike the mosque architecture of the Balkans and Istanbul. No such mosque graces the Warsaw skyline today.

Instead, the mosque in the northern port of Gdańsk is probably still among the most impressive recently built Islamic structures in the Baltic region. It is regarded as one of the northernmost beacons of the faith.

Lech Kurpiewski, in an article called 'The minarets of Lehistan', which first appeared in a special number devoted to the ties between the Poles and the Arabs in the Polish journal *La Pologne* (also published in *Contemporary Poland*, no 5, 1990) explained why it was decided to build a new Polish mosque in that particular location:

> Why, for the first time in two centuries, is there to be a new mosque in Gdańsk?
>
> The Muslim religious community of this town totals two hundred believers. The first Muslims to come to live on the Polish sea-coast were emigrants from Novohrudok (now in Belarus), Vilnius (the capital of Lithuania) and from Grodno/Hrodno (now in Belarus). They did so between 1920 and 1930. They were drawn to come there because of the construction of the port of Gdynia (adjoining Gdańsk).
>
> After the Second World War, they had fellow believers among those who were being repatriated from the east of Poland. But the Gdańsk mosque is not only destined to cater for Polish Muslims. The town has a port and it is visited by Muslim seamen and by numberless students from the Muslim countries, students who are in courses of study there. These students were those who began to raise funds that were needed. A very large sum was contributed by the Arab merchant, 'Alī 'Abd Turkī, who is likewise entrusted with the collecting of funds in the countries of the 'Persian' Gulf. Some diplomatic missions of the Islamic countries have equally promised their financial assistance. The authorities in our country (Poland) have given a favourable welcome to the project to construct a mosque. The State Treasury has supplied the land and a substantial grant of aid has been promised for the restoration and the reconstruction of the two (old) mosques that already exist (Bohoniki and Kruszyniany) as well as the Tatar cemetery, in Warsaw.
>
> The Gdańsk mosque – the project of Marian Wszelaki and 'Alī Muchla – will not only serve as a place of worship. It will equally shelter two rooms that are destined for courses in the Arabic language and for lectures on the history, culture and art of the Muslim

countries, as well as for lectures about Polish culture for the benefit of foreigners who are Muslim by confession.

The future mosque that is planned for Warsaw will not be solely used for prayer. It will become a centre for Muslim culture and will be endowed with halls that will include a library that will have its own lecture hall, an exhibition hall, classrooms and a room that will be used for multiple functions, in addition to the traditional rooms for reunions and similar functions. The Warsaw mosque will be sited on the right bank of the River Vistula. It will be in the Sasa Kepa Quarter, Bajonska Street. The project has been worked out in detail by Dr Wojciech Zablocki, a well-known architect, as directed by the Muslim Religious Association. Bogusław R. Zagorski, who is the director of the Warsaw Muslim Community, will supervise the construction from a religious perspective. The Muslim mosque is to evoke the architectonic style of Islamic art and architecture, it will be very characteristic of the style, both on account of the quality and the solution to its mouldings and construction technique as well as by its dimensions.

The prayer hall will be able to hold 500 worshippers, 200 in the gallery for women, 150 in the porch, 400 in the court. The mass occupied by the building will be 25,120m^3, the ground surface occupy 2,400m^2. The entire structure will have above it a minaret that will measure 51 metres in height.

But before the first stone of the mosque is laid in Poland's capital, the Gdańsk–Oliwa mosque will probably have opened its doors. It is located in Antoni Abraham Street, near to the Roman Catholic church of Saint Stanislas.

During the session which was organised by the Religious Association of Muslims, on the occasion of the ceremony of walling up the document of the act of erection of the Gdańsk mosque, on 29 September 1984, the engineer, Stefan Mustafa Bajraszewski, said in his lecture about the adepts of Islam, in Poland:

> The relations between Polish believers in Islam and the Roman Catholic Church, over the course of centuries, were generally good. These relations were upheld by the spirit of mutual respect that prevailed. Polish Muslims frequently gave gifts to the Church. Often, Catholic priests legalised the last wishes and wills of the Muslims. The generally good and long term relations between the Polish Muslim believers and the Catholic Church have continued up to the

present time. I have been personally invited to the ecumenical meeting with His Holiness, Pope John-Paul II. During the course of this meeting, his Holiness called for 'mutual respect, mutual awareness and a seeking for those things which unite the particular confessions, not for those things which divide them'.

It may well be that soon the faithful who will pass through Gdańsk along 'Abraham Street' and who will go, each one, respectively, to the church of Saint Stanislas, or to the mosque, – will hear the sound of the bells of the church at the same time as the call of the muezzin, 'Allahu Akbar', 'God is great'.

The mosque opened its doors to all believers and to welcomed visitors in June 1990. After 1995, its *Imām* has been Dr Selim Chazbijewicz.

The excitement and Muslim revival during the 1980s have been sympathetically documented in the important article by Gyorgy Lederer and I. Takacs, 'Chez les musulmans de Pologne'.[4]

The years of the late 1980s were also to have other impacts on the Polish Muslim community. These impacts included a new translation of the 'message of the Qur'ān', into Polish, namely Professor Jozef Bielawski's *Koran. Z arabskiego i komentarzem*.[5]

One cannot be sure when the 'first' translation was made. The translation that preceded Bielawski's was published in 1858.

As for the ecumenical goals of the Muslims and the Catholics, this led to further developments that were only dreamed of by its first promoters. They will be examined later in this chapter. Before this, it would seem appropriate to examine the revival of Islam amongst the Tatars in neighbouring Lithuania and in Belarus, and the Muslims in Estonia and in Latvia.

Muslim Tatar life in Lithuania in the twentieth century

The Tatars in Poland have always been the most studied representatives of the nation that claims descent from the 'Golden Horde' amongst the writings of Westerners in Europe, Great Britain and the United States. The same is also true in the Muslim World at large. Sir T.W. Arnold, in his *The Preaching of Islam, a History of the Propagation of the Muslim Faith* (Luzac, London, 1935), which predated the essay by Bohdanowich, referred to them as 'Tatars in Lithuania' (p. 245). However, he went on to remark, 'But they have been in the habit of marrying Lithuanian and Polish women, whose children were always brought up as Muslims, whereas no Muhammadan girl was permitted to marry a Christian.'

The reason for this imbalance in any description of Tatar communities in this same local region is not hard to explain.

For many years huge tracts of Lithuania, as we know it today, including Vilnius, its capital, the nearby town of Trakai (Troki), and the adjacent Tatar villages, were an integral part of Poland. Only Kaunas, the home of the sole surviving 'antique' stone mosque in this Tatar region, was to enjoy some degree of national identity. Frontiers were regularly changed. This was on account of the wars, the treaties and the 'ethnic cleansing' that were to follow during, and after, the war years. It is only recently that the indigenous Tatar communities in contemporary Lithuania, and also the almost forgotten community, in Belarus, are able to be visited and to be studied by researchers from the West and also by the Lithuanians. Here, there is almost a paradox, since the Tatars of Belarus considerably outnumber those in Poland and in Lithuania, and, in fact, it was through the scholastic endeavours of Dr G.M. Meredith-Owens and Father A. Nadson, and in the researches of Dr S. Akiner and P. Wexler in their *The Byelorussian Tatars and Their Writings*, *Oriental Borrowings in the Language of Byelorussian Tatars*, *The Vocabulary of a Byelorussian Kitab* and *Jewish, Tatar and Karaite Communal Dialects and Their Importance for Byelorussian Historical Linguistics* that these north-western, or 'Baltic Tatars', their literature and their culture were to become better known in academia and so arouse some interest and respect in Western Oriental and in Slavonic and Eastern European Studies.

It is very probable that the benchmark article 'Islam in Lithuania' by Gyorgy Lederer[6] has been the most widely known recent report on the cultural rebirth within the world of Muslim Lehistan outside Poland. His article broke new ground, since Lithuania, not to speak of its Muslim minority, were little known in Western publications. In this respect, the value of what he wrote surpassed his own, and Ibolya Takacs's, slightly earlier report on Islam in Poland entitled 'Amongst the Muslims in Poland'.[7] In the article, the joint authors wrote about the history of Tatar settlement in Lithuania and Poland, the distribution of the Polish Tatars, their federation (*Zwiazek*), the cultural significance of the 'Oriental days of Sókołka'(*Orient Sokolski*) and the important part which Imām Mahmūd Zūk, the leader of the Ahmadiyya sect in Poland, was playing in Poland at that time. Alhough Lederer's, 'Islam in Lithuania' appeared in the 1990s, its content described the great changes that had taken place in that country during the previous decade.

This decade was a time when Tatar intellectuals in the country seized the opportunity to save their secularised fellow Tatars from total assimilation. Their goals were not solely cultural. In 1988, the founders of the Cultural Society of Lithuanian Tatars (*Lietuvos Totoriu Kulturos Draugija, Obschina Kul'tury Litovskih Tatar*) were well aware that this could not be achieved without a revival of the faith that had fundamentally shaped their culture over past centuries. From the late 1980s, they began to declare themselves to be 'Lithuanian Tatars'. At the same time reconstruction of the country's few surviving mosques was at the top of their agenda.

Structurally, the most impressive of these was the Kaunas mosque, situated in the city's Rambyes Park. It is a brick building in a slightly 'Cairene' style built in 1933. The Soviets used it for secular purposes, including a sports club. Restoration began in late 1989. The dome, the doors, the floor and the painting were restored and carried out by the Museum of Fine Arts. The Kaunas Tatar community rewired the entire building, furnished the pulpit (*minbar*), and they purchased the carpets, and the banisters. In the interior, above the principal room is a balcony for women and children. The project was co-ordinated by Professor Jonas Ridzvanavichius who was born into a Tatar family in Alytus. The mosque was inaugurated and restored for use in June 1991. The opening ceremony was attended by the Lithuanian vice-president and Muslim guests from countries in Eastern Europe, Turkey, Jordan and the United Kingdom, and this entire ceremony was recorded by Saudi television. The ceremony was unattended by representatives of the Lithuanian churches.

Two other old mosques in the country were also restored at this time. One of these two was Raizai (Rejze), near to Alytus. It contains Lithuania's most antique Tatar pulpit, dating from 1686. The inauguration ceremony took place in October 1993. A similar restoration took place at Keturiasdešimt (Sorok Tatary, '40 Tatars'), a village not far from Trakai. The entire settlement is 600 years old, the plan of the existing village showing its Tatar origins. Foreign help was important in both these restorations. Financial help came from the Turkish Embassy in Lithuania, the Human Appeal Foundation of the United Arab Emirates and wealthy sponsors in the Gulf. The Lithuanian Tatars saw that the restoration of their mosques was a vital element in the assertion of their ethnic identity in the new Lithuania and in the new Europe. This assertion, at a religious level, is personified in the revival of the Muftiate and, at the same time, a project that has recently begun, namely to achieve a translation of the Qur'ān into the modern Lithuanian language. At a wider level, the Tatar's revival has been spearheaded by The Society of Lithuanian Tatars, who have also worked closely with the Karaims, both of them Qipčaqs (Qipchāqs), and both of them looking back to Duke Vytautas as the founder-patron of their medieval settlements.

Lederer has shown how this came about in the revolutionary movements of the late 1980s, led by Mensaid Bairasewski the first president of the 'Tatar Society'. He was replaced by Adas Jakubauskas, who was a Tatar poet and a scholar in Russian philological studies. Turkey actively sponsored this movement, both for pan-Turkic and for religious reasons. Another supporter was the Ahmadiyya Islamic movement (whose most active advocate in Poland has been *Imām* Tāhā Zūk, in Warsaw). A Lithuanian Tatar delegation visited London, in 1991, in order to meet the fourth 'Caliph', Hazrat Mirza Tāhir Ahmad. Ahmadiyya missionaries came to Alytus to found a centre, but their dreams of directing the Lithuanian Tatar's religious revival proved to be unsuccessful. Instead, the 'Tatar Society' renewed their long established relations with the Sunni Kazan Tatars, in Tatarstan, and also with the Crimean Tatars and with Mufti Talgat Tadjuddin of Ufa, in Russia. As in Poland, visiting Arab teachers, *imāms* from Bosnia, and devout Muslims from Azerbaijan and from Chechnya, have played an important part in the overall Muslim revival through regularly attending the mosques and teaching the faith particularly to the young. Vilnius, which once possessed a mosque of historical importance, is now in great need of a mosque to represent the Muslim community in Lithuania's capital. Its existence will be of importance in maintaining the links with Muslim congregations in Minsk, beyond the current bounds of the new Europe.

The future of the Tatars, in Lithuania, must also be seen within the context of the marked resurgence of interest, in Lithuanian academic circles, and especially centred within the University of Vilnius and in the Institute of Lithuanian History, in all the country's ethnic and religious minorities: Rabinnical Jews, the Yiddish language, the Karaims, the Tatars, the Old Believers and the Roma. The Tatars, and indeed the Muslims, in Lithuania, as elsewhere, are only one ethnic and confessional component. Inevitably, events have overtaken the predictions of Lederer, when he wrote that, 'The anti-Islamic xenophobia raging in Europe is not likely to affect the Lithuanian's benevolent indifference toward Islam even if their politicians are eager to join Europe and its international institutions. This requires an improvement in the legal and actual conditions of all minorities ... Despite certain nationalistic and conservative Catholic exclusivist tendencies in post-socialism, the Islamic experiment is nevertheless far from being conceived as an alien body in Lithuanian society, unlike that in some other countries of Eastern Europe' (pp. 446–7). However, with exceedingly few numbers, the Tatars enjoy many advantages over those other Muslims in Europe, who live in 'ghettos', or who have become the focus of militant Islamic movements seeking new recruits and new fields for missionary endeavours.

A note on Russian Kaliningrad

The *Oblast* of Kaliningrad is today part of Russia, but in the past it was known as 'East Prussia', or 'Little Lithuania'. It was the city of the famous philosopher Emmanuel Kant.

Islam is far from being unknown there. Indeed, Muslims are said to number more than 20,000. As elsewhere in the Baltic region their principal interest and concern is the construction of a mosque and the development of a deeper friendship and closer co-operation with the other non-Muslim communities amongst whom they live and work.

As planned, and approved, the proposed mosque would consist of a two-storeyed building, 46 metres in length and 36 metres in breadth. It would be able to accommodate 400 believers during Friday prayers and on major festive occasions. Its minaret would rise to a height of 28 metres above street level.

The Muslim leaders were given a plot in Dzerzhinsky Street, in August 2005. They had requested in 2004 that it should be built and the authorities in the city had approved the construction of an Islamic Centre not far from the Moscow Rayon Administrative Centre. Objections to its erection there followed at a later date. Instead, a site in a popular resort district had been proposed, but again the city authorities raised objections. As an alternative, the city officials proposed a site on Peace Prospect (*Prospekt Mira*). The decision was approved by Vladimir Yegorov, the governor of the *Oblast*. However, complaints continued to be aired about the locality and particularly strong opposition was expressed by the Russian Orthodox Bishop Seraphim of the Baltic. It was his firm conviction that the goal of the Muslim community was not only the building of their mosque but that it was also to be a 'spiritual centre', the aims and aspirations of which were far reaching. As for the mosque, he would raise no objections to its construction. However, he and his 'flock' insisted that it should be a 'modest mosque'. It should be sited near the very edge of the city and in a locality that reflected the numerically minority status of the Muslim community in Kaliningrad.

Once again, the local authorities reverted to their original proposal, made ten years previously, to construct a mosque near to the city centre.

To date, the opposition to the building is as strong as ever at a local level. It recalls the local opposition to the rebuilding of the Minsk mosque, in Belarus, in the heart of that city. The presence of a large Orthodox congregation in the close vicinity seems to be an important factor determining the suitability, or unsuitability, of the respective mosques whatever may be their size. There is also a fear of local terrorism. Some opposition was expressed in extreme terms that were heavily criticised by Yury Savenko, the mayor of Kaliningrad. It will take some time for these religious barriers to be removed.

The source of the above report is the Union of Councils for Jews (UCSJ) in the former Soviet Union. This Union has shown an active and very positive attitude and role in the Jewish community within Kaliningrad in support of the case of the Muslim community. It has done this by hosting interfaith gatherings in the city synagogue. It has been here that the representatives of Islam, the Russian Orthodox Church and Judaism have all agreed to meet regularly in order to discuss their common goals. They have included Orthodox Archpriest Maryan Pozun, Hakim Bekteyev of the Muslim Community, Rudolf Alexanyan of the Armenian Apostolic Church and Chief Rabbi David Shvedik of Kaliningrad.

So far the outcome of their deliberations has been fruitful and they have agreed upon a positive and common approach to communal religious problems. This activity does not seem out of place in the city of Immanuel Kant. Karen Armstrong made a pertinent observation in her *History of God* that:

> Like al-Ghazzali centuries earlier, he (Kant) argued that the traditional arguments for the existence of God were useless because our minds could only understand things in space or time and are not competent to consider realities that are beyond this category. But he allowed that humanity had a natural tendency to transgress these limits and seek a principal of unity that will give us a vision of reality as a coherent whole. This was the idea of God. It was not possible to prove God's existence logically but neither was it possible to disprove it. The idea of God was essential to us: it represented the ideal limit that enabled us to achieve a comprehensive idea of the world.[8]

In Kaliningrad the monotheistic religions had set aside their differences and they had unexpectedly set a positive example to the other peoples of the Baltic region.

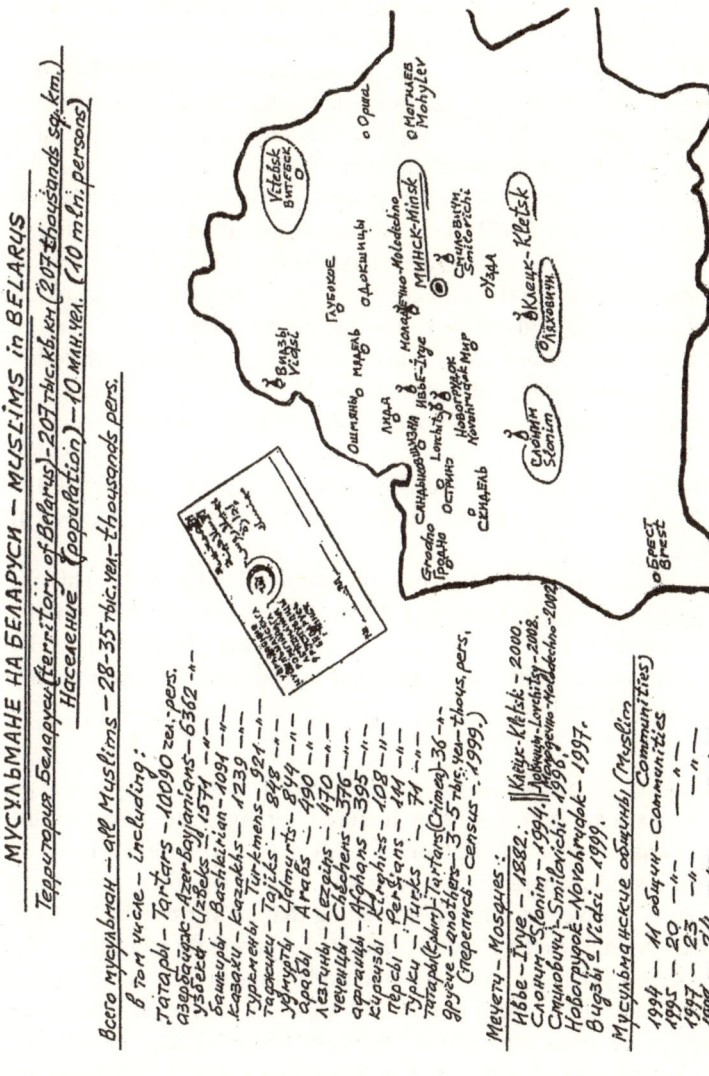

Figure 4 Map showing mosques in Belarus.

The Tatar Muslims amidst the mixed Muslim, the Christian and the 'neo-pagan' communities in Belarus

According to information given to the author by Mufti Ismael Alexandrovich, recent figures for the believers in Belarus reveal an interesting change in the balance of the Muslim community in that country. Out of the estimated total, 12,500 are now Tatars (from Belarus, Tatarstan and elsewhere). They are still the biggest group, but the figures suggest that they could be outnumbered by others in the multi-ethnic Muslim community in the relatively near future.

Dr Zorina Kanapacki is now engaged in making one of the first documented demographical studies of Belarusian Tatars. She has found that this community is widely dispersed. Some 8,337 of them live in towns and 1,762 live in the villages. The Tatar minority has shrunk, in size, between 1989 and 1999, and it has been decreasing by over 30 per cent, due to intermarriage and old age. Despite this, the direction of matters and policies that relate to the Muslim faith community in the country reflects the unique place the Tatars have always occupied within the religious history of Islam in Belarus. Other research taking place in this entire region includes a study into the genes of the Polish Tatars which is now currently in progress at the University of Białystok.

The first All Belarusian Muslim Congress was held in 1994. This led to the foundation of the 'Muslim Religious Community of the Republic of Belarus'. Its first head was Mufti Ismael Alexandrovich. It would appear that Lederer had initially planned to visit this Tatar community many years ago. He wrote:

> Minsk is probably too far for Lithuanian Tatars. They maintain relations with their couple of hundred coreligionists living on the Byelorussian side of the border in Ivje (*sic*) (İvye)/Iwie), in the Lyda district, where a mosque is still used. The other mosques in Byelorussia were destroyed, including that of Minsk which was in the centre of the city. New mosques were reportedly reopened in the western city of Novogrudok (Nowogrodek) and in Slonim. According to Mr Sabanović, there are 25,000 Muslims in Byelorussia (many immigrated from other parts of the former Soviet Union), a high figure indeed, and a Muslim youth organisation has been founded there, presumably by the numerous Arab youth studying in that country. He showed me one of their publications, a *Bayram Journal*. All the information on modern Islam in Byelorussia is to be checked and treated

Islam and the contemporary religious scene 91

in a separate study. This also applies to the Tatar Cultural Association of Grodno (Hrodno, near the Polish border) called 'Kitab' (a Tatar association in the Tsarist empire had the same name) and organized by the very active Mr Jusuf Ali Mirza Krinitsky.[9]

The above passage in Lederer's article mentioned a handful of rebuilt or newly established mosques. However, it furnished no details, nor photographs. Since he wrote, two outstanding 'catalogues' have been published in Warsaw. These allow one to see the remarkable restoration and reconstruction of several of the mosques in Belarus, alongside those which are to be found in Lithuania and in Poland. Furthermore the Belarus Muslim community has made impressive strides towards reshaping its identity within twenty-four Muslim communities. Far more mosques are functioning if one is to include 'house mosques' in several localities. These include: Iwie (İvye), a beautifully restored mosque, mostly dating from 1882, which is located in the middle of a largely Tatar village; Slonim, its new mosque having been built in 1994; Smilovichi, built in 1996; Novohrudok (Novogrudok), restored in 1997; Vidsi opened in 1999; Kletsi in 2000,; Lovchitsy in 2008; and Molodechno, in 2002. Scattered Muslims are located in Vitebsk and in several other important provincial towns.

The first of the catalogues, which have been published in Warsaw in 1999, is titled *Meczety i Cmentarz Tatarów polsko-litewskich* (Mosques and cemeteries of the Polish–Lithuanian Tatars).[10] Leading Belarus Tatars contributed to, and furnished, the illustrations for this sumptuous production, in colour. The photographs of the mosques of İvye, Novohrudok, and Smilovichi indicate how active the Belarusian Tatars have recently been in the repairing, refurbishing and rebuilding of their religious monuments of antiquity. A more recent volume, titled *Piśmiennictwo i muhiry Tatarów polsko-litewskich* (Manuscripts and Islamic pictures and hangings (*muhirs*) in mosques of the Polish–Lithuanian Tatars), with text contributed by the same authors was published in Warsaw in 2000.

This latter book is equally outstanding and comprehensive, with plates showing pages of manuscripts and *muhirs* from Belarus. There are some excellent examples from the latter. These publications enhance the modestly produced text of C.L. Dymin and Ibrahim Kanapacki's short, though unique, study of the Tatars in Belarus, *Belaruskiya Tatari: Minylae i Suchasnasch*, which was published in Minsk in 1993. Other works have been published since. These include: short monographs associated with the journal *Bayram*; Ibrahim Kanapcki and A.I. Cmolik's *History and Culture of the Belarusian Tatars (Gistoriya i Kultura Belaruskikh Tatar)*, published in Minsk in 2000; and *Belarusian Tatar Manuscripts of the End of the Seventeenth up to the Beginning of the 20th Centuries from the Collection of the Yakub Kolas Central Science Library of the National Academy of Sciences of Belarus*. The publication of this valuable catalogue was supported by the American Council of Learned Societies. A short book on the architecture of the Belarus mosques, *Berag Bandravannyay tsi Adkul u Belaruci Myachztsi*, was published in Minsk by A.I. Lakotka in 1994.

The Belarus Tatars have participated regularly in conferences on Tatar affairs in Vilnius and in Białystok.

A tour organised by Belintourist (2004), entitled 'Moslem Places in Belarus', and lasting five days, has enabled Muslims and other visitors to visit the principal mosques of historical interest and to meet the local Muslim communities.

The greatest dream of the Belarusian Tatars, in the near future, was to rebuild the city mosque in Minsk, which was destroyed in 1962. According to the plan, it would recapture the architectural elegance of its nineteenth-century predecessor, which, in its design, bore a resemblance to the mosque in Kaunas and to the Karaite *kenesa*, in Vilnius, in its Oriental architecture. Though it was planned to re-erect it elsewhere in the city, it would have eventually been equipped with far greater teaching facilities and with ample space for students and visitors, and it was to be surrounded by a beautiful garden. Other plans included the restoration of the ancient ruined mosque in Doubuchki, wooden parts of the old mosque having been currently preserved as a historical relic, and the acquisition of houses for prayers and social gatherings in Hrodno (Grodno), Glubokoye, Orsha, Uzda, Brest, Mogilev and Lida. There are also plans to stock Islamic 'Sunday schools' with Islamic books, to organise Muslim summer camps (*muhayyems*) for young people and to plan future international conferences in which participants will come from the other countries of Eastern Europe which have sizeable Muslim, especially Tatar, populations. It is a matter of great regret that all the efforts made by the late *Imām*, Dr Ibragim Kanapatski, to launch this project in 2005 were brought to a complete standstill for a number of reasons, though principally on account of disagreements and irregularities within the Muslim community itself and their failure to obtain financial support from sponsors and from funding within the Islamic World.

Dr Kanapatski had made every effort to acquire funding from the wider Islamic World and, according to Dr Zorina Kanapatskaya, had visited Tripoli on two or three occasions. He had been the guest of

President Muʻammar al-Qadhdhāfī and he had held lengthy discussions with him. At that time, the Libyan president had promised to help with the construction of the Minsk mosque. With the tragic early death of Dr Kanapatski there is, at the moment, no successor of the same calibre and commitment to renew the discussion of this Libyan offer.

All the facts that are known to us therefore indicate a sizeable, active and increasingly important mixed ethnic community of Muslims, both Sunnī and Shīʻite, including the long established Lithuanian Tatars, in Belarus today. There are four acting mosques in the country. Approval for the building of a mosque in Vidzy, in Braslav and Vitebsk district, has already been granted. Dr Ibrahim Kanapacki had also reported the presence already of a working mosque at Kletsk in Minsk district.

Belarus contains a large number of historical and newly built Orthodox, Catholic, Uniate and Protestant churches and Christian religious organisations, notwithstanding the Marxist image it still seeks to present to the outside world. To this may be noted the revival of allegedly 'pagan' cults. Though the centre of this movement is now in Lithuania, similar activities are to be found in Latvia, Poland and the Ukraine, as well as in Belarus. In the Baltic States the revival, which dates back to the Lithuanian mystic Wilhelm Storosta, or Vydunas, who was born in 1868, seeks inspiration in the beliefs of the extinct Prussians. Their religious beliefs have been revealed by archaeology and by linguistic studies combined with ideas of the 'New Age' movement in general. Followers hold pagan shrines in the Kaliningrad region as especially sacred. In Belarus, the 'pagan' movement is represented by the Centre of Ethnocosmology, in Minsk. Known as 'Krywya', it takes its name from the Krywiches, a tribe, part Balt, part Slav, which in ancient times populated the northern area of contemporary Belarus. Similarly, the Ukraine has its 'Union of Ukrainian Indigenous Faithful'. The groups, who are centred in Kyiv, publish the magazine entitled *Svarog*, the Slav god who represented the father of the sun, a god of fire and of battles.

Belarus, however, is overwhelmingly an Orthodox Christian country (some 50 per cent, although one figure maintains that 80 per cent are Orthodox). Orthodoxy reached the country around AD 900, though what survives of the early churches dates back no further than the twelfth century. The country has a substantial Catholic minority (some 30 per cent), as well as over 100,000 members of the Uniate (Greek Catholic) Church. Members are predominantly Ukrainians. Protestantism in Belarus was a result of the Renaissance. It reached its peak in the fifteenth and sixteenth centuries with sub-branches of it representing anti-Trinitarians and Unitarians (Socians). Today, there are to be found churches, both old and new, of every denomination. The Baptists have at least 200 churches and their numbers are continuously growing.

In Lithuania and in Poland, the dialogue of the Tatar Muslims has always been with Catholicism, or with Protestantism, or with the once very large Jewish community. In Belarus, their friendly co-existence (one can only speak of a relatively recent 'interfaith dialogue') with Orthodoxy, and with Jewry, has meant that their position has been closer to that of the Russian Tatars, those in Kazan, and those Orthodox and Armenians and Karaims who were established in the Crimea alongside the Turks and the Tatars during the Middle Ages. The Muslim Tatars of Belarus have shared with Christian neighbours in the dreadful consequences of the Chernobyl disaster, just over the border in the Ukraine, and deaths from radiation are to be found amongst them. Within the cemeteries where both Orthodox and Muslims are buried, each year half the fresh burials are of people whose ages range from between 20 and 30 years. In spring, after Easter, the Orthodox bereaved come to tend and to decorate the graves, to share their meals beside and upon the graves, and, in the spirit, to share their loss and separation with those who are buried there. This is during the still observed pre-Christian holiday of Radunitsa. Such visits are matched by those during the 'Āshūrā celebration amongst the Tatar Muslims. Dr Zorina Kanapatskaya has told the author how the Tatars in Belarus nowadays share the great festival customs of their Christian neighbours. Thus, in Iwie (İvye/Ivje) the Muslim Tatars celebrate the Catholic Easter, whereas those in the region of Minsk celebrate the Orthodox Easter. She has told the author how her grandmother still paints Easter eggs and on the same occasion she bakes Tatar cakes. The Tatars are very happy to celebrate both *Ramadan Bayram* and Easter.

Tatar and non-Tatar Muslims in Estonia in the twentieth century

Whatever may be the date of its sources, the Estonian folk-epic *The Kalevipoeg*, attributed to F.R. Kreutzwald (1853), has introduced the Tatars amongst the foes of Kalevi, the folk hero of the Estonians, fighting, as he did, against the Poles and the Lithuanians. In ballad XXX, vv. 407–34 the Estonian hero spares no quarter for his Polish and his Tatar foes in his combats with them in a district outside Pskov, beyond the eastern border of Estonia. This whole episode is almost a mirror image of the defeat of the Teutonic Knights by Alexander Nevsky, or, during another occasion, the defeat of the Livonian Order, at Tannenburg and Grunwald:

Then Olev constructed a bridge, like a great frame of wood,
The war crossed the bridge, the principal beams snapped and, at the
angles, the stones quaked and then crumbled.
Battalions of Poles, ranks of Tatar killers, a long train of
Lithuanians, according to the spies' reports,
Took up their station near to Pskov.
Once more the war began its course, the wagon of war wended its
advance,
The gallant son of Kalev set forth once more to smite the foe.
To condemn the Poles to perish for ever, to throw the Tatars
To the sod of the earth!
His wild sword, methinks, a scythe, felled bodies in that open field,
Severing Polish heads as berries in the depths of yonder woods,
Like fallen nuts under a hazel.
Like hail stones on fresh land amidst a clearing.
Corpses covered the ground, up to three cubits was their height,
A bloody torrent streamed forth from the piles,
Five spans it was,
On that morrow, the Tatars towards their death were swept away.[11]

Estonia has a substantial Muslim community that has been established in the country for a considerable period of time. As in Belarus, Lithuania and Poland, the Muslim community is predominantly Tatar, though they are not descendants of the Tatars and Karaites who originated in the Qipčaq (Qipchāq) steppes and who were once a part of the 'Golden Horde'. Here, their family roots are to be found in today's Tatarstan and in other regions of the former Soviet Union. Timur Seifullen, honorary president of the Estonian Union of National Minorities (*Eestimaa Rahvuste Ühendus*), has explained the reasons for their settlement in Estonia in a letter that he wrote to Mr Leopoldo J. Niilus of the Lutheran World Federation (Lutheranism being the national religion of the Estonians):

> The history of the current Tatar community in this country begins with the years following the Great Socialist October Revolution. When the Russian Empire, under the pretext of civil war, reached, with its conquering quests, the Tartar Republic and once again occupied it (in other words, instituted the Soviet regime there) massive repression took place. A common feature was the locking of intellectuals and religious leaders within the mosques and even to burn them alive. A wave of refugees fled from their homeland in the 1870s as its consequence. Tartars were scattered all over the world, and, amongst other

havens, they reached Finland and Estonia. In Estonia, the towns of Narva and Tallinn were to witness the main concentration of these refugees from the war. It was almost a miracle that these Tatars crossed through Russia alive. They were living in total deprivation and they were frequently very sick. Many of them – those from the rural districts and especially their women-folk – spoke no other language than that of the Tatars. Amongst their men-folk a little Russian was known but it was very faulty.

Although their faith was alien, the Estonians were tolerant. Separate cemeteries were appointed for the Tatars, in the Tallinn region and in Narva. Between 1920 and 1940 no restrictions were imposed on the Tatars. Some found employment while others became merchants. The youth reached a higher level of education and some of them even studied in the University of Tartu, the prime university within Estonia. The sufferings of the Tatars were experienced anew during, and after, the Second World War and the Soviet re-occupation.

Seifullen concluded his letter with a plea to the free Estonians:

> Today this faith community is registered again in the Republic of Estonia. As long as the Estonians remain the rulers in their own land we can rest assured that it (the faith) will not be forbidden once again. In the process of the registration and all the paper work related to it, we have had an immense amount of problems and questions to answer. The Department of Religious Affairs of the Republic of Estonia, and Chancellor Tiit Sepp, has not only shown a positive attitude towards our endeavours, but they (its members) have also actively assisted us in all kinds of ways. They have shown us their serious concern and they have spent much of their time for our benefit. The government of the Republic of Estonia, and its Prime Minister, Mr Mart Laar, are attempting to find possible ways to our request to build a house for the activities of our faith. It is obvious in this country it is commonly understood that if any 'European' is entitled to proclaim, with pride, that he or she is a Christian, then, likewise, any person of the Islamic faith, who has settled in Estonia, has the right, without shame, to call himself, or herself, a Muslim.

As in Belarus, the Muslim community has seen a change in the ethnic balance of the Muslim faithful.

According to the statistics that have been given to the author, and thankfully acknowledged by the Mufti of the Estonian Islamic association (*al-Jam'iyya al-Islāmiyya al-Īstōniyya*), Mr Ildar Muhhamedshin, the Tatar predominance is challenged by other ethnic groups. Out of a population count in Estonia (*kokku elanikke Eestis*), in 2000, 1,370,052, the figure for the Tatars was 2 per cent of the population, 2,582, a drop in number from 4,058, in 1989. Amongst the entire Muslim population the figure for 2000 is also significant. The Tatars total 2,582 (in 1989, they were 4,058, in 1997, 3,315), Azeris, who are predominantly Shī'ites, total 880 (1,238 in 1989), Bashkīrs, 152, Uzbeks 132, Chechens 48, Turkmen 36, Tajiks 35, Kirghiz 26, Turks 24, Arabs 19, Persians 14, Circassians 14 and Abkhazians 13. These latter are very low figures. The entire Muslim population in Estonia is estimated to be 3,975.

Within Estonia, these statistics are very loosely used. Thus, the 'Estonian Turkic School', the aim of which is to teach Turkic languages, in Tallinn, gives the following estimate of the Muslim minorities for whom it serves as 'about 2000 Azerbaijanis', 'about 4000 Tatars', and 'about 1,200 Chuvashes'. No figure is given for the other ethnic groups entered above. In the West the figures given exceed the above figures. Thus, in a map which illustrates 'The New Europe' published in the May 2004 edition of *Q News International*,[12] the Muslim population of Estonia is stated to be 10–20,000, mostly in Tallinn.

Some sharp debate has arisen in Estonia over the benefit of building of a mosque in Tallinn. One of these plans envisaged the construction of perhaps the largest mosque in the entire Nordic and Baltic area. The idea was supported by 30 per cent of the population, as opposed to 60 per cent against, according to a poll published by the daily *Eesti Päevaleht*. One reason for the opposition to its construction was its location since such an alien structure seemed incongruous amidst the grand medieval Gothic and the Hanseatic architectural skyline of this beautiful city. Member of Parliament and City Counsellor Liina Tönisson, of the Centre Party, was quoted as saying, 'I hope that for the building of the mosque the city will provide land in a less significant location.' Habib Gulijev, a wealthy Azeri, and an importer of pomegranate juice from Azerbaijan to Estonia, proposed a site in the district of Pinta, but his grandiose and costly scheme has alienated many Azeris. Timur Seifullen has opposed this plan. He confirmed this when the author spoke to him about the aspirations for the building of a mosque during the author's visit to Tallinn in autumn 2004. The demographic distribution of Muslims now favours the Shī'ites, though, in both Estonia and Latvia, the Sunnis still outnumber the Azeris.

A short history of the Muslim communities in Latvia[13]

Latvia's total population surpasses 2,700,000 souls. However, only 52 per cent of these are ethnically Latvian. The remainder are Russian 34 per cent, Belarusian 4.5 per cent, and Ukrainian 3.5 per cent. As for its cities, all seven of the largest among them contain Latvians who are in the minority. Rīga itself is no exception to this rule. It has a predominantly Russian population. Since the tiny and divided Muslim community lives within Rīga, with only a few living beyond its suburbs, there is an immense barrier to their participation in Latvian life and culture. Latvia today, culturally and linguistically, is a little like a nest of Russian dolls (*matrioška*). Its outermost 'doll', or 'shell', portrays the ideal national aim of the Latvians, namely, that their Baltic culture and language will ultimately truly reflect their national culture of the twenty-first century and that it will enshrine the personality of a people that has achieved a newly won independence after years of suppression. Latvians had, in the past, faced the near extinction that had once befallen their Prussian kinsfolk. This goal, this hope, will determine their ultimate place in the New Europe. Religious loyalties are divided. Out of some 800,000 to 900,000 nominal Christians, some 370,000 are Protestants, including Lutherans, and 350,000 are Catholics, who are at their strongest in the region of Latgale bordering Lithuania and Belarus.

If Latvia is the outermost 'doll', then the Russian 'doll', the Orthodox 'doll', is to be found immediately within it. The minute Muslim 'doll' is hidden, barely visible in fact, nestling deeply beneath those other 'dolls' that are overwhelmingly Russian or Balt-speaking. For this very reason they are helpless and alone. They are barely able to express themselves outside the circle of their formerly Soviet communities. Today, their customs are overwhelmingly 'Russian', in most aspects of their daily life, or else, they, as a community, would appear to imagine or find inspiration or cultural solace from the life of those territories of the former Soviet Union from whence they had originated: from Russia, from Belarus, from Tatarstan, from Bashkortostan, from the Ukraine, or from Armenia and from Georgia.

For this reason the Latvian Muslim community is divided and strikingly diverse, difficult to integrate, yet very conscious of its own Islamic identity. This situation will continue for some time, though the slowly growing number of believers from Africa, the sub-continent of India and Pakistan, from Turkey, the Middle East, or from Western Europe, will, in time, effect this prevailing situation, and, indeed, this is already producing radical changes and ideas. Mosques are almost non-existent, though the Latvian authorities have not rejected the Muslims' requests, they have rejected the original proposed site for a major mosque that, by chance, was discovered to lie in the path of the Via Baltica that is now under construction. This highroad will link Finland to central and southern Europe. But, as is the situation elsewhere in the Baltic, the money to build such a mosque is at present nowhere to be found, and for the foreseeable future the weekly prayers will be held in private homes, or in hired halls, or in the so-called 'Sunday Schools' for *Qur'ānic* study, or, during the summer, in camps (*lager*) for the young in which their faith can be taught and they can join together as a living Muslim community. As in other parts of the Baltic, the preservation of cultural and ethnic identity, at times, seems to take a priority over specifically Islamic loyalties and priorities, especially so where these apply to certain issues of faith. Thus, the cartoons of the Prophet Muhammad that were published in Denmark provoked only a limited response among the Muslims in Latvia. Years of an atheist system for many within the Soviet Union has conditioned these small communities to adopt a position of a reserved though pained displeasure, or of silent disapproval. This contrasts markedly with the violent reactions in Great Britain, Scandinavia, France, Spain, Africa, the Middle East and in Pakistan.

Veiled women are exceedingly few indeed in Rīga's streets, or, rather, there are so many Russian and other local women who wear types of headscarves that a Muslim *ḥijāb* is barely worthy of notice amongst them.

Immigrants from Africa are far more likely to be veiled. Even the most noteworthy 'Islamic' organisation today in Latvia, *Īmān*, has been markedly restrained in its response to international issues where the Latvian government and society have shown strong support for NATO intervention, for example in Afghanistan.[14]

Central amongst the priorities of these Muslim communities has been an active participation in the national organisation that has been established by the efforts of the dedicated, highly cultured and brilliant Armenian musician and pianist Raffi Harajanian. He is the director and co-ordinator of the Ita Kozakeviča's Society of the National Cultures Association of Latvia.[15] This society which is wide in its embrace, includes, 'Rīgas Ebreju Kopiena' (the Rīga Jewish Community), 'Dačija' (the Moldav-Romanian Society), 'Šamšoblo' (the Society of Georgians in Latvia), 'Lao' (the Society of Armenians in Latvia), and others that represent the Belarusians, Estonians, Germans, the provincial Latvian Latgalians, Lebanese (the Cultural Club (LLIKK)), Lithuanians, Gypsies

(Čigānu), Poles and Russians. Five others are solidly representative of the Muslim communities. They include 'Azeri' (the Latvian Azerbaijani Cultural Society[16]), 'Čišme' (the Latvian Baškīr-Tatar Cultural Society[17]), 'Nur' (the Latvian Uzbek Cultural Society[18]), and 'Idel' (the Latvian Tatar Society[19]).

These last four societies represent Muslim communities throughout Latvia. 'Azeri' was founded in 1988. Its chairman is Ulduzhan Ahmedov and it numbers some 2000 members who principally reside in Rīga, Ventspils, Daugavapils, Limbažos and Jelgavā. Central to its interests and its goals are Azeri culture, education, language, the defence of social and civil rights and the interests of Azerbaijanis in Latvian society. It fully supports the 'Sunday School' wherein Azeri children learn their native language, culture and the history of Azerbaijan.[20]

'Čišme' was also founded in 1988. It has, as its chairman, Zaki Zainuļļins, who is assisted by Ravils Kalinkins, Haris Fahrazijevs and Musavirs Šaripovs. In 2000, the Society (LTBKB) was established in Riga and became a member of the Society of Latvia's National Cultures. Amid the estimated total of Latvian Tatars, totalling 3,049, some 309 of these are Baškīrs. Branches outside Rīga include, Daugavpils and Ventspils. Besides its cultural goals and its interest in the integration of the Baškīrs into Latvian culture, the society also promotes Islamic faith and ethics. LTBKB actively upholds the celebration of the two major feasts of *Uruza-Bairam* and *Kurban Bairam*, in the Muslim calendar, amongst the Baškīr community. It also supports a chapel for prayer and study (*molelnaya komnata/lūgšanu istaba*) and also an Islamic camp for children (*islamskii lager/bērniem darbojas islama vasaras nometne*) during the summer months.[21] Russian Bashkhortostan, according to the Russian census of 2002, now has 4,100,000 Muslims forming 54 per cent of its population, approximately the same percentage as the Muslims in Russian Tatarstan.

'Nur' was registered within the Register of the Enterprises of the Latvian Republic as the 'Latvian Uzbek Cultural Society' on May 31 1993. Its chairman is Alim Abdusaidov, together with a board of guardians and honorary members and it numbers over 1000 persons. The vast majority live in Rīga, others are to be found in Ventspils, Daugavpils, Liepaja, Valmiera, Jelgava, Salaspils and elsewhere. Its aims are primarily the culture, education, the preservation of national traditions, customs, culture, language and education and 'love and pride of the ethnic motherland – Uzbekistan'. The Muslim faith is not mentioned amongst the above.[22]

Among these associations, it is 'Idel'[23] which places the Islamic faith at the very centre of its activities. It has the closest association with the

Tatars of Lithuania. The Tatars in Latvia whom it claims to represent (some 1,500) trace their arrival in Latvia to around the year 1897, though Tatars were present as far back as 1890 when a small Muslim cemetery alongside the Catholic cemetery existed. They established a cultural centre in Rīga in 1902. Its first *Imām* was Ibragim Davidov. The '*Občestvo Tatar Latvii*' was founded in November, 1988. Named 'Idel', it looked to Kazan, in Tatarstan, for its primary inspiration, and its religious goals were brought to the fore, alongside their traditional Tatar culture. This is still the case today. In 1994, a 'Sunday School', a '*maktab*', or '*madrasa*', was in existence in Rīga, in which Professor Nuri Usmanov, assisted by Arab and Arabic students, taught the Qur'ān and the Arabic language to novices.[24] In 2001, *Imām Muḥtasib*, and then *Mullah* Midhat Satdanov, assumed the position of being the leading Muslim figure in Latvia, and two years later 'Idel' joined *LNKBA* as the most representative Latvian Kazan Tatar body (*Latvijas tatāru biedrība*) that had come into existence over three generations.

These Tatar and non-Tatar societies have to some degree been superseded by a relatively new organisation that is called '*Īmān*', 'Faith'. Its current leader is the Chechen businessman Musans Macigovs, the former head of 'Vainah'. He is regarded by some as the current leading figure and the spokesman for Muslim opinion in Latvia.[25] '*Īmān*' has also been called 'Rīga's Muslim Parish' and in some respects it has subsumed the activities of the Tatar societies, named above. Its appeal is addressed to all Muslims, whatever their ethnicity may be, and it is open to contemporary influences from the Muslim World beyond the Baltic. Its headquarters is in Brīvības, 104.[26] The society to which he belongs is likewise known as 'the Rīga Muslim Community'. It transcends those ethnically centred societies mentioned above. The new president of this society, or congregation, '*Rīgas pilsētas musulmaņu draudzes padomes priekšsēdētāja*', is Dr Rufija Ševirjova, whose family comes from Tatarstan. She is a widely respected psychologist, and her son was educated and trained in the major Islamic madrasa in Ufa, the capital of Bashkortostan. Oļegs Ševirevs Muhammedgali, by name, is now the recognised Mufti of Latvia.[27]

Dr Rufiya Ševirjova is a lady who is greatly respected and she has many contacts with the Muslim communities in Russia and elsewhere outside Latvia. She participated in an important conference that was held in Rīga on 5 April 2006, 'Facing Islamophobia and Anti-Semitism',[28] though she did not present a paper herself. The papers covered a wide range of themes, Ilga Alpine chose the subject of 'Tolerance in the Latvian Community', Valts Apinis chose 'Tolerance in Judaism: Jews in relation to the World and the other', Uldis Bērziņš, leading Latvian poet, Orientalist and current translator of the Qur'ān into Latvian[29] (see below), spoke about 'Some remarks about tolerance in the Koran',[30] Deniss Hanovs spoke on '"Noble 'Enemy'": Image of the Muslim Culture in the European Opera', Ilze Brands-Kehre spoke on 'Muslims and Islamophobia in the European Union', Dmitrijs Oļehnovičs spoke on 'Anti-Semitic Propaganda in the Latvian Press, 1940–1945', and Valdis Tēraudkalns spoke on 'Islamophobia and Anti-Semitism in a contemporary Social-Political Context'. Common to all these themes was the accepted interconnection between anti–Semitism and Islamophobia, and the absence of any detailed discussion of the Muslims themselves and on ethnicity in Latvia other than the community statistics that were published in the paper that was presented by Ilze Brands-Kehre. The proceedings of this conference were published by The Latvian Bible Society (*Latvijas Bibeles biedriba*) in Rīga.

The Latvian poet and translator Uldis Bērziņš was born in 1944 and the first of his six volumes of poetry appeared in the 1980s. A polyglot, he has translated poems from Turkish, Persian and a number of European languages including Old Icelandic. He is well read in translations of the Qur'ān published in a number of European languages. He received the Literary Award of the Baltic Assembly in 1995 and the Order of the Three Stars in that same year. Uldis Bērziņš, besides his translation of the Qur'ān, is also actively engaged in a fresh translation of the Old Testament into Latvian. His former activity has recently drawn the attention of the media on account of an interview that accompanied the publication of translated passages from *Sūra* 13 in the Qur'ān, *Sūrat al-Ra'd* (The Chapter of the Thunder) – 'Pērkons', in Latvian – a Latvian translation of which appeared in the cultural paper *Kulturas Forums*, Rīga, 12–19 January 2007, on page 5. Indeed, a large part of this paper's number was devoted to his goals and his plans for the complete Qur'ān translation. This is now in progress, and it also challenges the importance of the message of the Holy Book to some Muslims in Latvia.

The first part of the published debate is an interview with Uldis Bērziņš. It reveals the poet's motives, his aims within his translation and what fired his inspiration for his task. The second part is a critical response to his translation and the third is a critique of the way that the interview was planned. It has produced a vigorous reply from Latvian Muslim Brālis Ahmed ('Brother Ahmed'). These parts are prefaced by a brief introduction, jointly written by Ilva Skulte (Rīgas Stradiņa Universitāte) and by Inga Šteimane. They emphasise that any interpretation, or translation of the Qur'ān is not only a revelatory verbal realisation of the

Divine word, but it can also be a 'poetic' translation, or interpretation, based on the existence of poetic foundations that some maintain form the basis for the structure of the world's religious literatures.

Uldis Bērziņš is quoted as saying in regard to his translation 'Religions are instruments we have fashioned.' 'In no way do I try – nor do I dare! – to "poeticise" the Text entrusted to me. But the Lord speaks to His lowly people – the proud Bedouin.'

This issue of 'poetry' is a very sensitive one, since, as Professor M.A.S. 'Abdel-Haleem points out, in his new translation of the Qur'ān, 'The Meccans dismissed the Qur'ān as poetry. After the Prophet moved to Medina, the Meccans commissioned poets to satirize the Muslims, and some Muslim poets counter-attacked'.[31]

It may be recalled that in general the Polish translation of the Qur'ān has not, in the past, provoked such unexpected criticisms, and, furthermore, that translation also entailed collaboration with Polish Tatars. Indeed, it has been quoted or copied by Muslim authors in Poland, for example, by Ali Abi Issa, who, in his *'Komentarz fragmentu LXX Sury STOPNIE w. 19–35' (Sūra 70, The Ways of Ascent (al-Ma'ārij), vv. 19–35)*,[32] published a full translation, side by side, of these verses, both in Arabic and in Polish. It was accompanied by a commentary, citing Ibn 'Abbās (d. c.688) extensively, this likewise in Polish.

Ms Marite Sapiets, of the School of Slavonic and East European Studies, University of London, has most kindly guided the author carefully through the content of the arguments and the misunderstandings that have arisen within this Qur'ānic debate in Latvia as it has been revealed in these Latvian articles.

It may be recalled that, within Islam, a clear distinction has been made between, first, an actual translation (*Tarjama*), claimed to be such, from the 'words of Allāh', in the Arabic language; words in the Qur'ān that are the revealed 'Word of God' in that holy Arabic language, and which, accordingly, are not to be translated into the tongues of men that are not heirs to the revelation in that language and are even opposed to its message, and, second, the liberty permitted to other categories of exposition. For example, this unconditional affirmation does not in any way apply to a sound commentary, a *Tafsīr*, the science of interpreting the sacred book. Approved commentaries are crucial works for its interpretation amongst all the believers, works such as the commentaries by al-Ṭabarī, al-Zamakhsharī, al Rāzī and al-Bayḍāwī. Popular commentaries in sundry tongues are to be found in the margins of manuscripts throughout the Muslim World. However, on occasions, the line that clearly distinguished 'Commentary' and 'Translation', in a language other than Arabic, has been undoubtedly crossed, and this to the extent that amongst the Moriscos, in Spain, and at times amongst the Tatars, the distinction between (a) *Tafsīr*, (b) *Ta'wīl* ('the turning a verse of the Ḳur-án from its apparent meaning to a meaning which it bears, or admits, when the latter is agreeable with the Scripture and the Sunneh', E.W. Lane's, *Lexicon*, Book 1, page 126) and (c) an effectively word for word 'Translation' (*Tarjama*) has been breached; these above distinctions having been overlooked or wilfully ignored. Indeed. Lane himself called his distinguished book of 1843, *Selections from the Ḳur-án, commonly called, in England, the Koran; with an Interwoven Commentary*. In choosing to do this he was conscious of his individuality of approach, in this work, a view that differed from acclaimed *Translations of the Qur'ān*, such as those offered by Sale, and by his other predecessors. Sensitivity marked Lane's treatment of holy writ. Even so, he remarked (p. v) that 'In translating my selections, I have had Sale's version constantly open by my side, and have always followed it when I have found reason to prefer it to my own.'

In the Qur'ānic debate in *Kultūras Forums*, both Uldis Bērziņš and Brother Ahmed were interviewed and questioned by Edvīns Raups. Introducing the current translation of the Qur'ān, the latter pointed out that Uldis Bērziņš had completed a translation of the Psalms fairly recently and that his current work on the Qur'ān translation had been preceded by a lengthy stay in Istanbul. According to Uldis Bērziņš, his complete translation of the 114 *Sūras* in the Qur'ān is to be published by Zinatne, as an 'academic edition', together with a commentary by his research editor. It will be accompanied by illustrations that will depict specific *Sūras*, and these will be by reproductions of verses of the Qur'ān that are to be seen in the Great Mosque in the Turkish city of Bursa. An abridged work entitled *The Kernel of the Qur'ān*, restricted to *Sūras 17–28*, will likewise be published in Latvia.

(a)

On the subject of poetry, Uldis Bērziņš defined his position by asserting that although the Qur'ānic text runs continuously, with numbered verses, it possesses its own rhythmic structure. He defined this as syntactical parallelism (an even form of rhyme). He had tried to keep to it, and even imitate it, although he had refrained from imposing and inserting his own rhyming pattern on the authoritative text. He flatly rejected the assertion that he had 'poeticised' the text. He had avoided a plethora of exclamation marks, since 'the Lord speaks to His people in His own way'.

He was questioned whether it were possible that his translation could be used by Latvian-speaking Muslims when at prayer. Uldis Bērziņš replied that he had received an email from Latvian Muslims requesting information about whether his research editor, Jānis Ešots, was a professing Muslim, and whether he would agree to the editing of his translation (in matters of dogma) so that it could be used in Muslim congregational worship. Uldis Bērziņš had refrained to comment on the beliefs of Ešots. However, he would feel honoured 'as a writer' to allow Latvians who were 'seekers after God' to use his translation if such matters of style could be resolved: 'For me, that is the main heavenly message – style!' It was the power of the word, of style, of 'super logic' that addressed millions and that had founded Islamic civilisation.

E. Raupes had asked him, in fact had almost baited him, in regard to *Sūra 13*, 'Thunder' (*al-Ra'd*), the same *Sūra* that was published in the same number of *Kultūras Forums*: 'What was the significance of thunder to the Arab Muslims?' Uldis Bērziņš answered that thunder was mentioned, praising God, together with the angels, because lightning is sent down by God. He made clear that the ancient belief in Latvia in the thunder God 'Perkons' (*Perkūnas* in Lithuania) had no relevance whatsoever to any non-Muslim Latvian's appreciation of the spiritual vision that was conveyed in, or by, the Qur'ānic verses. He also switched to the topic of the angelic female beings who were called by the pagan Arabs as 'the daughters of God', a term that in pagan Latvian belief and in folk songs were described as 'daughters of the Sun' and the 'offspring of God'.

Uldis Bērziņš confirmed to his interviewer that he believed that the Old Testament was the seed of the growth not only of Christianity and the 'many branched Talmud' but also the Qur'ān. He stressed that this was not the view of a Muslim believer for whom God's message to His chosen Prophet Muhammad was the final message. God's earlier messages to Moses, David and Jesus had been distorted by scribes, monks and popes, but the text of the final message sent to Muhammad was easy to learn by heart and to repeat, and this, in itself, was a proof of its divine nature.

E. Raups asked Uldis Bērziņš whether a 'New Qur'ān' was a possibility and the latter repeated the accepted Muslim belief that a sequel was inconceivable. One who might claim to have a fresh divine message would be condemned, an example of this being the fate of the Bahai sect in Iran.

In the interview Uldis Bērziņš attempted to present the Muslim attitude to Jews and Christians and its objections to their beliefs. He described the Jews as 'the Creator's first experiment ... though not entirely successful'.

They are referred to by the Islamic name of '*al-Yahūd*', etymologically signifying 'those led by God'. However as it seems they had not kept to the simple faith of Abraham (Ibrāhīm al-Khalīl), or Moses, and had opposed God's will, they are also referred to in the introductory *Sūra* of the Qur'ān as 'those against whom there is anger'. Christians are referred to in the Qur'ān as 'those who are deceived', since they have presumed to attribute a son to God – 'the honest Prophet Jesus', the Anointed, born of a virgin, who on the Day of Judgement will punish those who have misused his name to blaspheme against the Creator. To Muslims, the concept of the Trinity is irritating – as God is One! However, 'they do not understand it in the same way as the Christians'. It is seen as a 'divine family'; God the Father, the Mother of God and God the Son.

E. Raups found it unbearable to see disputes, viewed as unnecessary, between the two faiths, or civilisations, in the twenty-first century. Uldis Bērziņš reminded him of the differences between the Christian denominations, the Catholics and the Orthodox, which had led to cruel wars and the sufferings of the martyrs and the heroes. He also drew attention to the current, but historic, dispute between Sunnīs and Shī'ites within Islam.

E. Raups enquired whether it was not God who had died, but religions as they existed and still exist. What should society do to regain the equilibrium in the world that the religions are trying to destroy?

Uldis Bērziņš concluded the interview with his personal view of religion: 'Religion may be seen as the highest form of literature'. He did not feel that he could speak for those who could not recognise 'the hard bliss and misery of the relativism of our consciousness of the divine and our own basic lack of knowledge'.

Those who believe that 'God believes what I believe' are like he, himself, as he once was, at the age of ten. He referred to the dispute which he had with Christian clergyman Aleksandrs Bite – 'if this man had been born in the Muslim district of the Caucasus would he have been an Islamic radical, though he insists that he would have found his way to Jesus?'

> Now, when humanity is finally getting to know itself, as we get to know each other, we can no longer refuse to recognise that religions are instruments fashioned by ourselves (or given to us as gifts) whereby we are seeking our Creator? or are finding our way in the Cosmos? If, and when, we can agree on this, it only remains for us to compare our instruments as to talent and effectiveness.

(b)

Below is the second article by Brother Ahmed, entitled 'The interpretation of the Qur'ān by Uldis Bērziņš from the viewpoint of a Latvian Muslim'.

> What is the Qur'ān? The Qur'ān in Latvian is not the Qur'ān. It is only the translator's interpretation of the Qur'ān. The Qur'ān is the original blueprint. It is in the Arabic language alone, namely the words of God sent to His last Prophet Muhammad (may peace and God's blessing be upon him). They were revealed over twenty-three years. Its meaning cannot be fully expressed in another language. The Qur'ān is God's message to the whole of humanity. He has promised to preserve it from changes, from alterations and from additions. Thus, the Muslims possess the original message of God, unlike the texts that are found in the Bible.
>
> I shall give below a few examples of words in the Qur'ān which have more than one meaning and which lose certain of their nuances in translation. Firstly, the word, *kufr* (*kāfir*) – unbelief (unbeliever), which can also mean 'ingratitude', or 'cover' (a derivation of the English word (*sic?*)). 'Unbeliever' is closer in meaning to 'rejecter' than to 'infidel'. The 'Unbelievers' are also 'the ungrateful', who are hiding from the Truth. Secondly, '*Dīn*' is a word meaning 'religion', 'way of life' or 'path'. It is very important in Islam but it cannot be translated by one word alone. It is also used in a verse (*āya/ājat*) in the most important *Sūra* [the first]: *Mālik Yawmi d-Dīni* (the Ruler of the Day of al-Dīn). Uldis Bērziņš chooses to translate it as 'The Ruler of the Last Day'. But '*Dīn*' does not mean 'last'. Another meaning (but not a precise translation) would be 'The Day of Judgement', or 'The Day of the Resurrection', but this phrase cannot be truly translated and should be left un-translated. Thirdly, there are also difficulties in translating all the nuances of such words as '*Rabb*' ('Lord'), or '*Rahmān*' and '*Rahīm*' ('the Merciful', 'the Compassionate') since their meanings are diminished when translated. If the word '*āya/ājat*' is translated as 'verse', this leaves out its other meaning of 'sign'. In giving mankind verses God also gave them signs. In fact, a large number of words that have been translated from the Qur'ān should be followed by the original in brackets plus an explanatory note. 'But that does not form a part of Uldis Bērziņš's idea of a successful achievement'.
>
> Another problem, in interpreting the Qur'ān, is that of the interpreter's own knowledge and understanding of it (there are disputes

about a meaning even amongst the experts). 'Rewriting' the Qur'ān from the original becomes a human achievement, reflecting the author's own times and knowledge, thus risking the loss of the original meaning. Academic religious commentaries (*Tafsīrs*) are essential to readers of the Qur'ān, but even a grammatical term chosen by an interpreter/author is a comment, explanation, or retelling of the Qur'ān. It is not God's Word.

Nevertheless, though an interpretation is not the Qur'ān itself, some interpretations of the Qur'ān can be meaningfully used by Muslims. The use of interpretations is not permitted in Muslim religious worship, as the Prophet Muhammad laid down which prayers could be said in one's own language (these did not include excerpts from the Qur'ān). However, they can be used to help gaining knowledge of Islam (the translation into Persian of the first *Sūra* by Salmān, the Persian, was because the Persians did not know Arabic), but must be used together with the original Qur'ān and commentaries. Interpretation can also be used as part of the Friday sermon, to explain an *āya/ājat* to an audience unacquainted with Arabic. They can also be useful in communicating with non-Arab non-Muslims (as they do not require the reader to be in a state of ritual cleanliness and can be given to non-Muslims without concern for future use).

However, the difference between the work of Uldis Bērziņš and the interpretations of the Qur'ān that have been approved by Muslim scholars, for example, the English version by Abdulla Yusuf Ali , or the Russian one, by Elmir Kuliyev, is that their aim was to reflect the actual meaning of the verses of the Qur'ān, whereas Uldis Bērziņš wants to demonstrate the poetic beauty of the Qur'ān in the Latvian language. Concern must be expressed over the final version, especially following the severe criticism by the Research Editor, Jānis Ešots. Nor does the interview above give hope of something that could be offered to a non-Muslim without disquiet, namely as an impression of the original Qur'ān.

There are two ways in which Uldis Bērziņš's work could be used for good. Firstly, to correct a Latvian reader's mistaken view of Islam as an evil, terrorist cult. Secondly, though the interview raises doubts about this, Latvian Muslims could produce a re-edited version to help them in educational work about Islam. However, Muslims have a deep mistrust of any work by a non-Muslim about the Qur'ān, partly because of previous works by 'pseudo-academic Orientalists', which are unable to be objective and which pour out hatred and invented absurdities, related to Western policies, partly because of the

Islam and the contemporary religious scene 109

scepticism of non-Muslims who reject Islam. Uldis Bērziņš refers to the Qur'ān as a humanly created communication with God and he avoids answering the question of Islam being 'Submission to God'. Serious concern must be caused by his understanding of the Qur'ān, as revealed in the interview, which includes so many absurd statements and flippant and disdainful attitudes that Muslims could end up by feeling indignant and disillusioned.

(c)

The comment and critique by Brother Ahmed on E. Raups's interview with Uldis Bērziņš.

'If one out of 100 children wrongly copies out a multiplication table and the teacher crosses it out, it does not mean that an alternative multiplication table was crossed out'.

Both the interviewer and the man interviewed here make statements that mislead the reader, partly due to ignorance, or a disdainful attitude towards Islam, partly because of their personal beliefs. Misleading statements typical of incompetent Orientalism are, for example, that Muhammad was a 'Bedouin Prophet', or that the angels are supposedly seen as feminine beings in the Qur'ān, whereas Islam asserts that angels have no gender.

Standard libels about Islam are also reflected in the interview: that Islam was spread abroad by the sword, whereas forced conversion is condemned in the Qur'ān. This is a mediaeval myth spread by the Church, which refused to accept that the Christians of the Near East chose Islam, though minorities who did not still remain. Historically, the Byzantine Empire attacked the Arabs.

An unusual theological myth is expressed by Uldis Bērziņš. The Qur'ān, in his view, is apparently suggesting that the Trinity is a 'divine family', namely God, the Father, the Mother of God and God, the Son. This would imply that the Qur'ān was the invention of an ignorant individual. In reality, no such incorrect view of 'the Trinity' can be perceived. The Trinity itself is a human invention and the expression is not specifically mentioned by name in the Bible itself. It is refuted by the First Commandment, and the Qur'ān nowhere refers to the Trinity as composing three persons, namely God, Jesus and Mary [and here I quote three Qur'ānic references; Jesus says that he never told anyone to worship him and his mother (*Sūra* 5, verse 116), 'Do not say Three, God is one God ... too exalted to have a son (*Sūra*

4, verse 171), and that it is a blasphemy to say that God is one of three persons (*Sūra* verse 73)].

Definitions that are precise and, likewise principles, in regard to the Qur'ān are ignored. The Qur'ān is not a 'fundamental collection of texts' (unlike the Bible). It is God's word to mankind. These 'texts' are not the words of the Prophet Muhammad himself. His sayings and his acts are in the Collections of *Ḥadīth* (the Islamic text second only to the Qur'ān) It is also most offensive to ignore the word, 'Muslims' (those who practise Islam) and to call them 'Mohammedans', implying the worship of Muhammad, just like the followers of Paul being worshippers of Jesus (though Jesus and all the Prophets have said emphatically that only God must be worshipped).

God's message to the Prophets was one and the same message. This is why there are so many similarities between the Bible and the Qur'ān. The religion sent by God was Islam. Other religions have turned away from this message. It consists of five injunctions, five meanings; submission to God, devotion and obedience to God, faithfully obeying His will and being at peace with God and with oneself. God promised that he would guard that message He gave to His last Prophet from any alteration and any distortion. It is accordingly available to humanity in its pristine form, in the Qur'ān. The message of the Bible is not available in its original form, since Jesus did not speak Greek or Latvian. The expressions and terms, un-clearly expressed, regarding the 'unification', or otherwise, of the Qur'ān were in themselves absurd. There never was a destruction of alternative or variant versions of the Qur'ān. Only mistakenly recorded quotations were thus treated. The Qur'ān is the original (see my quotation, above regarding a child's incorrect multiplication table).

Some of the questions that were asked appear to have been posed by voices from outer space. What is the meaning of 'thunder' to the Arabs? Several assertions were made that were offensive to Latvian Muslims. For example, it was said that the latter had sent an email to Uldis Bērziņš, suggesting that his interpretation of the Qur'ān in Latvian might be used in Muslim worship. No such email was ever sent by Latvian Muslims. 'Latvian Muslim Congregations' do not exist; they are not based upon any ethnicity. To replace the Qur'ān, the Word of God, in ritual prayer by some other words, such as those of Uldis Bērziņš, would be blasphemous.

I regard as absurd many of the assertions made by Uldis Bērziņš that were based upon his personal view of God and religion. That God could ever have 'changed His mind' about the end of the World is a nightmarish vision (I cite the *Book of Numbers*, Chapter 23, verse 19, 'God is not a mortal that He should lie'). Only God knows when the End of the World will be. To use the phrase, 'The Jews were an 'unsuccessful experiment' runs counter to the Omniscience of God. Everything that happens accords with His will; however human beings have a free will to reject God's lordship.

In sum, both the interviewer and Uldis Bērziņš expressed unsubstantiated opinions, fantasies and an attitude contemptuous towards Islam. They include the reference, made by E. Raups, to the Qur'ān as the weak imagination of the opposition (meaning what?) and to religions facing extinction and 'destroying the equilibrium' in the world (meaning what?). It is a fantasy and a speculation of Uldis Bērziņš to declare that humanity is 'beginning to get to know itself' and that it 'cannot fail to recognise' that 'religions are instruments fashioned by ourselves'.

In conclusion, the interview was a disappointment. As regards the 'fundamental limitations of the religious point of view' I would respond 'Human understanding may be limited, but not God's instructions to mankind on how to live'.

The history of the Latvian Muslims

The pioneer research undertaken by Valters Ščerbinskis, which has been published in his book entitled *Newcomers from Remoteness*[33] has enabled us to obtain a clearer understanding of the history of the present day Muslim societies in Latvia and about the arrival of their forebears in that country from the East. His research has revealed a tiny Tatar community in Latvia's towns during the latter part of the nineteenth century. Despite an important presence of Karaites and Armenians in Rīga, the Tatars had no close contacts with the long-settled Lithuanian Qipčaq (Qipchāq) Tatar communities to the South, to the East, and to the West.

However, in the last fifty years, Tatar numbers have first declined, and have later grown, and this is principally due to migrants who have come from the former Soviet Union.[34] Most recently, Rīga's Muslim community has been increased by a small company of Africans, including Chadians and Sudanese, and Pakistanis, most of them students in Rīga's colleges and universities, who, together with Arabs and Turks, Chechens and Balkan Muslims, are currently playing an increasingly important role in the religious education of the existing Latvian Muslim community in the twenty-first century.

Up to the end of the nineteenth century there were few Tatars other than small units attached to the Russian army. At the close of the century, Muslims had already established a small community in Rīga. In 1890 there was found a Muslim cemetery alongside the Catholic, and, in 1902, the Rīga Muslim Congregation was officially recognised. Ibragim Davidov was elected as their *Imām* and a little later an oratory for prayers was opened. In 1897, there were 536 Muslims in Livland (a district shared by both Latvians and Estonians). However, there were 596 Muslims in Courland (today the district of Kurzeme). Of these Muslims, the Tatars formed the greater part, some 1,000 of them, and the majority of them served in the Russian army. They were largely illiterate and of peasant stock. After their military service they left Latvia. According to the census of Vitebsk (now a town in Belarus) of 1897, 564 out of 574 Muslims, 560 of them Tatars, lived in Daugavpils, in Latgale, where the Russian army had a major military fortress (*cietoksnis*). It had been built there in 1810. This base existed until 1993 and it was there that the famous Tatar poet Musa Jalil was held as an inmate during September and October 1942. At that time it was a Nazi concentration camp, known as Stalag 340.

In 1913, in Rīga and in its suburbs, there were 510 Muslims. Some 434 of these lived in the Maskava district of the city, and 406 of them were either Tatar or Turkish speakers. In 1914 there were 1,000 members in their congregation. Most of these emigrated from Rīga during the First World War.

The War of Latvian Independence took place in 1919. A few Muslims were in the army of the Republic of Latvia. In 1920, the commander-in-chief issued an order that serving Muslims were to be allowed three days leave during '*Kurban Bairam*'. Following that war, a Tatar named Hasan Haretdinov-Konikov,[35] on behalf of the Finnish Muslims, came to Rīga from Helsinki in 1920, and he requested permission to open a new building for statutory prayers. He based his case on the grounds that Finland had become the place of asylum for the Muslims of Rīga. This case was rejected by the Latvian Department of Religious Affairs on the grounds that the Muslim congregation in Rīga had never been officially closed down and that once life had returned to normal there was no valid reason preventing them from returning to their original homes.

In 1920, the Rīga Muslims selected as their acting *Imām*, the owner of a Turkish café and bakery, Šakirs Husnetdinov.[36] Eight years later the Muslim Congregation requested the Department of Religious Affairs to officially appoint him to be the permanent *Imām* of Rīga district. Their request was approved and he fulfilled his duties until 1940.

Throughout the years of Latvian Independence the number and the ethnic origin of the Latvian Muslims were to remain substantially unchanged. They were predominantly Tatars, or Turks. In 1920, there were 162 Muslims. This number was reduced to sixty-six by 1935. Only forty-two members of the Rīga Muslim Congregation were left and, of these, thirty-two had been born in Rīga. Four large families of Tatar origin formed the congregation. These families had members who bore either 'Turk' or 'Tatar' nationalities as shown in their passports. Muslim families were large, sometimes numbering seven or more persons. Religious sentiments were strong amongst the Tatars and they lacked the strong cultural life that characterised the Caucasians, both Armenians and Georgians, in Rīga.

The Soviet occupation of Latvia entailed the repression of both Latvians and ethnic minorities. A Tatar, Abdula Husnetdinov, disappeared, and this ethnic repression did not change with the Nazi occupation. By 1943, as Valters Ščerbinskis has shown from information that he has obtained from the Board of Statistics within Latvian territory,[37] the representatives of the minority nationalities were few, though varied, and they included Caucasians, Tatars, Turks, Assyrians and Uzbeks. There were also Islamic peoples amongst workers who had been displaced from Russia. The previous Mullah of Rīga, Š. Eriss (Husnetdinovs), had, in his assemblies for prayer, both local and displaced Muslims during the Russian and German occupations. After the end of the German occupation many left with only a tiny remnant remaining behind to face the Soviet occupation. Many Slavs were encouraged to enter Latvia as a work force in order to settle there.

During the 1950s, minority peoples began a modest return to Latvia. Some twenty Crimean Tatars were among them. This return continued during the 1970s and the 1980s. By 1979, there were 3,764 Tatars and they out numbered the Estonians in Latvia. The influx reached its peak in the 1980s. By 1989 the Tatar total reached 4,800.

Latvia's principal cities and towns, Rīga in particular, housed 88 per cent of the Tatars. The need for employment, and retirement from Soviet military service were the two important factors for this movement of labour. Possibly the higher living standards was the principal magnet that drew these Orientals to make their home in Latvia.

The movement spurred the Tatar community into selecting a Mullah to run their affairs. The failure of Russification revived interest in national traditions, in culture and in native languages. A reaction to this led to measures that were to curb this tendency and which, in the course of time, favoured a policy of repatriation. Even so, by this time the total number of Tatars had risen to some 5,000. In certain respects this figure was deceptive since, as Valters Ščerbinskis has shown,[38] statistical data has revealed that, in 1989, 2,505 out of 4,828 Tatars considered Russian to be their native language and only 2,257 claimed it to be Tatar. It should be recalled that there was a marked contrast between this tiny figure and the situation that existed in Lithuania and Poland, and to some extent in Belarus, where the assimilated Qipčaq (Qipchāq) Tatars had lost all knowledge of their mother tongue by the end of the medieval period. On the other hand, in Latvia, of the 1,454 Azeris who lived in Rīga, only 367 Azeris acknowledged Russian to be their native tongue.

In the post-Soviet period Latvia's Muslims are today facing the challenge of integration within Latvian society, and the replacement of Russian by the Latvian language. Some knowledge of this is essential to the granting of Latvian nationality. But it is a sign of the times that Latvian Radio regularly broadcasts half-hour and hour-long programmes in Azeri, Armenian, Georgian and Tatar. The existence of societies of national cultures, and the convening of regular 'Sunday Schools', is another development of our times. Here the history of the people in question and the history of Latvia is taught side by side. Time is also spent on native languages, folk traditions and songs, dances and folk music. One such school is specifically Islamic in character. It is provided for the Muslims in particular. Within it the Arabic language is taught, together with a comprehensive course of Islamic studies.

Religious institutions are further encouraged. This applies to the Muslim community that, in the beginning, was principally the society of 'Idel', together with the Latvian Tatar community. Later, its membership was widened, and, now, two Sunni Muslim congregations are to be found – one in Rīga and the other in Daugavpils.

The five daily prayers are said, weekly, at gatherings in Rīga, though, as Rufija Ševirjova told the author, small prayer groups in private houses is far more the common practice. The gathering for '*Kurban Bairam*' took place for the first time in the summer of 1991. By February 1997, the gathering for the celebration of '*Uraz Bairam*' attracted 450 believers. Apart from prayer, a public assembling of the believers also takes place at the Muslim cemetery on certain occasions and also at the newly approved Muslim section at the Jaunciems cemetery in Rīga. There are also cemeteries elsewhere, for example, in Valmiera, where much older graves and tombstones of the Turkish soldiery are also located.

On the question of integration, Valters Ščerbinskis has concluded his study on an optimistic note:[39]

One cannot fail to notice that a large part of eastern and southern people has chosen the way of integration. Integration takes place in the society of the state as a whole, as well as by gradual consolidation of the national groups in national communities. Studies show that the majority of children of small minorities continue assimilation in the Russian environment, by attending schools with Russian language teaching, and their number, contrary to spread opinions, has not changed considerably during recent years. It is characteristic that integration in the Latvian civic society and the Latvian environment is more rapid and successful in those cases where people have managed to preserve their ethnic identity. Noteworthy is also the fact, unlike the many immigrants, who can be considered as completely (or almost) Russified, their attitude to Latvia as a national country is understanding and thus positive. Now it is difficult to answer the question, to what extent members of national groups have come to the dominating either Russian or Latvian integration spheres. Yet it should be admitted, that regardless of their small number, members of national groups of eastern or southern origin in whole have not lost their national consciousness, and thus they take a definite place in the society of Latvia.

Even so, there is still a long way to go. In the *Distribution of the Population by Citizenship and Ethnicity, March, 1995*[40] published by the Latvian government in the Latvian *Human Development Report*,[41] amongst the number of Tatars listed, out of a total of 3,553, only 151 were listed as citizens, 3,402 were listed as non-citizens, some 0.01 per cent of the Total Citizenry. The figure for Azeris gives a total of 1,630, of which 162 were listed as citizens, 1,468 non-citizens, also some 0.01 per cent of the Total Citizenry. The smaller Chuvash population of 1,085, were registered as 25 citizens, 1,060 non-citizens, 0.00 per cent of the Total Citizenry. Other Muslim communities did not figure in the statistics. Yet, despite this tiny figure the administrative leader of the Rīga Muslims is represented in the Advisory Council of Nations of the President of the Republic of Latvia.

Islam in the Baltic as viewed from Scandinavia

Finland, and in particular its Tatar community, has acted as a 'bridge' between the Muslim communities of Eastern Europe and Scandinavia.[42] In Sweden, and in Denmark, the Muslim communities, their size and their composition are noteworthy on account of their very varied multiculturalism.

Sweden

A curious report in the second volume of F.W. Hasluck's *Christianity and Islam under the Sultans*[43] is his reference to one of the 'seven tombs' of the holy dervish Sari Saltik – a well-known dervish figure in the Balkans, especially so amongst the Bektāshī Sufi Brotherhood. An even greater curiosity is Hasluck's locating it at 'Bivanjah', an unidentified place name that Hasluck had accepted was to be found somewhere in Sweden. Poland is mentioned (Gdańsk) and also Bohemia, but why did he mention this tomb in Sweden? Who was the first to site it there, and where was its location anyway? Elsewhere in his work he attributes this information to the seventeenth-century Turkish traveller and writer Evliye (Çelebi) Efendi, 'on the authority of the dervishes of Kilgra' (Kaliakra).[44]

This location is a name that is quite possibly imaginary, or its spelling may be garbled, or it has been misplaced. The most likely locations in Sweden are Lake Båven (Sari Saltik's presence was sometimes associated with lakes). This lake is to be found to the south-west of Stockholm, and it is placed due south of Sparreholm. An even larger lake is to the east of Gothenburg, named Vänern. The greatest goal of pilgrims in medieval Sweden, 'the stone house beside the water', Vadstena, where the tomb and convent of holy St Birgitta Birgersdotter was consecrated in 1384, is also located by a lake – Lake Vättern. One recalls that Sweden in days past had been a great northern European power. It had expanded into the Baltic States, it had fought in Poland, and beyond, in eastern Europe. Between 1587 and 1660, Sweden had earned the unenviable reputation as being 'the plunderer of Europe'. In this 'plundering' both Poland and the Baltic States were to figure prominently. In 1561 this invasion was centred on Estonia, nominally ceded to Poland in 1598. In 1629, Livonia was occupied by Sweden, though it was a Polish fief between 1561 and 1660. Between 1655 and 1657 there was a major Swedish invasion to conquer the Baltic provinces of Poland. One may envisage that at some point in time the Swedes must have encountered Tatar units and individual Tatars who had fought within the Polish army. It seems improbable that Tatar Muslims had not been brought to Sweden at times, and this apart from the Swedish relations with the Ottomans over the centuries.

In fact, as Jonas Otterbeck has shown in his most informative article about the Tatars in Sweden,[45] it was they, the Tatars, who in fact had planted the Muslim faith in that country, though they had done so relatively recently, long after Hasluck's days. A few Tatar families from Finland had settled in borrowed summerhouses in Viggbyholm, near to Stockholm, and then, at the end of the Second World War, had moved to the part of Vasastaden called 'Sibirien'. They were to be joined by other Tatar families from Finland and from Estonia. In 1948 or 1949, the Tatars formed the first Muslim 'Parish' (*församling*) in Sweden. They had gathered together in a coffee house in Berger Jarlsgatan, known as *Kjellsons konditori*. This location had been a meeting place before for Tatars, Turks and Arabs, who were employed in foreign embassies. The initiative to form a 'Parish' was taken by Ali Zakhrov from Tallinn, Estonia, by Akif Arhan and by Osman Soukkan, who, in his roots, was part Turk, part Tatar. The latter became the first *Imām* of this tiny 'Parish'.

The two great Muslim feasts (*ajit* in Tatar) provided opportunities for larger gatherings: the first, *Korbanjıtı*, and the second, *Ramazan Bayram*. Traditional Sunni rules were observed, the recitation being in Arabic. The sermon (*khuṭba*) was delivered in Tatar. It was the Tatar community who, in 1950, were the first to apply for permission to build a mosque in Sweden. Permission was not granted, though it was during this period that the association of the 'Parish' changed its name to 'The Islamic Association of Sweden'.[46] This association bought the first graves for Muslims within the Sgoskyrkogården cemetery in Stockholm. A Tatar *ziyara*, or visit of respect, for the upkeep of the graves, and for general maintenance, took place twice annually during the *ajit* celebrations. A similar *ziyara* had been observed over the centuries by Tatars in Belarus, Lithuania and Poland.

After 1960, the Tatar character of Swedish Islam was altered. This was on account of the influx of Turks and of refugees from Bosnia and from Kosovo and from elsewhere. In order to preserve their heritage, the Swedish Tatars looked to the Finnish Tatars for support.

Unlike many of the newcomers, the Tatar Muslims had become well integrated into Swedish life, especially in the education system and in trade, notably the fur trade. As a consequence many of them today occupy posts in education, law and engineering, and they are employed as social workers. A biographical account of one Tatar who succeeded, namely Didar Samaletdin, and who has frankly written about her life and her experiences, is to be found in Otterbeck's article.[47] She, like many Tatars elsewhere in the Baltic, are fearful of ultimate extinction due to their few numbers; now less than one hundred souls in Sweden.

Otterbeck highlights the contribution of these Tatars to the Swedish Muslim community:[48]

a   They were probably influential in bringing about major changes to the national curriculum in 1962 and in 1969, in regard to religious instruction in Sweden. Since that time, an objective study of religions, alongside Christianity, still the primary interest, has become the general practice.

b Unlike other Muslims, the Tatars have escaped the restrictions that have been applied to their fellow believers. Otterbeck illustrates this with one example in regard to ritual slaughter 'Since the Tatars according to Didar, did not bother about *halal* (lawful), slaughtered meat, this cannot be seen as discriminating laws for the Tatar group'. Didar had also mentioned that the Swedish Tatars, like those in Poland and elsewhere, paid little attention to the Ramaḍān fast, though the feast that followed was joyfully observed. Other Tatar requirements, such as the necessity for a twenty-four hour burial time limit, to be followed by ritual commemorations after certain specified intervals, was almost impossible to square with the common Swedish postponement of burials, often up to a fortnight.

Otherwise, amidst the growing Muslim community of Iranians, Bosnians, Turks, Middle Eastern Arabs, Somalis and South Asians, Chechens, Scandinavian converts, and sundry others since the 1990s, the Tatars have had to face the current paradoxes of multiculturalism throughout contemporary Scandinavia. They have also had to face the depiction of Muslims, with little distinction, as one and all potentially sympathetic to international terrorism. Nor can it be said that integration, in general, within Sweden, has been a success even though the very different situation that applies to the Tatars has not escaped public notice. As has been the case of the Tatars in Lithuania and Poland for many centuries, the Tatar language, in general, has no longer remained a basis for everyday communication. The risk of being 'absorbed' by the 'Turks' – it is a very real possibility, for example, in Romania – is by no means unthinkable amongst the Tatar remnant amongst the Swedish Muslims. The Tatars in Estonia, in Belarus, even in Poland, will face this same possible problem in the future.

Denmark

Irrespective of the crisis brought about by the scandal of the cartoons of the Prophet Muhammad in the newspaper *Jyllands Posten* and its bitter aftermath, Denmark, in contrast to Sweden, has far more ruthlessly pursued a policy of Muslim integration. Furthermore, there have been no Eurasian Tatars within that community who might have had historical and cultural ties of any kind with their new Scandinavian homeland. The

Islam and the contemporary religious scene 119

few Arab visitors and merchants to Hedeby during the Viking Age have no relevance whatsoever for the rigidly conformist Denmark of today.

A visit to Bazar Vest,[49] in Århus,[50] is an exotic experience, since here one may find an Oriental bazaar filled with signs written in Arabic and Persian calligraphy, quotations from the Qur'ān, stalls with sellers of vegetables, small shops displaying Oriental wares, *ḥalāl* butchers, coffee houses stacked with hubble-bubbles, barbers, colourful shops displaying Oriental silks and carpets, all owned, or served, or enjoyed, by Africans and Asians, a *sūq* that is constantly visited by Danish families who go there for the purchase of vegetables and fruit, or of household items, or gifts, or out of sheer curiosity or who had arrived there by curiosity or by a mere chance during a visit to Århus. In large markets in Poland, or the Baltic States, the few Tatar purchasers are indistinguishable from the throng. The headscarves hide, or mask, identities rather than, though perchance unintentionally, openly asserting the 'otherness' of Muslim believers among the sea of infidels.

The Muslim community in Århus[51]

The Muslim community in this city is extremely diverse and multicultural. It has been well described and presented in Lene Kühle's 'Islam i Århus' in *Religious Multiplicity* (*Religiøs mangfoldighed*).[52] For any researcher into the variety of the Islamic community in Århus, *Religious Multiplicity* furnishes a wealth of insight and information on all the religions that are to be found in the communities.

Kühle's chapter is sub-divided into a series of descriptions of the diverse Muslim population, together with the associations, fraternities and 'parishes' into which it is divided. These are:

1   The Alevite, or Alawi, Association in Århus.[53] This was first formed in 1994 as the *Haci Bektashi Kulturforeningen*. The chief association in the city for the cultural and spiritual needs of the one hundred, or so, Alevis.
2   The Arab Cultural Association.[54] Founded in in 1988, it contains upwards of 170 members – men, women and children. Principally Shāfʿīs and Ḥanafīs, its activities are centred around the five pillars of Islam, including *ṣalāt* and *zakāt*.
3   The Iraqi Cultural Centre (*al-Zahra*).[55] This is an association of Iraqi Shīʿites. In 1980 moves were made to form an association for this community, but al-Zahra – a secondary name of Fāṭima, the daughter of the Prophet and wife of ʿAlī – was officially founded in 2002. It

has a membership amongst the young and in all it numbers over 120 persons. Particular importance is given to fasts and feasts of special meaning to Shī'ites, including those associated with al-'Āshūrā' and the mourning for the martyrdom of al-Ḥusain.

4. The Islamic Cultural Centre.[56] This was first established in 1979 in Christiansgade and, in time, was granted official status. By 1992, after some difficulties, it had become the most representative of associations with an appeal to multicultural and multiethnic Muslims in the city, having upward of 120 members. Used as a mosque, in 1992, the Turkish Embassy was approached to appoint an *imām*. Support was forthcoming from its members and from the Danish State and Århus Amt and Århus Kommune.

5. The Islamic Congregation in Århus, the Sultan Ayyūb Mosque.[57] Its name derives from that of a famous Kurd, the father of Saladin. The association is primarily for Sunni Muslims, especially for Turks and numbering some eighty members. Its mosque building, with facilities for Qur'ān teaching is to be found in Nørre Allé and it is well furnished with a billiard table, and with television, computers, the internet and a café.

6. The Muslim conformists, fraternities and brotherhoods (*ribāṭāt* or possibly *ikhwān*).[58] An association with many social activities. The first mosque in Århus was the Islamic Cultural Centre but this mosque serves the Muslims who live in the district of Brabrand. The society promotes strict religious principles and the observance of major feasts and traditional Islamic practice and belief. Journalists are not welcome but the congregation have good relations with Gellerup Church.

7. The School of Islamic Sufism,[59] the *Tarighat* (*Tarīqa*) of *Oveyssi Shahmaghsoudi* (*Uways al-Qaranī*).[60] The Sufi movement in Århus has been in existence since 1993. Named after Uways al-Qaranī, perhaps the earliest Sufi known, who was a contemporary of the Prophet Muhammad, and Shaykh Shamaghsoudi, the Sufi master of a world following of members who number some 400,000 souls. He brought the *Maktab Tarighat Oveyssi Shahmaghsoudi* (MTO) to Denmark, whilst its effective founder in the city, Dr Mehdi Safaye, has established it as a 'Sufi beacon' in Scandinavia. Apart from attendance at the *Zikr/Zekr* and regular Islamic festivities, the Sunday school has acted as a cultural centre for between forty and fifty members, disciples, students and enquirers from the Danish community itself. Here the Qur'ān is studied, likewise *Ḥadīth*, Arabic, Persian, the power to heal, music, the arts and crafts and the practice of meditation.

8   The Somali Family Association.[61] This association for Somalis, for men and women and for small infants and school children, is located in Eckersbergsgade. It was started in 1993 and was officially operating in January 1994. Its membership has varied between eighty and ninety though beyond this number it has contact with the substantial Somali community in the city. Its premises have been awarded a ten-year lease and education figures prominently in its activities as well as sewing, knitting and computer use in many activities. By religion, the Somalis are entirely Sunnis, the overwhelming number of them from the Shāfi'ī school. Religion figures high in its purpose and mission, though this is not an official view of the faith wherein theological issues are debated and questioned. Arabic is taught, likewise the Qur'ān and Hadīth and it is a location where the annual Islamic feasts are celebrated. In Århus, this association has contacts with the Somali diaspora as a whole. Somalis, including whole families, are frequent passengers on the Ryanair flights that link Stansted, Heathrow and Århus, hence they routinely travel to and fro to other Somali communities elsewhere in Europe.

9   The Association of Turkish Immigrants.[62] This group formed in 1986. Since 1989 it has been centred in Ormslevvej in Viby. Its active membership varies between 120 and 130, though at times this may reach twenty-five. The association is primarily interested in family welfare in both Denmark and Turkey and it places great emphasis on the study of the Qur'ān, children's activities, sport included, and in the promotion of the pilgrimage to Mecca. Founded by Necattin Kiyak as well as others, its *imām* (*hoja*), Dursun Kekec, is effectively now its head. Weekly Qur'ānic classes are held and during *Bayram*, at the end of Ramadan, its mosque is well filled. Paid by its members and by monthly local grant from the local community, it places high priority to the promotion of integration and the teaching of Danish culture and language. Discrimination against members is relatively rare in Århus. This association has a close relationship with the community in Copenhagen.

10 The Turkish Cultural Association.[63] Many of the activities of this association are similar to (9) above. The association has close links with (4), (5), (7) and (9) and also cooperates with Gellerup church. Situated in Brabrand, Silkerborgvej, it was begun by the *D. Türk Diyanet Wakfı ulu Camii* and is principally a mosque centred within a converted building with catering, recreation and teaching facilities. It has some 155 paying members and, in total, it caters for a community of some 300 family members. Its activities are centred

in the mosque and on certain festive occasions there may assemble some 200 to 250 people. Its *imām* has been fully trained in Turkey in Islamic theology and the association is financed by the Turkish state notwithstanding the secular nature of that state, and also annually by Århus Kommun.

One is at once struck by the difference between the ethnic representation within this community, the variety of its Islamic priorities and its affiliations, the developed administrative machinery that it employs in order to function and to achieve its political and social goals. Amongst the countries in this Muslim community are to be found Afghanistan, Albania, Djibouti, Indonesia, Malaysia, as well as leading Arab states.[64] The relative number of these communities is also important. In July 2003, there were 4,189 Lebanese (some Christian), 3,839 Turks, 3,147 Somalis, 2,184 Iraqis and 2,167 Iranians.

The contrast with the Baltic States, and even with Poland, is striking, underlining further current distinctions between the Western and Eastern Baltic communities.

The new movement for Catholic and Muslim dialogue amongst the Tatars in contemporary Poland

We have seen that Muslim Tartars have been present and influential in Belarus, in Lithuania and in Poland for over six hundred years. Despite some eras when their survival was in doubt, be it through forcible religious conversion, or by total assimilation, or an enforced atheism under Communist rule, their co-existence with Catholic, Orthodox or Jew has been a rare example of a continuous dialogue and a stable observed and mutually desired tradition of respect for each other's faiths. The Tatars contributed their own units to the Polish army and, over the centuries, they participated in those national movements which were to lead to the establishment of the Polish Republic; events such as the Confederation of Bar (1768–72), Kosciuzko's insurrection in 1794, and the November and January Uprisings. The unity of all Poles against Communism that was preceded by the horrendous events of the holocaust and the gas chambers have been memories which have brought together all the faiths that are present within the Polish nation.

Dialogues between Protestant and Catholic clergy and divines and with Tatar *imāms* and scholars have already been mentioned. It is now believed that translations of entire *sūras* and passages of the Qur'ān existed in

Poland prior to the landmark translation of the sacred text from French into Polish by the Polish Muslim Jan Murza Tarak-Buczacki, in 1858. As has been mentioned, the late Professor Jozef Bielawski produced the first complete translation of the Qur'ān, from Arabic into Polish. It was published and printed by the State Publishing Institute, in Warsaw, in 1986. However, already plans are being made by the Polish Muslims to publish a fresh, and in their view, far closer, Polish translation. This move is in the light of the 'newer Islam' now being proclaimed in Poland. 'New Islam' is marked by a return to the text of the Qur'ān. Its programme has been influenced by the Middle East and the Arab-financed missions that have been established in Poland, as elsewhere throughout Europe.

On the Polish Muslim side, there have now been decades of close contact between *Imām* Mahmūd Tāhā Zūk and Nazīm Barber, the *imām* of the accredited diplomats of the embassies of the Arab Muslim countries in Poland. In 1995, the Polish Tatars and Polish Shī'ites took part in the ceremonies that commemorated the fiftieth anniversary of the liberation of Auschwitz. These were organised by the then Polish president, Lech Wałesa. The *Imām* of Gdańsk, Selim Chazbiewicz, prayed on behalf of the Polish Muslims during the unveiling of a monument that was dedicated to the citizens of Poland who were murdered under Stalin's regime. This took place in September of that same year. It was the occasion of the fiftieth anniversary of the launching of the attack of the USSR against Poland.

Other joint meetings have been held in mosques and in churches and both faiths have established committees and organisations which have been formed explicitly to promote further 'dialogue' and mutual Catholic and Muslim attendance at religious services, in public, in Catholic churches and in the mosques. According to Zdizław Bielecki, the co-president of the 'Common Council of Catholics and Muslims' (established in the Warsaw Centre for Islam on 13 June 1997), and also active in the fund 'The Work to Restore Love, *DOM Foundation*', a council met Pope John Paul II, in Drohiczyn, in 1999: 'In 2001, the Polish Bishops proclaimed the 26 January to be the day of Islam in the Catholic Church, in Poland.'

> In 2002, the central celebration of the Mass for the Day of Islam was held in the Sanctuary of St Andrew of Bobola, in Warsaw. It was a prayer meeting, introduced by the reading of His Holiness the Pope's speech that had been delivered in the Umayyad mosque, in Damascus. In the introduction, Bishop Piotr Libera, the General Secretary of the 'Conference of the Episcopate of Poland', said that 'the Day of Islam

inspires to a fuller vision of reality, a new relationship to God and to other people'. The prayers were led by Bishop Tadeusz Pikus and by the President of the Council of Polish *imāms*, Tomasz Miskiewicz, After the recitation, in Arabic, of the Qur'ānic passage describing the Angelic Annunciation to Holy Mary, the same passage was read in Polish, and also, analogously, the words telling of the Annunciation, in the Gospel of St Luke, was read in Polish as well as in Arabic. After the Believer's Prayer, prepared and read by Zdisław Bielecki, the co-President of the Council, from the Catholic side, speeches were delivered by the Ambassador of Pakistan, Khālid Mahmūd and by Bishop Tadeusz Pikus.[65]

One of the most recent joint events of this kind took place in spring 2003, on 18 May. On this occasion it was held both within and outside the most prestigious of Poland's historic mosques, Kruszyniany. The proceedings were led by *Imām* Tomasz Miskiewicz.

It was a moving occasion. Besides the presence of several Polish *imāms*, Tatars from the area of Białystok, Warsaw, Gdańsk and other Muslims now living in Poland, some from Morocco, Chechnya and neighbouring countries in Eastern Europe, the occasion was also graced by the attendance of the ambassador of Indonesia and the lady ambassador of Pakistan, and by Zdisław Bielecki, senior Catholic clergy, and the local Greek Catholic priest from the village. Each delivered addresses. Further messages of support were read to the gathering by *Imām* Tomasz Miskiewicz. He gave all those who were present a warm welcome. Prayers were said for peace. Following a short service within the mosque, a lunch, prepared by local Tatar ladies, was eaten out of doors under canvas. Young Tatar men and women walked freely amongst the gathering in their national dress. Many who were present also paid a visit to the nearby cemetery (*mizar*) in order to visit the graves of relations and friends, or else to show their respects to the relatives of the deceased who had attended the ceremony.

To accompany the celebration, pictures of the mosque were distributed, together with passages from the Qur'ān and a small leaflet which contained a prayer 'for peace and for justice' (*Modlitwa o Pokoj Sprawiedliwosc*). The text expressed the prayers of the Tatars who were present:

> We, Polish Muslims, pray for the reign of justice, peace and love in our fatherland and all over the world. We pray for weak and exhausted nations – decaying amidst hunger and sickness, oppressed by wars,

ethnic and religious quarrels – so that they can create their own countries based upon peace and justice.

Several passages from the Qur'ān were quoted in this sheet, both in Polish and in English. Prominent amongst these was a quote from *Sūra* 4, 'Women' (*al-Nisā'*), verse 135: 'You who believe, uphold justice and bear witness to God, even if it is against yourselves, your parents, or your close relatives. Whether the person is rich or poor, God can best take care of both. Refrain from following your own desire, so that you can act justly – if you distort or neglect justice, God is fully aware of what you do.'[66]

To the above is added the comment, 'Let us pray for the speedy ending of all wars and military conflicts. Let us try to look at evil with eyes of people who love peace. Let us bring all quarrels and conflicts to an end. Let justice, brotherhood, love and peace reign all over the world.'

Another Qur'ānic passage was taken from *Sūra* 49, 'The Private Rooms' (*al-Hujurāt*), verses 11–13:

> Believers, no one group of men should jeer at another, who may after all be better than them; no one group of women should jeer at another, who may after all be better than them, do not speak ill of one another; do not use offensive nicknames for one another. How bad it is to be called a mischief-maker after accepting faith! Those who do not repent of this behaviour are evildoers. Believers, avoid making too many assumptions – some assumptions are sinful – and do not spy on one another or speak ill of people behind their backs: would any of you like to eat the flesh of your dead brother? No, you would hate it. So be mindful of God: God is ever relenting, most merciful. People, We created you from a single man and a single woman, and made you into races and tribes so that you should recognize one another. In God's eyes, the most honoured of you are the ones most mindful of Him: God is all knowing, all aware.[67]

To the above is added the comment, 'Let us pray for victims of wars, terror, dictatorship, violence and injustice all over the world ... let us pray for the full engagement of all religions in creating peace all over the world. Let us pray so that peaceful co-existence, respect for human rights and religious tolerance may be the foundations of the unity of Europe and of the whole world.'

In such words the deep longings that are expressed by the Lehistan Tatars were addressed, on that occasion, not only to the West, but were also directed towards the World of Islam. In spirit, they expressed the emotions of several peoples who were, for long periods, under a harsh yoke amidst these steppes and these forests, ravaged by war and now menaced by new man-made political barriers. The tumult of their fellow believers in many far-flung corners of the globe, to the south and to the east, is as remote from them as is their frontier environment, yet many of their fellow brethren amongst the Tatars have a unique knowledge of both the heartlands of Islam, of Cairo and Medina, or of Kazan, Bukhara, Simferopol and Bachshiserai, or of the Eurasian steppes and of the economic, political and religious implications of the European Union of the future which now includes Estonia, Latvia, Lithuania and Poland. The borders of Europe will be fixed little further than beyond the eastern outskirts of Kruszyniany village itself. The Tatars, like the Karaims, face both West and East. Poland's eastern borders may, in future, be a barrier and a 'fence' dividing the Tatars. The Tatars and the Karaims – the descendants of the medieval Qipchāqs, are a human bridge. They will surely play a role in the future as they once played in the past, in the days of Gediminas and Vytautas (Vita'ut, in Belarus), when they were citizens of a part 'pagan', yet tolerant realm, a culture, a haven for numerous religious survivals. This haven once extended from the Baltic to the Black Sea.

Flexibility marked its frontiers, both earthly and spiritual. A tolerance marked the great Dukes of medieval Lithuania. Early in his reign, Duke Gediminas invited tradesman, artisans and peasant families as well as priests, monks and even bishops to settle in Lithuania. In an epistle he wrote, 'I don not forbid the Christians to worship God as their faith requires of them. This is likewise the choice of both Russians and Poles. Such be it, though we ourselves will worship the Deity according to our own customs.'

Recent trends amongst the Muslim communities in the Baltic region

A renewed religious zeal is to be witnessed amongst the Tatar and non-Tatar Muslims between the Baltic and the Black Sea. Spurred on by the entry of the Baltic States and Poland into the European Union, and closer contact with Scandinavia, the Tatars have been encouraged to pursue a regional reorganization within the Muslim communities. Added to this is the fact that Sweden has, in all probability, the largest Muslim minority in the entire world of the North, the total of believers reaching hundreds of thousands and containing not only Muslims from former Soviet

Republics, but others from Albania, from Bosnia and Kosovo, and from the Indian sub-continent.

At the village level new associations have been formed. One example is a rural community near Kielce, in Poland, which, following a mass revival of Muslim commitment and observance, formed an 'Organisation for Muslim Unity' (*Jednosc Muzulmanska*). These small revivals characterise the entire Muslim community, especially the Tatars in this region. Regional cooperation, joint congresses, tourism, Muslim youth camps (*muhayyems*), may be found throughout. More significant for the future is the founding of a Baltic regional movement, The Muslim Confederation of the Baltic Sea (MCBS).

The unofficial headquarters of this organisation is in the joint city of Gdańsk–Gdynia. It does not confine its 'parish' to the Tatar Muslims, Middle Eastern and Russian Muslims, or local converts, but it seeks to cooperate with Muslim centres and organisations in Germany, Denmark, Sweden and Finland. The Muslims in Gdańsk have a special role to play. They have the largest mosque; a former *imām*, Dr Selim Chazbijewicz, is the editor of the journal *Muslim Life*. He is the chairman of the Polish Muslim Heritage Foundation and has worked tirelessly for Catholic–Muslim cooperation. Other more radical Islamic movements, the *da'wa* and the members of the *Ikhwān* (*ahretni bracia*) have their important centres in Gdańsk. Another important centre is the city of Białystok, situated close to the border with Belarus and the Ukraine and hence it is uniquely placed, geographically, to bridge the divide between the 'New Europe' and its Eastern neighbours.

More radicals and ambitious goals are sought after by another organisation in Gdańsk – the Muslim Revival Movement (MRM). This has, as its aims, the restoration of the Caliphate and it has branches in the Russian republics of Tatarstan, Bashkortostan, Dagestan, amongst the Chechens and Ingush, the Idel-Ural and the Crimean Republics. Its appeal is primarily addressed to Tatars, Turks and Caucasian Muslims. The long-lasting tensions between the pan-Islamic and pan-Turkic movements lie at the heart of this stirring within the heart of these Muslim communities. Within Poland and the Baltic States such tensions are also openly discussed. It is an issue that often concerns the Polish Tatars, particularly those of the older generation and the Polish and Belarusian converts to Islam, who, though respectful of the Tatar heritage which marks their faith, view their faith of Islam as the flag to which they owe their first allegiance. Whatever the future may have in store for the Tatars, be they Qipčaq (Qipchāq), or Kazan, or Baškīr Tatars, Islam as a faith in the Baltic region will certainly survive.

The Muslims in Belarus have suffered some severe setbacks and loss during the past three years, although at the same time new opportunities have arisen.

Since the writing of this book, the following events have taken place:

1. The distinguished Belarusian scholar Dr Ibragim Kanapatski died in tragic circumstances. As a consequence, the rebuilding of the planned replica of the Minsk mosque has had to be abandoned – and its future indefinitely postponed. In place of it, an entirely new mosque is currently being erected through support and funding from the Tatars of Tatarstan where mosque building is taking place on a large scale, not only in Kazan but throughout that Russian Republic. Dr Kanapatski is greatly missed. He was born in the large village of Smilovichi, an hour's drive by car from Minsk, and he is buried in the Mizar, which is situated in a small wood in open country outside the village. The mosque in the village is a part of his legacy to the Muslims in Belarus.
2. A new Tatar Mufti from Iwie has been appointed.
3. A major conference has recently taken place in Minsk devoted to interfaith dialogue, a subject that was dear to the heart of Dr Kanapatski. It was strongly backed by the Orthodox Metropolitan of Minsk and Slutsk, Philaret, the Patriarchal Exarch of all Belarus. The title of this international conference was 'Dialogue between Christianity and Islam in conditions of Globalization'. The Conference was organised by the Institute for Religious Dialogue and Interconfessional Communications under the Exarchate of the Belarusian Orthodox Church, and the International Voluntary Association Saints' Methodius and Cyril Christian Educational Centre. It was organised in detail by Professors Andrey Danilov and Gregori Dovgyuallo respectively.[68]

The conference took place between 25 and 26 October 2007. The sessions covered a wide range of themes and topics: the history of the Christian–Muslim dialogue, the theological basis of the Christian–Muslim dialogue, the borders of this dialogue?, faith, truth and tolerance, the hermeneutics of the mutual perception, Christian and Islamic understanding of globalisation, new social teaching of Christianity and Islam as an answer to globalization, the image of religions in a world of globalization, the responsibility of Christians and Muslims for creation, a round-table discussion on the theme 'Violence and Terrorism' under the mask of religion. The debate on these issues was frank and constructive.[69]

The speakers included representatives from the Vatican and the Orthodox Church, including Philaret who took the chair on occasions. The Mufti of Belarus also took the chair. Other participants included: Monsignor and Dr Khaled b. Akasheh, head officer for Islam, Pontifical Council for Interrreligious Dialogue, Vatican City; the Rev. Dr Risto Cantell, executive director of the Evangelical Lutherans of Finland; Abdalla. M. Almaghrawi, the Libyan ambassador in Belarus, the head of the Palestinian Community of Belarus; and Dr Sinaşi Gündüz, professor of the History of Religion in the Faculty of Theology of Istanbul University. Parts of this conference were shown on Belarusian television, participants were interviewed and much public interest was reported. Several of the participants were received by President Alexander Lukashenko who had given strong support for the aims and goals of this conference.

Latvia was represented at the conference by Professor Leons Teivans of Riga University. He informed the participants, when questioned, that the Latvian government had now taken the necessary steps to sponser and assist in the publication of a definitive translation of the Holy Qur'an into Latvian. This has been given the full support of the Latvian Muslim community. From this item of news it was clear that the extensive criticism of the translation attempted by Uldis Beržinŝ had been a major factor for this decision and for taking this step.

It should be mentioned that a remarkable concert took place on 26 November at the Belarusian State Philarmonic. It was performed by the Choir and Orchestra of the National Academic Great Opera Theatre of the Republic of Belarus. Performers included the international contests' winner, the organist Konstantin Sharov, the 'Norus' Choir, the Boys' Choir of the Music Lycée of the Conservatoire, the Opera Theatre, Mariinsky Theatre, St Petersburg, the Opera Theatre, Poznán, Poland, and soloists of the Opera Theatre, Kazan, Tatarstan.

The theme of this concert was truly remarkable. It was an act of homage to the three 'Abrahamic Faiths' and to the conference that had just taken place. The concert hall was packed to the doors.

G. Harbuson's *Abraham* began the concert. It was performed for the first time in Belarus and, indeed, the first time in Eastern Europe. It formed a bridge between the three faiths.

It was followed by P. Chesnokov's 'Let my prayer be set forth' and G.Caccini's *Ave Maria*, the emphasis here being the joint honour shown to Our Lady in Catholicism, Islam and Orthodoxy. Next came three dances, Arabian, Turkish and Caucasian Lezghinka from the opera, *Ruslan and Ludmilla* by Mikhail Glinka (1804–57) who had been born in Novospasskoi, outside Smolensk, a city in Russia just beyond the current eastern frontier of Belarus. Next followed Rimsky-Korsakov's *Easter Festival Overture* followed by Mozart's *Requiem* and Verdi's Chorus from the opera *Nabucco*. This dialogue between faiths stamped every work performed that night.

Patriarch Philaret and the Mufti sat side by side in a box that overlooked the performance and the speeches that accompanied it. Where else in the world, be it in Christendom or in Dār al-Islām, could such a concert of praise to the One God take place today?

Addendum

On 18 January 2008, in Minsk, Aleksander Sdvizhkov, editor of the now closed independent weekly *Zgoda* (the Consensus) newspaper, was charged with 'incitement of religious hatred' and was sentenced to three years' imprisonment in a high-security prison. This arose due to his reprinting of the controversial Danish cartoons of the Prophet Muhammad, first published in *Jyllands Posten* in 2006. The trial was held 'in camera'. There were calls for his immediate release. The former editor-in-chief of *Zgoda*, Aleksei Korol, expressed his view, strongly, that the court ruling was disproportionate to the action that he had committed. However, Korol acknowledged that he had disagreed with Sdvizhkov's decision to reprint the cartoons alongside the paper's article that had given an account of the uproar in Denmark and in the Muslim World. He added that the staff of *Zgoda* had apologised to the Belarusian Muslim community. The leader of that community, Ismail Voronovich, expressed the view that he had hoped for a reprimand and not an imprisonment. When questioned, he is alleged to have remarked that, 'I thought that this case had been closed and that this newspaper was printing once again.' This is probably the most serious response to the publication of the Danish cartoons in any European country where Muslims have been shocked and hurt. 'Incitement to religious hatred' is viewed as an extremely serious offence within Belarus. This is in stark contrast to the ridicule and indifference that it received in certain EU countries.

Conclusion

In Belarus, the Baltic States, and in Poland, as in many Tatar- and Turkic-inhabited regions of the World of Islam, the daily practice of the faith has, over the centuries, suffered the influence of popular beliefs. Some of these may be traced to the ancient Shamanism of Eurasian peoples, or, again, it may be traced to popular Catholic, Orthodox and even Calvinistic Protestant beliefs, or ideas which were derived from those Arian Unitarians (the Socians) who were to be found in several parts of Eastern Europe. Concepts of the Divinity display these influences, likewise the rituals, and so too the status of the Muslim hierarchy, Muslim social activities and many past superstitions. However lofty and distinguished were, and are, the Tatar *Muftis* and *imāms* and scholars, the life of a small minority cannot be divorced from centuries-old pagan and Christian beliefs which preceded their settlement, nor would a goodly number amongst the Tatars wish for a cultural divorce from their non-Muslim neighbours ever to come about.

Their beliefs are accepted as having been inherited, in part, from this 'paganism', or having been borrowed from the cherished Christian faith of their neighbours, heretical or heterodox though that faith may have become. The pagan faith of Lithuania once fought tenaciously against the Teutonic Knights, yet it consciously, or unconsciously, ensured the survival of a Balt, and a Muslim Slav, and a Tatar, national identity. As has been seen, this Muslim Tatar identity was also one which shared many common values with Catholic, Eastern Orthodox, Uniates (Greek-Catholic), Jewish and Karaim communities, with whom, and beside whom, they, as Muslims, lived and worked, and with whom they have intermarried at times in their history. The Karaite community shared many common traditions with the Tatars: not only a common history that dates back to the time of Duke Vytautas, but likewise in the way that the religious communities were administered and served.

This was the view of the noted *Hakham* of the Karaites, the Orientalist Seraya Szapszal (1873–1961). His views were typed out in a document that is still preserved within the library of the Lithuanian Academy of Sciences. They demonstrated how the religious duties within the Karaite Jewish community in both Poland and Lithuania matched those within the Muslim Tatar community.[1] In that document he described the character of the 'Religious Union of the Muslims and Karaims'. It was one that had been established in Poland in 1936. This was particularly true of Vilnius district, which, at that time, was a Polish city. Each community was under the jurisdiction of their own spiritual and administrative superiors. He went to considerable trouble to explain the historical circumstances that had brought the Karaims and the Tatars together in the region. He also showed, in a historical survey in that document, how the Karaims had traced their teachings to Iraq in the age of the 'Abbāsids, thus further emphasising their common Oriental cultural roots. Turning to the history of the Karaite *kenesa*, or synagogue, in Trakai, together with its school, he mentioned how King Kazimierza (Casimir), in 1665, had given his permission for their erection as a reward for 'the gallant military service of the Karaims'. He added that the Tatars, too, had all their rights recognised in the seventeenth century and that a statute had also guaranteed all these religious rights and national freedoms. Furthermore, both had been granted total autonomy from any religious hierarchy, be it the Caliphate, or in the case of the Karaims, the Crimean Khānate.

In his document, he then outlined the common structure that characterised both communities and the parallels that applied in both their hierarchies:

> At the head of a Muslim religious body stands a Mufti. His position corresponds to that of the *Hachana* [*Hakham*]. *Imāms* among the Muslims correspond to *Hazzanas*, and *Muezzins* to *Szamasz*. Both the Mufti and the *Hachana* have their seats in Vilnius. A second religious organization, which supports the Muftiate in the government of the Muslim Religious Organization, is the Supreme College of the Muslims. This consists of the Mufti and his chairman, who is second to him in authority, and four other members, two of them religious and two of them secular (article 10). The Advisory Religious Body to the *Hachana* is the Karaim Religious Organization. This consists of two representatives from active *Hazzanas* (article 11).
>
> These articles have been approved by the Ministry of Religious Beliefs and of Public Education, together with the cooperation of the *Mufti* and the *Hachana*. Its declarations have been accepted by the

Polish government and by the Muslims and Karaims, in Poland. The special efforts of the director of the Department for Religious Beliefs, Franciska Potocki, deserves to be acknowledged.[2]

To this day, that Christian faith – be it Orthodox, or Catholic, – still encompasses Islam, and in the Lithuanian Polish case, the Karaims, on every side in the Baltic region, whether it be in a shared rural or in an urban environment. This environment may be a small village or it may be in a major modern city such as Gdańsk, or in Warsaw, in Minsk, or in Vilnius. More and more both faiths are centred within urban districts.

It should be recalled that mention has been made of the fact that the culture of the Muslim East for long had a special fascination for the Poles. It influenced them in many ways: in their aesthetic taste, their way of life, artistic imagination, many customs, language and in weaponry and armour. This was to a degree that far surpassed most of the lands of Western Europe, Spain included, and it was a totally different influence from that which was to be found in England during the heyday of the Indian Empire. Islamic influences could be found in every strata of society and it was to be found at an age that began way back in the later Medieval Ages. The inventories of residences which were located at Nieborow and Arkadia, which in 1774 became a part of the estate of the Radziwill family list, among other sundry items: Turkish curtains, Turkish settees, Turkish slippers, small sofas which were upholstered in Turkish fabrics, a Turkish saddle made from wood, a Turkish longbow, a Turkish sabre, Turkish coffee pots, Turkish cutlery, Turkish bedclothes, Turkish quilts, Turkish carpets and clothes and embroidered Turkish tablecloths. Some of these Oriental artistic influences were brought to Poland by the Armenians. The name of *Allāh*, written in Kūfic script, could be found on liturgical vestments of the Catholic Church. Christian and Muslim symbols were combined. A statuette of the Mother of God was set up upon a crescent on the top of a minaret erected by the Turks at the Cathedral of Kamienice Podolski, in the Ukraine, following its capture by the triumphant Poles.

The crescent and the star are, of course, by no means an exclusively Islamic symbolic logo of identity. In Białystok, close to today's border between Poland and Belarus, is one modern example. In Rocha district, Our Lady stands aloft upon a crescent moon above the city's most conspicuous church, gazing way below at the stream of cars and trolly-buses which characterise working daylight hours in that city. An Orthodox multi-pointed cross may share a prominent place beside a wooden Muslim chapel in the very same village street. One may wander in the depths of limitless pinewoods or expanses of silver birch, or upon sandy heaths, but the local villager or the wayfarer whom one greets may be a Christian, or he may be a Muslim. To this day, at Bohoniki, in Poland, within a few miles of the frontier with Belarus, a simple wooden mosque stands amidst a village of painted and thatched cottages and farmsteads. These cottages are usually indistinguishable, in design, from those others, in adjacent villages, where no mosque is to be seen today, nor, indeed ever, in the past, housed one family, or many, of Tatar Muslims. However, at Bohiniki, for example, a neighbouring house makes no attempt to conceal its ardent Catholicism. A statue of Our Lady, in a conspicuous position in the garden, greets, or confronts, the few Tatars, who, on a Friday, tread the path leading to the porch of this mosque.

The mosque has a *miḥrāb*, in wood. It faces south towards Mecca and its interior is covered with carpets and felts and hanging *muhirs*, namely, sacred pictures and Qur'ānic texts and calligraphic affirmations of faith. Yet, in many other respects, it can hardly be distinguished, in its exterior architecture, its woodwork and in some of its furnishings, from an Orthodox or Uniate church, or from a former synagogue, although the turreted and hollow ornamental stunted minaret that peeps above its roof recalls the Muslim Orient. The mosque is still a mosque, but within its structure certain of its furniture show influences from the places of worship of other faiths. In such wooden Polish, or Lithuanian, mosques, candles burn in fine candlesticks, just as they burn in front of a statue of Our Lady. Womenfolk may sit in galleries or in separate enclosures. The Qur'ānic text, which at times is hung in frames along the walls, is intoned melodically during prayers, and, just as the sacred scriptures are lovingly chanted in the Karaim Qipčaq (Qipchāq) tongue, in the *kenesa*, the Arabic sentences have a solemn and ancient sound of chanting to Western ears. The Muslim worshippers intone in a manner that recalls the Lithuanian and Polish Catholics, and even those who belong to the Orthodox faith. Were one to remove the minarets, the shared architectural heritage of Bulghār on the Volga, and of Kyiv and Byzantium often stands revealed.

In all the Baltic countries today, the Muslims, Tatar and non-Tatar long for the construction of a major mosque, their mosque, be it in a capital city or beyond. Opposition is faced from many quarters. However, above all it is the shortage of money to erect such mosques that brings home to them that they are on the edge of the continent, they border the 'Sea of Darkness'. They appeal for funds and support, they plead their case in the richer nations of the World of Islam to their south.

One example is the appeal that was made by former Mufti of Belarus

Ismael Alexandrovich and from the Muslims of Belarus to the leaders of the Islamic countries, organisations, funds and Islamic centres of the World:[3]

> Peace be with you and the mercy of God!
>
> The Muslims of Belarus, the basic part of whom are Tatars, started their national and religious revival in 1990. The Republic of Belarus, the territory of which is 208,000 sq kms, is situated in the centre of Europe. Its population is 10 million people. The Islamic religion started at the time when the Muslim Tatars (originally from the Crimea) arrived here at the end of the fourteenth century. In 1997 we celebrated the 600th anniversary. Six centuries ago the first mosques appeared in Belarus. In the sixteenth century here lived 40,000 Tatars and there were 60 mosques.
>
> But later came difficult times, and, during the Communist era (1917–1990) Islam suffered its serious setback. Many mosques were closed down and used for other purposes. Teaching children was strictly forbidden. Despite all this, religion could not be destroyed, but it became very difficult to practice it. Before the beginning of the Second World War in Belarus there were 19 mosques and after the War there remained only ONE – one for about 12.5 thousand Tatars and 30–35 thousand Muslims from other countries living and studying in Balarus. The mosque in Minsk was destroyed in 1962.
>
> Now there is a law that guarantees the freedom of religion. There is a possibility of Muslims gathering for 'ṣalāt' and for teaching Islam to our children; we can fulfill Islamic ceremonies, we can publish our newspaper and magazine, organize Islamic youth camps. We are presently doing all this, but we are experiencing the problem of having no mosques and schools (or rooms) for teaching Islamic studies and a basic problem in the absence of financial facilities.
>
> In January 1994, a joint Muslim Association was formed at the first Congress of Belarusian Muslims. At this conference, the Mufti of the Belarusian Muslims was elected. The Muslim Association was legally registered by the Government on 20th February, 1994. The Muslim Congress of Belarus entrusted the Mufti with the task of finding ways of establishing mutual contacts with the aim of getting assistance for the revival of Islam on the Belarusian land. At present the economic situation in our country is very difficult and there are no possibilities of getting material assistance either from the state or from the Tatar population of the Republic of Belarus to satisfy our spiritual needs.

> Under the present circumstances the important thing for us is to build four or five mosques in different regions of Belarus where Muslims live.
>
> The most important for us is the construction of a mosque in Minsk.
>
> We have already acquired land in Minsk for the construction of the mosque and the project design is complete, but the commencement of the construction is not within our financial competence (2 mln. USD).
>
> The Muslims of Belarus are hereby seeking your financial assistance for the construction of the Mosque in Minsk, for the acquisition of houses or rooms for thanksgiving and teaching, for organizing Islamic youth camps, for issuing an Islamic newspaper and magazine – all for the revival and preservation of Islam in Belarus.
>
> We hope that, with the help of ALLAH, the Great, our appeal will be listened to by the Muslims of the World. May ALLAH'S Blessing be upon you all! May ALLAH, the Most Supreme, be pleased with us for our endeavour![4]

The Tatar peoples of Eastern Europe have some of their roots in a Christian past, but the Christians themselves are aware of their own ancestral inheritance from the 'pagan' peoples who were their ancestors. The Shamans, the priests and the priestesses have long vanished from Lithuania, but they had formerly worshipped in the darkness of the forests or along the shores of the sandy spit in the Baltic Sea, and ceremonies which take place on the eve of Midsummer day are central to the annual calendar of the modern Lithuanians. Christianity has been compelled to absorb ancient cultures and these ancient cults. No geographical barrier stood in the way of the divine beings that had come into mythology from distant Asia.[5] The cult of fire was widespread.[6] Gods and goddesses were transplanted within Eastern Europe. Borders were open, steppes were vast, rivers could be navigated, and this had a particular relevance for such countries as Belarus, Lithuania, Poland and even more so beyond them in the Ukraine.

Anne Applebaum in her remarkable book, *Between East and West* wrote that:

> The borderlands lie in a flat plain, crushed between the civilizations of Europe and those of Asia. East of Poland, west of Russia, their lack of mountains, seas, deserts, and canyons has always made the borderlands easy to conquer. Five centuries ago, an army on horseback

could march from a castle on the Baltic to a fort on the Black Sea without meeting a physical obstacle greater than a fast-running river or a wide forest.⁷

She further adds:

> The waves of invasion created odd hybrids: the cathedral with a minaret in Kamenets Podolsky, or the town of Trakai, where five religions (Catholic, Orthodox, Jewish, Moslem, Karaim) once set up their houses of worship around a single lake. Apart from the huge Jewish population in these territories, 'Scattered among all of these peoples there were others; colonies of Armenians, Greeks, and Hungarians, Tartars and Karaites, the descendants of war prisoners or merchants or heretics or criminals. For a thousand years the peoples of the borderlands spoke their dialects and worshipped their gods, while the waves of invaders washed over them, mingled with them, receded, and then washed over them again.⁸

All these cultures and faiths left their mark. The influences from the ancients also left an indelible mark upon the men of faith amongst the Christians and Muslims who shepherded the human flocks who were to follow them. This influence, in Lithuania, particularly struck Anne Applebaum when she discussed religion with a. young Franciscan brother in the Lithuanian monastery of Dotnuva. She enquired as to why he had taken his vows in order to help the godless in his motherland.

He replied:

> 'It all started with a simple question. Every day, I woke up and asked myself: Why did Christianity come to our people so late? For a long time, I worried that it was because we were somehow lower in the eyes of God. I worried that Lithuanians were not so blessed as other nations. I worried that our nation had somehow sinned in the years of its infancy, and that the sin had prevented us from conversion until the fourteenth century'.
>
> Brother Francis stopped abruptly in front of a broad oak tree, stared at it for a second, and then turned his gaze on me.
>
> 'But one summer, after much meditation, I divined the real reason. I understood that the spirit of God has always lain deep within the Lithuanian soul. You see, our pagan religion was concerned not with the worship of idols, but with the worship of trees. We spoke to the

trees, we believed that God lived in the trees – and I believe that we knew Christ through the trees. We understood Him through what He had created.'

Brother Francis glanced at the tree again, and continued walking.

'I believe that our late conversion was a blessing. Because of it, Lithuanians have a clearer understanding of Christ than other nations. We are a simpler people, we are closer to His truths, just as Christ is closer to the simple people than He is to intellectuals. The day that I understood this was the day I decided to take my vows. I wanted to devote myself to God's people, to the simple people, to the Lithuanians.'[9]

A sense of identity with a 'pagan' and Christian past and, especially the causes and ideals of the heroic figures of Duke Gediminas and Duke Vytautas have also for many centuries preoccupied the once refugee, or captive, Tatar peasants, nobles, and the *imāms*.

Selim Chazbijewicz is a respected representative of those Polish Tatars for whom 'Tatar identity' and the multi-religious past of the peoples of the Grand Duchy of Lithuania and of contemporary Poland, Lithuania and Belarus cannot be disassociated from the Islamic heritage of his forebears, many of them Muslim scholars and distinguished *imāms*. When asked about the 'sons of Toqtamish', he proudly claims that he is amongst that hero's lineal descendants.

Selim Chazbijewicz was born in 1955. Described as an essayist, a poet, an *imām* in Gdańsk, a lecturer and a scholar in Philology and in History and, currently on the staff of the University of Olsztyn (once in former East Prussia), he was, between 1986 and 1991, the editor of the quarterly *Muslim Life* (*Życie Muzulmanskie*). He is currently editor of *The Polish Tatar Annual* (*Rocznik Tatarów Polskich*). He is a respected figure in Muslim life in Poland and he has journeyed in the Middle East, having performed the Meccan pilgrimage with his son, Olgierd. He has paid regular visits to his fellow Tatars who are now returning to the Crimean peninsula from Central Asia. He is a prolific author. To him his loyalty to his faith is matched by his strong loyalty to Muslim and Catholic dialogue, in Poland. As a consequence of Poland's entry into Europe, and with a border that, at the moment, may threaten to partially seal off his fellow Tatars in Belarus, he is a passionate believer and worker for the maintenance of close cultural contact with all his Tatar brothers, including those in Kazan, in Ufa, in Simferopol and in Bachshisarai in the Crimea. Tatar 'nationalism', to him, is synonymous with unity in the faith with all Muslim believers. In the same way, many Lithuanian and

Polish Karaims reject the call to 'return to Israel'. They too are Qipchāqs, first and last. Selim Chazbijewicz is also strongly drawn to Turkish Sufism and he dearly wishes to see a Tatar 'brotherhood' (*ṭarīqa*) founded in his homeland. However, this Sufism should not disavow those other streams of belief and spiritual quest which once marked the Islam of the Tatars, especially the mystical heritage of ancient 'Shamanism', the belief in Almighty *Tengri*, the presence of the divine in the forests, the heaths, the steppes and also within the blooming cities now inhabited by Tatars; Baltic cities which are the historic legacy of Vytautas (Witold), of Jagielo, of the Karaims, of the merchants of the Hanseatic League, of the Armenians and of the great Jewish tradition of scholarship and culture within this Baltic 'Tatar world'. That Baltic world is full of hope, but it is also a world that was once exposed to a militant Crusader movement that threatened its survival from without and from within. That threat, the threat of '*l'Homme Armé*', still remains, and it haunts the memories of the Qipchāqs and the non-Qipchāqs alike.

Appendix

A Tatar document in Arabic script from the Department of Rarities, the Latvian National Library (Latvijas Nacionālā, Bibliotēka, Rīga)[1]

This document (which possibly in its style is the closest to the genre known as a *dałavar* or to the *Chama'il*) bears the Library Catalogue number n28, A 222S (no 28 Austrumtautu/Oriental). It has 176 pages and is written on very small sheets of paper. It was brought to Latvia from St Petersburg and dates from 1885, though other dates are shown on a separate page that is included within the document. These dates extend back to 1835. The document is in vocalised Arabic script throughout, although despite being conscientious and systematic, this vocalisation is invariably faulty, at times unreadable, furthermore some grammatical constructions (e.g. double definition – the prefixing of the Arabic definite article is frequently to be found before a word that is also defined by a pronominal suffix) are inexplicable. The bulk of this work is in this deformed Arabic, although it also contains sub-headings and quite extensive passages of text in Byelorussian and what appears to be a Tatar language. The latter has its own grammar and forms of Arabic letters, denoting non-Arabic consonants and vowels. Each one is written in Arabic script, though the author has frequently used an ink of a far lighter colour. Notwithstanding its numerous linguistic mistakes, one is at once struck by the fervour, the sincerity and the piety of its author. That author appears to have been a certain Salayman (Sulaymān) Bogdanov Abraham (Ibrāhīm).

It opens, on pages 2 and 3, with a passionate prayer:

> In the name of God, the Compassionate and Most Merciful and peace be upon the Messenger of God. O God, open for me the gates

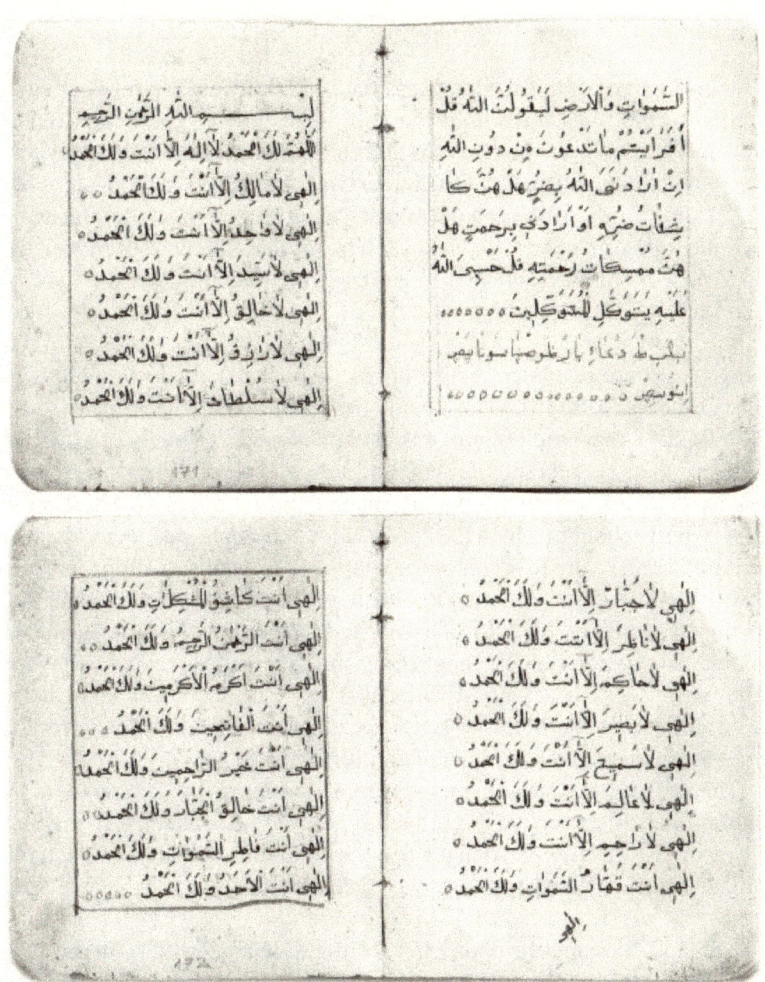

Figure 5 A Tatar manuscript from Rīga, no 28, A 222S (no 28 Austrumtautu/ Oriental), pages 171 and 172

of Thy Mercy and the gates of Thy grace and Thy favour through Thy munificence, O Most Merciful of the merciful. All praise be given to God, the Lord of the Worlds. O Lord, pardon and show mercy. Thou art the best of those who show mercy, Praise be to God, the Lord of the Worlds. O God, receive from us, by the sacredness of the *Fātiḥa*.[2]

The text continues, in Arabic, following a passage in Tatar:

> In the name of the all Compassionate and the Most Merciful, O Thou who ever lives and who is the Self Subsisting, O Thou, the Creator and Designer of the Heavens and the Earth. O Lord of Majesty and Greatness and Bounty. O Thou, O God, Almighty, no God exists but Thou. Verily, I beseech Thee that you always revivify my heart by the light of Thy knowledge, by God, through Thy mercy, O Thou, the Most Merciful of the merciful. Praise be given to God, the Lord of the Worlds.

This is a Sunnī document and it opens with the names and qualities of the 'Orthodox' Caliphs, whose names are occasionally spelt incorrectly: Abū Bakr, 'Umar (spelt 'Ummara), 'Uthmān (spelt 'Ushmān), 'Alī (spelt A'lāya), then Ḥasan (spelt Ḥasana) b. 'Alī, and so on. These names are followed by a list of the Orthodox schools of law in Islam, Abū Ḥanīfa (the Ḥanafī school to which the Tatars belong, though spelt, occasionally, as Abū Ḥanūf). The text continues with lists of names of Prophets from the Bible and from the Qur'ān and it is followed by an introduction to the 'five pillars' (arkān) of Islam and an outline of what a Muslim should believe and how he should pray and live with his fellow believers. The entire work is a kind of 'breviary', or 'catechism', or manual for instruction in the faith. It is either for personal use, by an imām, or for the private and personal use of the author himself and his family.

There is a passage later in the text (pp. 158–62), again often remarkably ungrammatical and erroneous in spelling and in its vocabulary. It provides a prayer list of holy personages for whom divine blessings are sought. This list includes Archangels as well as Prophets:

> O God, blessings be upon Michael, the Archangel of Thy mercy, who was created for the service of Thy high status. He it is who seeks Thy pleasure and pardon in respect to Thy obedience. O God, blessings be upon Isrā'fīl,[3] he who holds and blows the last trump, he who awaits Thy commands and who is on the watch for, and from, Thy wrath. O God. Blessings be upon 'Azrā'īl,[4] he who bears aloft Thy throne and who is the righteous steward for Thy sake and for Thy honour, O Master of majesty and generosity.
>
> O God, blessings be upon all angels and upon Thy Prophet and other prophets; upon Ādam, the wondrous being of Thy Creation whom Thou hast granted a favour, namely, the prostration of the angels before him, (though) he was rejected[5] from Thy Paradise.

O God, blessings be upon Āmina, a soul urbane and refined, who was pure from uncleanness, hounded and banished from humanity, wandering to and fro while bearing within her womb the holy one (Muḥammad).[6] O God, blessings be upon Muḥammad and upon his family, blessings be upon Abel,[7] and upon Shīth[8], and upon Idrīs,[9] and upon Noah, and upon Hūd[10] and upon Ṣāliḥ[11] and upon Abraham and Ishmael and upon Isaac and upon Jacob, and upon Joseph and the Children of Israel, and upon Moses and Aaron, and upon al-Khaḍir[12] and upon Elias, and upon Alexander the Great (Dhū'l-Qarnayn),[13] and upon Jonah, and upon Job, and upon Lot, and upon Elijah, and upon David and upon Solomon, and upon Zachariah, and upon John the Baptist, and upon Jesus, and upon Joshua, and upon Shu'ayb,[14] and upon Shiqq/Shikk,[15] and upon Simeon, and upon the disciples of Jesus, and upon those who followed thereafter. O God, blessings be for ever upon Muḥammad and upon the Prophet's household, so too prayers and God's peace and blessings, and mercy be upon Abraham and upon the household of Abraham in both worlds. Our Lord, Thou art worthy of highest praise in Thy glory. O God, blessings be upon Muḥammad and the household of Muḥammad, upon the household of true guidance and upon righteous substitutes and upon men of high rank and upon the women who are pious and God's servants and those who abstain and are prudent and those folk who are stubborn in adversity and in the fight for righteousness (*al-ijtihād*), in particular.

This kind of document is not unusual amongst the Tatar literature in north-eastern Europe, though it is not in any way typical of the far higher quality of the major genres that may be found in that Tatar literature, namely the *Kitābs*, the *Chamā'il* and the *Tefsīrs*, the commentaries on the Holy Qur'ān. Very fine examples of these latter works are to be found in libraries and in museums in Belarus, Lithuania and in Poland, as well as in London.

This document most closely resembles types of *Chamails* that are to be found in the Seraya Szapszal's Collection of Karaim and Tatar manuscripts in the Library of the National Museum of Lithuania.[16] These are catalogued as: '698, Short Arabic-Russian prayer book (*molitvenniik*), dating from the nineteenth century, in Russian and in Arabic', and, also, '711, List of 40 prophets, Islam figures and other persons to be prayed for while reading the 36th *Sūra* of the *Qur'ān*, *Yā'Sīn*, in Polish and Arabic, written on the 26 February, 1795'. Such books and manuscripts cannot be included in their quality within the same genres as the *Kitābs* and *Chamā'il*.

Typical of these texts are the passages that are to be found on in the opening pages and in pages 159–62 of the Rīga text. In it one may read the passage that is translated above.

Also to be noted is the appearance of names from the Bible that are rarely to be found, if at all, in the Qur'ān, or in other Muslim writings. This is quite common amongst Tatar writings and it is probably explained by the contact between them and the Christian literature in Belarus, Lithuania and in Poland.

Dr Adrzej Drozd has made a special study of the exchanges that took place, and especially the works from Old Polish literature that were borrowed by the Polish Tatars and that are to be observed in passages in their literature, especially in their *Kitābs*[17] The use of Arabic script for recording Byelorussian and Polish language content is known from the latter half of the sixteenth century. Biblical personalities and chosen events that are to be found in the Old Testament were matched to the apocryphal material that was to be found in such Arabic works as *Qiṣaṣ al-Anbiyā'* and *'al-Awliyā'* (*Opowieści o prorokach*), the 'stories of the miraculous lives of the Prophets and the saints'. Drawing upon these influences of the Reformation and the Renaissance, the Tatars were frequently familiar with relatively obscure and even minor personalities who are only to be found in the Bible. Such references may be compared with the text of the Qur'ān that was, in all likelihood, translated into Polish by the end of the sixteenth century. The Tatars principally used the Polish translation made by the Arians, or the Unitarians, principally that of Szymon Budny, dating from 1572. Bible quotations were used by the Tatars in their case for the truth of the abrogation of the preceding scriptures that Islam afforded. All kinds of Bible themes from sundry sources were not excluded as well.[18]

A note on the homelands of the Cumans and the Qipčāqs in south-eastern Europe

Throughout the content of this book, the Lithuanian Tatars, the Karaims of Lithuania and Poland, and other Turkic peoples of Muslim faith figure on every page. A short description of the geographical setting of their homelands in eastern Europe is the necessary background to their faiths, their history and their literary accomplishments, something of which is presented in my chapters. In the south of the Ukraine, the Crimean peninsula is the home of the Crimean Tatars who have returned there following their expulsion under orders of Stalin. The exiles have resettled and now number some 350,000 Tatars. However, their years in exile, in Central Asia and in Turkey, have meant that many of their old villages and homes have since been settled by others. Most of the older mosques, *madrasas* and graveyards have been obliterated A few of the finest have been restored. Only now is painstaking research bringing to light the ancient Turkic toponyms. The cultural roots and the historical memories of the pre-war Tatars have only a limited significance to those of a younger generation. The contrast between the Ottoman character of Bakhshiserai, recalling picturesque towns in Turkey, or in Albania and Bosnia, and the new settlements, on new sites and with mosques which have lost the centuries old architectural features of Ottoman mosques (although the mosques in Feodosiya and in Yevpatoriya, which have been tastefully restored, are notable exceptions), is to be observed almost everywhere throughout the length and the breadth of Respublika Krym. Few Karaims remain in the peninsula, although the dramatic site of Čufut-Kalé defies the ravages of time. For both communities, and for their relations in the Baltic region, the Crimean peninsula will always remain a spiritual home in which are concealed their extremely ancient cultural roots. Many Tatars and Karaims in both Lithuania and in Poland regard the Crimea as the key to their identity before their forebears were transferred northwards into the Baltic region in the days of the Lithuanian Grand Duke Vytautas.

The geographical heartland of this book is situated on the borders between Belarus, Lithuania and the Podlasie region of eastern Poland.

Here are to be found situated some of the oldest settlements of 'Lithuanian Tatars', who are lost in a countryside of forest and heath, reminiscent in places of the Norfolk and Suffolk Breckland, though on a far vaster scale. At the very heart of this landscape is situated the Pushcha Reserve, part of which is in Poland and part in Belarus, a unique and unspoilt region of Europe, where rare species survive and where wild bison may still be found. In these districts, apart from such old Tatar mosques as Kryszyniany, built with the approval of Jan Sobieski III, are found ancient synagogues with their graveyards which are not dissimilar to those of the Tatars, for example at Krynki, and also frequented churches and sites of pilgrimages for the Orthodox and the Greek Catholic Uniates, such as Grabarka. This landscape is filled with relics of a multi-faith society which has lasted for centuries. However, this study of the Qipčaqs, both Tatars and Karaims, and their faith and their culture, also includes other parts of eastern Europe. It refers, in passing, to the Crimean peninsula, in particular the southern districts, the towns of Sudak (Surdaq), Feodosija (Kaffa), Yevpotoria, Bakhshiserai, and the ancient mountain fastness of Čufut-Kalé, a hallowed place with ancient graves and proud historical memories for both Karaims and Tatars. The daughter of Toqtamish is buried in a *türbe* there. It is not possible to understand the past and the cultural heritage of the Tatars and the Karaims of the northern, the Baltic regions, without considering the far earlier historical events in the Crimea and the steppes to the north of that peninsula. The medieval Moroccan traveller Ibn Battūta has left in his *Riḥla* valuable details about Turkish and Tatar life in the peninsula. These should not be overlooked. The regions from the Baltic to the Black Sea have shaped their identities. Eastern Europe extending from the borders of Scandinavia to the Azov Sea is the geographical stage for the dramas which are recorded in all of my chapters. For a while, the Crimean region once formed part of the 'Grand Duchy of Lithuania'. It is the legendary memory of Grand Duke Vytautas which unites these vast and undefined borders of eastern Europe. It also unites Qipčaq Tatar and Karaim, Balt, Slav, Armenian and Greek. At the heart of this book is the achievement of one great man, one point in time. It is his memory, be it recorded in history, or in folk epic, which spans both the history and the vast expanses of Europe's now newly drawn borderlands.

Notes and references

Chapter 1

1 The substance of this chapter formed part of a lecture delivered in Rīga, in October 2006, to a class of second-year students in the Faculty of Modern Languages, Department of Asian Studies of the University. I am grateful to Professor Leons Taivans for arranging this.
2 Translated from the Finnish by F.W. Kirby, London and New York, 1951, vol. 2, p. 39, vv. 277–90.
3 For background reading on this topic, see *A Description of Europe, and the Voyages of Ohthere and Wulfstan*, edited and translated by J. Bosworth, London, 1855, and G. Jacob, *Arabische Berichte von Gesandten an germanische Furstenhofe aus dem 9. und 10 Jahrhundert*, Berlin and Leipzig, 1927 and, likewise by Jacob, *Der Nordische-baltische Handel der Araber im Mittelalter*, Leipzig, 1887.
4 On this poet, see, M.M. Badawi, *An Anthology of Modern Arabic Verse*, OUP, 1970, p. xxiii.
5 Pp. 6 and 7 of the Arabic text. It has been freely translated here and condensed into a selection of three of its verses.
6 This passage from Ibn Fadlān may be read with full notes in *Ibn Fadlān, Voyage chez les Bulgares de la Volga*, translated by Marius Canard, Paris, 1988, pp. 38, 57–8, and pp. 111–12, n. 174. The Viking dimension to Ibn Fadlān's account may be examined further in the comment of Jørgen Bæk Simonsen, in his *Vikingerne ved Volga*, Wormianum, Hojberg and Århus, Denmark, 1981.
7 *Selected Poems from the Divani Shamsi Tabriz*, edited and translated with an introduction, notes and appendices, by Reynold. A. Nicholson, New Delhi, 1898 (second edition. 1994), Appendix II, p. 344.
8 *Religious Art in Finland during the Middle Ages*, Helsingfors, 1921, p. xvii.
9 Arguably, the most thorough examination of this whole story in relation to the Baltic may be read in T. Lewicki's 'Ponocna kraina Amazonek w opisach sredniowiecznych geografow arabskich', in *Odbicie ze Sprawozdan Polskiej Akademii Umiej*, Tom 49 (1948), nr. 7, str. 352, pp. 352–5.
10 The 'Island of Women' and the 'Lands of the Amazons' are sited in various parts of the globe in Arabic accounts and are not only in the far North. Sundry

texts locate them in the Far East, East Africa, the Caucasus and in remote Pacific islands, to quote a few examples.
11 Ḥudūd al-'Ālam, *'The Regions of the World', A Persian Geography 372 A.H.–982 A.D.*, translated and explained by V. Minorsky, second edition, with a preface by V.V. Barthold translated from the Russian and with additional material by the late Professor Minorsky, edited by C.E. Bosworth, 'E.J.W. Gibb Memorial', London, 1970, pp. 58–9. The number of rivers, thirty-six as opposed to three, seems to confirm the view that the 'Island of Men' was believed to be a far larger land mass than the 'Island of Women'.
12 O.J. Tallgren-Tuulio and A.M. Tallgren, *Idrisi, La Finlande et les autres pays baltiques orientaux* (Géographie, VII 4), Edition Critique, Studia Orientalia, 111, Helsingfors, 1930, furnishes full details, and Abdurrahman li El-Hajji, *The Geography of al-Andalus and Europe from the Book 'Al-Masālik wal-Mamālik'* (The Routes and the Countries) by Abû 'Ubayd al-Bakri (d. 487/1094), Beirut, 1387/1968, in particular pp. 169 ff., where al-Turtūshī is extensively quoted.
13 O. Klindt Jensen, *The Vikings in England*, Copenhagen, 1948, pp. 23–4.
14 O.J. Tallgren-Tuulio and A.M. Tallgren, ibid, where the references, by al-Idrīsī, are discussed with great thoroughness throughout the monograph.
15 Al-Idrīsī refers to the river Niemen (Nīmiya), namely the major river Nemunas, in Lithuania. This fact is cited as evidence by Tallgren-Tuulio and Tallgrento in order to prove that the city of Kaunas, today Lithuania's second largest city, was already a town of importance. 'Note 4, Je pense qu'il pourrait s'agir de l'actuel Kaunas, Kovno. Ce ne serait pas la première fois qu'Idrisi appliquât le nom d'un fleuve à la principale des villes situées sur ce fleuve.' Their same approach also applies to Tallinn, which has sometimes been identified with the port (spelt 'Qlwrī' in the published text, though there are other variant Arabic readings). According to al-Idrīsī, 'among Astlanda's towns there is also Qlwrī. This is a small town like a large castle', a description which is true of Tallinn today. It is doubtful however that Qlwrī is the correct Arabic reading. This ought to be closer to Kolõvani (Koluvaniga the ancient name for Tallinn). A known variant reading of 'Qulūwnī', in fact achieves this. See Ivar Leemus, Jaak Mäll and Erki Russow, *Origines Revaliae, Esmakordset Tallinnas ja Tallinnast*, Eesti Ajaloomuseum, Tallinn, 2004, pp. 3 and 4.
16 Curland and Courland, the sandy Curonian spit which today links Lithuania with the Russian Oblast of Kaliningrad, formerly East Prussia. The name also appears in Latvia in the province of Kurzeme.
17 The Scandinavian name for the large islands surrounding Estonia.
18 See Abū 'Ubayd al-Bakrī (d. 487/1094) *The Geography of al-Andalus and Europe from the Book "al-Masālik wal-Mamālik"* (The Routes and the Countries), critical edition by Abdurrahman Ali El-Hajji, Beirut, 1387/1968, op. cit., pp. 166–8, and Francis Dvornik, *The Slavs, Their Early History and Civilisation, Boston*, 1956. Page 110 ff. sums up the historical importance of this Polish ruler:

> 'The other important factor emerging at this period was the Polish Duke, Mieszko 1. He is introduced into the annals of history by the chronicler, Thietmar of Meresburg and by the contemporary Arab writer Ibn Jakub, According to these two authors, Mieszko – of the dynasty founded by

Piast – was a mighty ruler commanding a standing army of 3,000 men whom he paid in minted money. He appears to have been master of a strong federation of Slavic tribes known since then as the Poles (Polane) after the most powerful amongst them, and the center of his realm was Gniezno (Genesen).'

This is in the region of Poznań. Ahmed Nazmi, in his *Commercial Relations between Arabs and Slavs (9th–11th Centuries)*, Warsaw, 1998, p. 241, discusses how the unclear Arabic expression 'murqūtiyya' should be interpreted. Mithqāl is a synonym for the golden Muslim dīnār (a unit of weight equal to 4.25/88 grammes) and he interprets 'murqūtiyya' as a distortion of 'bīzanṭiyya', Byzantine. He adds that with the coming of the eleventh century it would seem that the flow of Islamic silver coins to Poland had stopped completely.

On the relationship between Ibrāhīm b. Yaʻqūb and Poland, see Tadeusz Kowalski, *Relacja Ibrahima z podrozy do krajow slowianskich w przekazie Al-Bekriego*, Krákow, 1946.

19 In this context the 'Russian Vikings' are clearly meant.
20 The ancient Prussians, the descendants of the Aestians, the Galindians and Sudovians, who were conquered by the Crusaders in the thirteenth century and who are now extinct, were the third of the three principal Baltic peoples. Only the Latvians and Lithuanians survive today.
21 Prussian, as a western Baltic language was spoken at that time. Only a few written records have survived. Such are described, and illustrated, in Zigmas Zinkevičius, Aleksiejus Luchtanas and Gintautas Česnys, *Where We Come From*, Vilnius, 2005, pp. 78 [79]. See also, the articles on the Prussians by Valdis Muktupāvels, Rita Grāvere, Kaspars Kļaviņs and Letas Palmaitis in 'Western Balts: A Historical Perspective', 3 (49)/2006, *Humanities and Social Sciences*, Latvia, University of Latvia, pp. 4–67.
22 On the respective distinction between these names see Ahmad Nazmi, *Commercial Relations between Arabs and Slavs*, Warsaw 1998, op. cit., pp. 89–100 and Warang, pp. 32, 87, 95, 96 and 97, likewise, *Where We Come From*, ibid., n. 19, pp. 104 [105], especially CVIII, The Water Route of the Varangians.
23 An attack on the coastline of Prussia and Lithuania from the west would suggest, here, that the Scandinavian Vikings are meant, although the geographical points of the compass in these Arabic accounts are unreliable.
24 a While both the tales of an island or peninsula, or city, which was the exclusive home of womenfolk, Amazon, or otherwise, is a widespread fable in the Middle Ages in both East and West, we are to understand from Ibrāhīm al-Turtūshī, al-Bakrī and al-Idrīsī, that the incentive to their inclusion of it in their geographical works was the interest in it in Christendom at that time, especially in Germany.

Magdeburg contained the name of 'civitas virginem', see Tadeusz Kowalski, ibid., p. 93. Al-Idrīsī sees fit to show its outline upon his map, furthermore, he provides us with names of ports and other locations which assist in plotting the location of this legandary island. Unfortunately, those who have studied the text are themselves confused as to the identity of the ports.

Al-Hajji, op. cit., in a footnote, on pp. 169 and 170 furnishes a text based on the manuscript in Paris, No 2221, folio 344. It refers to directions to the neighbouring 'Island of Men'. The way into them, namely their island, is at its closest, via Anhu, the distance between them being three days sailing. They may be entered via the town of Falmar (Qalmar or Kalmar) and via the town of Dāghūda'. These names are corrupted and where there are plausible grounds for their identification, Tallgren and Tallgren, op. cit., locates most of them, rightly or wrongly, in Estonia. Falmar/Qalmar is an interesting reading since it suggests the important port and region of southeastern Sweden, which is called Kalmar, saw the launch of Viking raids on the opposite coast of the Baltic and which faces the two major Baltic islands, Œland and Gotland.

b The 'Island or City of Women' is associated with three major marvels: the pairing of the women Amazons with slaves, serfs or lower beings in order to breed offspring, the mass slaughter of males when they are born, and some kind of annual festival in spring which brings their partners to the island for the purpose of procreation. Today, in the Baltic States, the midsummer solstice, with all its sun rituals, is the 'mating season'.

It is by no means impossible that in Europe and in the Muslim world, snippets from Baltic fairy tales, which may not have survived, suggested some of the details of these stories. Mention has been made of the Amazon motif in Northern sagas. There are reports that as late as the wars with the Teutonic Knights, Baltic women warriors entered battle with their menfolk. However, as this is reported in other cultures it can hardly be described as an unusual characteristic of pagan Baltic culture. The Lithuanians have many folktales which would appear to be ancient and which date from the pre-Christian era. Traces of these legends might be discovered in future research.

Two that are well known are, first, the legend of the goddess Jurate (*jura* is 'the sea' in Lithuanian) and Kastytis. Jurate was betrothed to the water-god, but she fell in love with a fisherman whom she carried to an amber castle on the seabed. Full of wrath, the god, Perkūnas, destroyed this castle. All the amber which is collected in the sea and on the Baltic shore is all that is left of that castle. A second legend is that of Egle, the Queen of the grass-snakes. After swimming in the Baltic, she found a grass-snake lying curled in her shirt's sleeve. It swore to return the shirt if she would marry him. She agreed, and left her parent's house with a retinue of grass-snakes. When she reached the shore, she was met by a handsome man who, in fact, was a transformation of that same grass-snake whom she had promised to marry. They crossed to an island and from it they descended into a palace where they were married amidst great rejoicing. Life in the palace was so enjoyable that Egle forgot her parents altogether. She gave birth to three sons: Azuolas (Oak tree), Ousis (Ash tree) and Berzas (Birch-tree) and a daughter called Drebule (Asp). She was the youngest. After nine years had passed Egle's eldest son asked Egle about her parents and he expressed a wish to visit them. Egle's husband refused her request unless she fulfilled three tasks, amongst them the wearing of iron shoes until they were no longer wearable. Having accomplished these near impossible tasks, she said farewell to her spouse. It was agreed that, on her way back, she would call her husband with a special 'code word' whereupon he would emerge from its waters.

Egle enjoyed her stay and was determined that her daughter would remain with her parents. Egle wished to kill her husband but she failed to obtain the password from her sons who kept it secret. Threatened with a flogging, her daughter, Drebule, disclosed it, but when the party reached the shore they were confronted by blood coloured waves and they heard the grass-snake's voice crying from the seabed, lamenting how he had been betrayed. Egle, who was heart-broken, turned her sons into trees, oak, ash and birch, and her daughter into an asp. She transformed herself into a fir tree.

Other legends of a similar kind are told about women who once lived in the area of the Curonian Spit.

25 On the importance of Otto 1 in the history of the Slavs and Baltic peoples, see Francis Dvornik, op. cit., pp. 108–9.
26 See al-Bakrī (Critical edition by Abdurrahman Ali al-Hajji, op. cit., pp. 174–5). Despite al-Hajji's suggestion that 'Wulīnānā' might be the correct spelling, hence the possibility of Vironia, the region of Reval, or Tallinn, Waltāba, or Wołyn, Volhynie, would seem to be the closest reading. Professor T. Lewicki, in his contrbution to the al-Mas'ūdī Millenary Commemoration Volume, edited by S. Maqbul Ahmad and A. Rahman, India, 1960, p. 12 remarks, 'The Slavs living westwards of the Odra river, the so called WALITAB or WELETABE (Veletians or Liutice). Their former prince, Magik (MAzaKZ) had previously been the ruler of all the Slavs in the earlier days'. Francis Dvornik, op. cit., has much to say about the Veletians, the temple of Radgosc (spelt Radegast in Rimsky Korsakov's opera, *Mlada*), the magnificent temple of Svantevit on the island of Rügen, due south of southern Sweden, and, arguably, to be 'The Island of (Amazonian) men'. His observations are on pp. 298–307. If all the above facts are taken into account, and a glance paid to the curious coastline and its islands as shown in the map of al-Idrīsī, one observes some similarities in shape to the so-called 'Fyra Horn' map, a map of the four corners of the Østersøen which links southern Skåne, in Sweden, with Bornholm, with Rügen and with Świnoujście (Wolinski Pn), now included within the extreme north-western point of Poland, including Wolin. These peninsulas and islands were linked by shipping lanes for sailing boats engaged in commerce, and with harbours.

There was much cultural borrowing and exchange, including art and architecture, dress and social habits.

Professor David Lang, in his article, 'The Slavs', in *Mythology*, edited by Richard Cavendish, Orbis, London. 1980, p. 195, remarks, 'This cult of idols was also widespread among the western Slavs, right up to the twelfth century. The Danish chronicler Saxo Grammaticus (1150–1206) records King Waldemar's destruction of the Slavonic pagan temple of Svantevit or Svyatovit on the island of Rügen in the Baltic Sea. The huge idol stood on a sunken base in an inner sanctuary, hung with purple rugs. The statue held in its right hand a drinking horn into which wine was poured at the harvest festival, to enable prophecies and divinations to be made regarding next year's crops. Other idols destroyed by King Waldemar were those of Rugievet (patron deity of Rügen island), Porevit and Porenut.

However much zealous converts like Vladimir or King Waldemar might rant against the Slavonic idols and physically destroy them, the people obstinately refused to abandon them. Perun, whom we have mentioned, was reincarnated in Russia as Elijah or St Elias. In the Baltic region, Perun is re-embodied in the popular Lithuanian deity, Perkūnas, portrayed in folk mythology as a vigorous man holding an axe or hammer. He is a purifier and a fructifier and lives in a castle on a stone hill. If Perkūnas strikes a tree, a rock or a man with lightening, the object becomes sacred, for the heavenly fire remains inside it. As late as 1652, we read of an old man travelling in Western Lithuania in a thunderstorm and actually eating the ashes of a leather saddle which had been burnt up by lightening: to him, this meant immunity against illness, the gift of oracular powers and the ability to conjure up fire.'

The description, in al-Bakrī's text, also recalls the legendary settlement of Wolin/Wollin/Jomsberg (Vineta) in the land of the Baltic and Slavonic Wends, in this same region. According to the account of the Jomsvikinga saga, which matches al-Bakrī's account, the Jomsvikings lived a monastic kind of existence though they voyaged far into the Baltic. They built a giant harbour which sheltered 360 longboats. The harbour entrance had a stone arch, iron doors and a great tower in which catapults were installed (see N.F. Blake, *The Saga of the Jomsvikings*, London, 1962, pp. viii, xi and 18). In al-Bakrī's (al-Turtūshī's) account, the city was out to sea in al-Baḥr al-Muḥīṭ. It had twelve gates and a harbour. In the Jomsviking saga, none must have a woman in the city (it was the mirror image of the 'City of Women') and none must be absent from the city for more than three days. Every summer they went on a raiding expedition.

27 Al-Hajji has a problem in translating '*shuṭūr-an ḥarl-an*', which may, in his view, refer to some method of twisting ropes (possibly for boats or for moorage). E.W. Lane in his Arabic Lexicon, London, 1863, has no entry under '*ḥarl-an*' though under '*ḥarīd-an*' (a possible reading), p. 544, he has 'an uneven rope or a bow string having one or more of the several portions of which (by their being twisted together) it is composed longer than others'. 'Halves' might somehow be a way of describing such ropes. Al-Hajji is equally dissatisfied by this meaning and he suggests instead '*adīlan*', or '*qawā'id 'adīla*', 'just' or 'equitable rules', instead of '*ḥarl-an*'.

In this reading he is closer to the Jomsviking saga, in which the mythical leader of the Jomsborg community, Palna-Toki, enforced such equalitarian rules upon his warriors. Tadeusz Kowalski, who is far more concerned with alternative readings in the Arabic text, printed, with alternative readings in his article, does not speculate on these lines and he gives consideration to a reading of the text as '*shuṭūr ajdhal*' – in the sense of '*jadhl*' being translated as a wooden trunk of a tree, or 'timber', hence conveying the idea of a 'half timbered' construction, or a construction with split tree trunks.

28 According to al-Bakrī, 'only elders (shuyūkh) are their chiefs'. According to Francis Dvornik, op. cit., p. 295, 'The State of the Veletians was a kind of republic of federated tribes and it varied in size at different periods.'

29 Tallgren and Tallgren, op. cit., together with maps, attempt to locate many of these localities. More recent research has done much to focus attention on more plausible identifications. As far back as 1954, H. Birkeland published *Nordens Historiae i Middlealderen etter Arabiske Kilder*, Skrifter Utgift av

Det Norske Videnskaps-Akademi i Oslo, H, Histo-Filos Klasse, 1954, No 2, Oslo I Kommisjon Hos Jacob Dybwad, and Scandinavian place names in Arabic texts are discussed. Extensive archaeological research has taken place in the Baltic States and much of the findings of Latvian and Lithuanian archeologists has been referred to in this chapter. As has been pointed out, the *Kalevala* cites the 'Island of Women' in a region of lakes and not out in a sea. The major importance of settlements on an island inland is exemplified by Trakai, which became the supreme fortified centre for the Lithuanian Duchy, for the Lithuanian population and for the Karaims and Tatars who were brought to the land to serve it, to defend it and to participate in a cause which had as its aim the continued identity of the Lithuanians, as a people.

30 See *Where We Come From*, op. cit., 'Neighbours and Loan Words', pp. 62[63]–74[75].

31 The Daugava valley region, particularly localities and sites inland and to the north-east in the Tallgrens' study (op. cit.), is an important river which divides the Baltic peoples, see in particular, pp. 129–30. However, their map also draws attention to two particular regions where al-Idrīsī concentrates a large number of his toponyms: the peninsula of Jutland, extending north-east in the region of southern Sweden (Kalmar is shown as no (O) 29, on this map) and south-western Finland extending deep into Estonia (Estlanda), the most easterly inland locality being Palamuse (no (O)7) on his map. As a consequence, al-Idrīsī's directions to the siting of the 'Island of Women', or their city, whether out to sea or in an inland location of lakes and rivers, as far east as lake Peipus, favour an Estonian-centred setting for this legend.

32 See *Where We Come From*, op. cit., p. 112[113], where the Quedlingburg Chronicles are quoted, 'St Bruno, who is called Boniface, archbishop and monk, in the eleventh year of his monkhood, on the border between Rus [perhaps Prus, i.e. Prussia] and Lithuania, was beheaded by the pagans, with eighteen companions on March 9 [i.e. February 14] 1009, departed to heaven'.

The name of 'Lithuania' therefore precedes in time the description of the southern Baltic coastlands, by both al-Bakrī and al-Idrīsī. The substance of their accounts would be negligible without borrowed or expanded quotations from Ismā'īl al-Ṭurṭūshī, plus al-Bakrī's individual glosses on his observations. What survives, therefore, is, with the exception of the details in regard to Miezsko 1, only relevant to the life in those regions a century prior to their records, that is, to an age when trade and exchange with Arabic and Islamic coinage were the only meaningful channels of communication between the peoples of the North and the lands of the Caliphate. If any Islamic scholars who had happened to glean the writings left by Muslim geographers had accompanied the first Tatar settlement in Lithuania, Poland and Belarus in the fourteenth century, it is possible that this meagre record would have been the maximum background information which they could have read about, in all Arabic literature, or had access to, at the time when Tatar settlement began within the realms of Vytautas.

33 Stasys Samalavicius, *An Outline of Lithuanian History*, Vilnius, 1995, pp. 13–15.

34 Ibid, p. 21.

35 Ibid, pp. 22–3.

Chapter 2

1. The highland situated in the eastern part of Lithuania, the area between the towns of Utena, Ignalina and Švenčionys. Within its present borders is located the Aukštaitijas Nacionalinis Parkas, covering some 300 square miles. It is heavily wooded with pine, spruce and deciduous forests inhabited by elk, deer and wild boar. The region has several lakes and contains a number of eighteenth-century villages.
2. Stasys Samalavičius, *An Outline of Lithuanian History*, 1995, pp. 26–7.
3. Zigmantas Kiaupa, *The History of Lithuania*, 2002/2004, p. 38.
4. Agnius Urbanavičius, *Vilniaus Naujieji Miestiečiai*, 2005, pp. 205, 208, 212, 214, 216, 225, 233.
5. Zigmantas Kiaupa, op. cit., p. 56 and Stasys Samalavičius, op. cit., p. 31.
6. Ibid., pp. 66–77.
7. See Professor David Bivar, 'The Portrait and Career of Mohammed 'Ali, son of Kazem Beg: Scottish Missionaries and Russian Orientalism', *Bulletin of the School of Oriental and African Studies*, Vol. LVII, part 2, 1994, pp. 300–1.
8. Gyorgy Kara (ed.), *Between the Danube and the Caucasus, a collection of papers concerning Oriental sources on the History of the peoples of Central and South-Eastern Europe*, Budapest, 1987, pp. 86, 87, 93 and passim. These edicts date from around 1381 when the headquarters of Toqtamish was located at the middle course of the Don.
9. Zigmantas Kiaupa, op. cit., pp. 56–8. This tactical withdrawal is discussed in detail by S. Ekdahl, 'Der Flucht der Litauer in der Schlacht bei Tannenberg', *Zeitschrift für Ostforshung*, 1963, t. 12 , pp. 11–19 and *Žalgiris. Siandienos žvilgsnis* (Žalgiris. A Contemporary View), Vilnius, 1999.
10. Salkhat, today Staryi Krym, in Mamlūk times was the Tatar Golden Horde capital in the Crimean Peninsula.
11. Ghillebert de Lannoy, *Voyageur, Diplomate et Moraliste, recuillies et publiées par Ch. Potvin avec des notes géographiques et une carte par J.-C. Houzeau*, Louvain, 1878, p. 38.
12. Ibid., p. 39. The first cathedral in the city was made of wood, but St Nicholas' Church, founded by German merchants, dates from 1320.
13. Ibid., p. 40.
14. Ibid., pp. 40–1. Trancquenne is recognisably Trakai (Troki) as we know it today with its massive castle out in the lake.
15. Ibid. The fact that the Tatar language was still spoken in 1414 is an important detail that is furnished in this account.
16. Ibid. It is unclear whether the Jews to whom he refers spoke Hebrew or whether it was the Qipchāq language of the Karaites.
17. Sasys Samalavičius, op. cit., p. 40.
18. Ghillebert de Lannoy, op. cit., pp. 55–6.
19. Ibid., pp. 57.
20. Here is confirmation that the sway of authority of Vytautas (Witold) was acknowledged at this time as far as the Black Sea.
21. Here indicating the river Dnister.
22. Ghillebert de Lannoy, op. cit., pp. 60–1.
23. Ibid., pp. 64–5.

24 Jurgita Šiaučiūnaitė Verbickienė, 'The Tatars', in *The Peoples of the Grand Duchy of Lithuania*, edited by Grigorius Potašenko, 2002, p. 74.
25 Ibid., p. 75.

Chapter 3

1 A historical novel by Henryk Sienkiewicz, Edinburgh, 1943, p. 80.
2 For the term 'Lipqa' see Glossary in this book, and 'Lipka' by Z. Abrahamowicz and J. Reychmen in *The Encyclopaedia of Islam*, 2nd edition, pp. 765–62.
3 Geoffrey Chaucer, *The Canterbury Tales*, translated into Modern English by Nevil Coghill, Penguin Books, 1974, p. 407. Tsarev is, without doubt, Saray. Cambusksan, as Coghill explains, p. 520, is generally thought to be a corruption of 'Genghis Khan', though the character who is described matches that of Qubilai Qa'an (Khān) better. It might be pointed out that when Chaucer was busy writing the Tales, Toqtamish Khān was the ruler of Saray. Chaucer refers, in passing, to Lithuania in his Prologue (p. 20). His was the time when the Union between Poland and Lithuania was proclaimed.

There is also the distinct possibility that news of the family of Toqtogha, the predecessor of Uzbek Khān, came to the West via Franciscan and other Christian sources who were present in the realm of the Golden Horde. Their claims to successful conversions included 'emperor Coktaganus' (Toqtogha), his mother Thododothelia and three sons (Chaucer has two sons and a daughter called Canace). The third son was called 'Abusta', recorded elsewhere as 'Abuscan' (compare Chaucer's Cambuskan, above). Chaucer ends his tale with the statement that Cambuskan overran cities and that he had a son called Algarsayf (probably a star name) who, gave aid with his flying horse of brass, which had been given to him by the 'King of India and Araby', something won, like his wife, Theodora (compare with Thododothelia above). Although no clear preference can be made amongst these names, they lend support for those who would argue for a Franciscan influence on Chaucer's tale, see Devin De Weese, *Islamization and Native Religion in the Golden Horde*, op. cit., pp. 97–9.

4 For an account of the setting up of the dual monarchy of the Grand Duchy of Lithuania and the Kingdom of Poland, see Stephen C. Rowell 'Forging a Union? Some Reflections on the Early Jagiellonian Monarchy', *Lithuanian Historical Studies*, 1, Lithuanian Institute of History, Vilnius, 1996, pp. 6–21.
5 See note 6, below.
6 See the entry on the Karaites (Karaims) in the Glossary.
7 Lithuanian 'Paganism' is admirably summarised in Eric Christiansen's book *The Northern Crusades (The Baltic and the Catholic Frontier 1100–1525)*, pp. 137–8: 'Both Prussians and Lithuanians worshipped "a god of ill fortune", a "far spirit" protecting the dead, a sky ruler, and a goddess of the forest. When in 1258 a force of Lithuanians was disappointed at a chance to loot a town, "they grieved and spat, shouting 'yanda', invokimg their gods Andai and Diveriks and others". And both they and the Prussians were also reported to venerate Percunos, ruler of fire and lightning, Picollos, ruler of the underworld, and Porimpo, god of rivers and springs. A seventeenth-century

collector, Hartknoch, was able to list thirteen separate categories of minor gods, and folklore preserved details of what they were supposed to look like, although they were never worshipped in idol shape.'

8 S.C. Rowell, *Lithuania Ascending, a Pagan Empire within East-Central Europe, 1295–1345*, Cambridge University Press, 1994, p. 18. The exact relationship between the Duchy of Lithuania and the Tatars of the Golden Horde merits clarification. Contacts between Tatars and Lithuanians predated the reign of Vytautas and his immediate predecessors. During the reign of Mindaugas (d. 1263), the Lithuanians regarded the Golden Horde as a threat. South-eastern Lithuania was devastated in 1258–9. The Tatars made a number of unsuccessful expeditions. However, in 1274–5, they plundered the upper Nemunas and burnt the settlement of Naugurdukas. Under Duke Algirdas (1345–77), the help of the Tatars was sought in 1349 against the growing power of Muscovy. Algirdas sent his brother Karijotas to Janibeg Khān with a proposal to form a Lithuanian–Tatar alliance. The Khān declined. After successes, including the capture of Kiev, in 1363, Algirdas defeated the Tatars at 'Blue Waters' (Sinie Vody). Khān Mamay made an agreement with Jogaila (1377–92) for a joint invasion of Muscovy. Mamay, however, was defeated by the Russians in the battle of Kulikovo (1380). The policy of the capture, and later, resettlement, of Tatars by Vytautas began during the latter's campaign to help the unseated Khān Toqtamish against Tīmūr Qutlugh and Edigey. Despite the pagan background of many of his warriors, Vytautas regarded his efforts as a 'Crusade' and he asked for a blessing from Pope Boniface IX. He even had the moral backing of the Teutonic Knights. Despite the defeat of Vytautas, at Vorskala (1399), he later re-established his position against the Eastern Tatars. In 1419, after the battle of Grunwald, Edigey made peace with Vytautas and he sent him three camels and twenty horses. A brief account about the methods which were adopted by Vytautas to control the Tatars of the Golden Horde in the region of the Black Sea and in eastern Ukraine is described by Mykhailo Hruchevsky, in his *History of Ukraine-Rus*, Vol. 7, 'The Cossack Age to 1625', Canadian Institute of Ukrainian Studies Press, Edmonton, Toronto, 1999, pp. 7–8.

9 W.E.D. Allen, *A History of the Georgian People from the beginning down to the Russian Conquest in the Nineteenth Century*, London, Kegan Paul, 1932, pp. 99–100. Dr Andrew Peacock has also drawn my notice to the article by P. Golden, 1984: 'Cumanica 1: the Qipčaqs in Georgia', *Archivum Eurasiae Medii Aevi*, 4: 45–87. Reprinted in idem *Nomads and their Neighbours in the Russian Steppe: Turks, Khazars and Qipchaqs*, Aldershot, 2003, Study XI.

10 By the eighteenth century there is clearer evidence of the demographic distribution of Tatars in both Belarus and Lithuania. According to Dr Tamara Bairašauskaité, 'The Lithuanian Tatars in the Nineteenth Century' (summary of the research report presented for habilitation, *Humanities*, Lithuanian Institute of History, Vytautas magnus University, Vilnius, 1998), pp. 37–8: 'The incomplete data about the census of the population (revision), in 1795, made it possible to determine the area inhabited by the Tatars. It stretched as a narrow belt through the southeast lands of present Lithuania, and North-West territories of present Belarus. In the west it was bordered by Grodno and Brest, north-Alytus, Kaunas, Trakai and Vilnius, northeast-Postavy, south-Minsk environs, Nieswiez, Slonim. At the end of the eighteenth–beginning of

Notes and references 157

the nineteenth century this area was extended into the New Eastern Prussia. These boundaries of the area remained unchanged throughout the whole researched period. The Tatar migration took place within the defined area; with the exception of cases when the Tatars moved to the central provinces of the Russian Empire.' For a detailed account of the Polish and Belarus frontier region, together with maps showing Tatar villages, a number of which have disappeared, see Jerzy Wisniewski, 'Ocadnictwo Tatarskie w Sokólskiem i na Pólnocnym Podlasiu (English summary, pp. 403–5), *Rocznik Białostocki*, Tome XVI, Museum Okregowe w Białymstoku, Warsaw, 1991, pp. 325–405. On the wider question of Tatar assimilation in Poland, between the sixteenth and eighteenth centuries, see Andrzej B. Zakrzewski, 'Assimilation of Tartars within the Polish Commonwealth, 16th–18th centuries, *Acta Polonia Historica*, 55, 1987, pp. 86–106.

11 It is not clear whether the Qipchāq language was extensively spoken, in Lithuania, or Poland, by this date, or only by a few, or whether it were at all possible to meaningfully distinguish amongst the Qipchāqs between the Karaims and the Muslim Tatars. On the relationship between the Qipchāq/Khifchakh/Polovtsi/Qomans to other Turkic and Tatar peoples, including their languages, see V. Minorsky, 'Ḥudūd al-'Ālam', *The Regions of the World, A Persian Geography, 372 A.H.–982 A.D.*, E.J.W. Gibb Memorial, London, 1970, pp. 315–17. Though the date of 1398 must be accepted as the most correct year for the Tatar settlement, nevertheless, Tatars, in very small numbers indeed, came to Lithuania at varied times. The Tatar numbers were of no significance, at some time prior to 1398. There is a persistent tradition that amongst the first Tatar settlers were fugitives from the forced Islamisation policy of Uzbek Khan. Many were probably pagans and a few may have been Christians. The presence of Christians amongst the Qipchāqs in the Crimea is confirmed in a passage in Ibn Battūta's *Voyage (Riḥla)*. On p. 322 (Beirut edition, 1379/1960), he remarks, 'When the morrow came, following our arrival at this harbour, one of the merchants from among our companions betook himself to those in the desert from amongst the group known as the Qipchāqs. They are Christians. He hired a horse-drawn wagon from them. We rode in it and we arrived at the town of Kaffa.' These Qipchāqs could have been converts to Catholicism, or have been mixed with Armenians, or they could have been Karaims whom Ibn Battūta mistook for Christians. All of this might have been a factor in the decline of their Qipchāq language in the steppes and to their rapid assimilation. Those who came with Toqtamish were probably nominally Muslims. So also were Tatar exiles from Saray, and others from the Kazan Khanate (after 1552), from Astrakhan (after 1554), from the Crimea, and from small groups of Nogai Tatars who originated in other parts of Russia and the Caucasus. It is also likely that the Tatars established strings of settlements to the south of Poland. The location of these is uncertain today.

12 Correspondence between Jogaila and Toqtamish has survived. It includes a letter, in Uyghur script, from Toqtamish, dated 1392–93, 'Yarlik Khana zolotoi ordy Tokhtamysh k pol'skom korolyo Yagailu', which was published in Kazan by the noted Orientalist M.A. Kazem-Beg in 1850. See, Professor David Bivar, 'The portrait and career of Mohammed Ali, son of Kazem Beg: Scottish missionaries and Russian Orientalism', *Bulletin of the School*

of *Oriental and African Studies*, Vol. LVll, Part 2, 1994, pp. 300–1. Other examples of correspondence and edicts of Toqtamish may be found in Gyorgy Kara (ed.), *Between the Danube and the Caucasus, A collection of Papers concerning Oriental Sources on the History of the peoples of Central and South-Eastern Europe*, Budapest, 1987, pp. 86, 87, 93, and passim. These edicts date from around 1381, when the headquarters of Toqtamish were at the middle course of the Don.

13 A detailed biography of the author, his life, his works and his contribution to Tatar and to Russian, Arabic and Turkish historiography has been written by Professor Ahmet Temir, in his 'Dogumunnn 130 ve Olomunum 50, Yili Dolayisilya Kazanli Tarihci Murad Remzi (1854–1934)', in *Bulletin* (Ankara), vol. 50, August, 1986, No 197, pp. 495–505.

14 For these passages in regard to the Polish and Lithuanian Tatars in Muhammad Ramzī's writings, see, Muhammad Ramzī (1854–1934), *Talfīq al-Akhbār wa-talqīḥ al-āthār fī waqā'i' Qāzān wa-Bulghār wa-Mulūk al-Tātār*, 'The embellishment of reports and consideration of the effects of the events which took place in Kazan and Bulghār and among the Tatar kings', Orenburg, 1908, vol. l, p. 629–30 and 638–9.

15 The title of Shihāb al-Dīn al-Marjānī's pioneer work may be freely translated as 'The reported (and profitable) accounts and chronicles regarding the circumstances and vicissitudes (even, the 'years that have passed' – if *aḥwāl* is plural of *ḥawl* and not *ḥāl*) of Kazan and Bulghar'. A short biography of this author and distinguished Tatar scholar-theologian may be read in Jemaleddin Velidov's *Outline of the History of Education and Literature of the Tatars before the Revolution of 1917 (with Russian text)*, The Society of Central Asian Studies, Report No 11, Oxford, 1986, pp. 199–201. A very detailed assessment of Marjānī, as a teacher, writer and thinker, may be found in *Mardzaniy ucheniey, misliitel, prosvetiitel*, published by the Academy of Sciences of the USSR, The Institute of Languages, Literature and History of Tatarstan, Kazan, 1990, especially two essays on this specific historical work, by Abdullin, Khayrallin and Khakov, pp. 146–59. Both Ramzī and Marjāni are appraised, especially the latter, in Uli Schamiloglu, 'The formation of a Tatar Historical Consciousness: Sihabaddin Marcani and the image of the Golden Horde', in *Central Asian Survey*, Oxford, vol. 9, no 2, 1990, pp. 39–40. On p. 48, note 10, the author describes M. Ramzī's work, *Talfīq al-Akhbār*, as 'an example of an outstanding historical work written in Arabic', adding that the work was 'virtually unknown today but found useful by Spuler in his "Die Golden Horde. Die Mongolen in Russland, 1223–1502"'. One of the latest studies of Marjānī's masterpiece is to be found in Allen J. Frank's *Islamic Historiography and Bulghar Identity among the Tatars and Bashkirs of Russia*, Brill, Leiden, 1998, pp. 149–57.

16 See Ramzī, op. cit., pp. 638–9 in particular.

17 George Vernadsky, *The Mongols and Russia*, Yale, 1953, p. 281.

18 See Ahmet Kanlidere, *Reform within Islam, the Tajdid and Jadid movement among the Kazan Tatars (1809–1917) Conciliation or Conflict?*, Eren Publishers, Istanbul, 1997, chs 1 and 5 (pp. 129–39 in particular).

19 The tribulations of the Baltic Tatars during different periods of their history in Lithuania and Poland are described in Piotr Borawski's article, 'Religious tolerance and the Tatar population in the Grand Duchy of Lithuania 16th to

18th century', *Journal of the Institute of Muslim Minority Affairs, London*, vol. 9, 1 January, 1988, pp. 119–33. We have some idea of a contemporary view that was held in regard to the faith of the incoming Lithuanian Tatars from the writings of Michalonis Lituani. His views were expressed in the tenth section of his *De Moribus Tartorum Lituanorum et Moschorom* (Basle, 1614, Moscow University edition, 1994, pp. 103–6). It was appreciated that the local Tatars were linked, in their history, to the Jewish Karaims. It was also believed that they were descended from the 'Scythians', or from a kindred 'barbarous' stock. The latter formed part of a people of historical importance who dwelt in the northern Balkans, in Russia and in Central Asia. Their habits contained things that were praiseworthy, spiritually benighted though they might be in certain other respects. To Michalonis Lituani, in the sixteenth century, the religion of the Tatars was also that of the Turks. It was an offshoot of that belief which was commonly held by the Saracens. It had the 'savour' of Judaism and also of the Nestorian heresy (et haeresim quondam Nestorianam). In the Lithuanian translation this reads 'Totoriu su turkais ir kitais saracenais religija ta pati, panasi I zydu tikejima ir Nestorijaus erezija'. The Tatars expressed a belief in One God, Christ is held to be a Prophet of God and to be the future Judge of the World. The Virgin is pure and undefiled. Circumcision is observed, established by Ishmael, and the rites are centred upon the city of Mecca, in Arabia. Thus, to him, and no doubt to other Catholic Lithuanians, Islam was viewed as a 'heresy', rather than as a distinct and alien faith. All this, of course, seemed less strange, in view of the Mongol's earlier support for the Nestorian sect. It was the opinion of Michalonis Lituani, and also that of George Sale (1697–1736), that the root disagreement of faiths was based upon the marked divergencies of the two faiths where they were centred upon the historical account of the Crucifixion, not, however, on the single nature debate, this latter being a matter of primary concern for the Nestorians. In the same category were certain other sectaries, heretics who were subsequently confounded. They included the Basilidians, the Corinthians, and the Carporcrations who had espoused some substitution theory. These, it was believed, were the likely sources of Islam. The above opinions indicate that Michalonis Lituani held fast to a view that was no doubt widely held in Lithuania during the centuries old encounter, face to face, and in everyday life, between the Tatars and the Catholic Lithuanians and the Poles. The Karaims, and their relationship with the Tatars is not commented upon.

20 See Stefan Reichmuth, *The Interplay of Local Developments and Transnational Relations in the Islamic World: Perceptions and Perspectives, in Muslim Culture in Russia and Central Asia from the Eighteenth to the early 20th Centuries*, vol. 2, Inter-Regional and Inter-Ethnic Relations, edited by Anke von Kügelgen, Michael Kemper, Allen J. Frank, Islamkundliche Untersuchungen, Band 216, Klaus Scwarz Verlag, Berlin, 1998, pp. 5–38.

21 Allen J. Frank, *Muslim Sacred History and the 1905 Revolution in a Sufi History of Astrakhan, Studies on Central Asian History in Honor of Yuri Bregel*, edited by Devin De Weese, Indiana University Research Institute for Inner Asian Studies, Bloomington, Indiana, 2001, pp. 300, 302, 306, 316–17.

22 Andrzej B. Zakrzewski, 'Assimilation of Tartars within the Polish Commonwealth, sixteenth–eighteenth centuries', *Acta Poloniae Historica*, 55, 1987, pp. 85–106.

23 Ibid., pp. 88–94, see in particular p. 88, note 14.
24 Ibid., p. 95.
25 T.W. Arnold, *The Preaching of Islam, A History of the Propagation of the Muslim Faith*, Luzac, London, 1935, p. 245.
26 See Zakrzewski, op. cit., p. 100.
27 This is conveniently summarised in Dr Tamara Bairašauskaité, 'The Lithuanian Tatars in the Nineteenth Century, Summary of the research report presented for habitation', *Humanities*, 05 H History, Lithuanian Institute of History, Vytautas Magnus University, Vilnius, 1998, and in *Muslim Culture in Russia and Central Asia from the eighteenth to the early 20th Centuries*, op. cit., pp. 313–35, under the title, 'Politische Integration und religiöse Eigenständigkeit der litauischen Tataren im 19. Jahrhundert'.
28 Quoted from a personal communication sent to the author by Dr Zorina Kanapatskaya.
29 Mrs Dżemila Smajkiewicz-Murman, and her family, were my hosts in Gdańsk during my first visit to the Tatars in Poland. This was part of her address during the official opening of the mosque in Gdańsk in 1990. Work on its construction had begun in the late 1880s. I have visited the family since. During my last visit she kindly gave me approval to quote this, her deeply felt speech, in my book.

Chapter 4

1 There are passing references to Sufi-influenced customs in Tatar life and literature in earlier publications of *Rocznik Tatarski*, first published in Vilnius and more recently in Gdańsk. The subject was touched upon by J. Szymkiewicz, and by M. Aleksandrowicz, 'Legendy, znachorstwo, wrozby i guala ludu muzulmanskiego w Polace (Légendes, sorcelleries, augures et sortilèges du peuple musulman en Pologne)', *Rocznik Tatarski*, vol. 2, Zamosc, 1935, pp. 368–369 and also in Stanisław Kryczyński, *Tatarzy Litewscy* (Les Tatars lithuaniens), Warsaw, 1938, 2000, pp. 245–68.
2 The Polish *imāms*, who are Hanafīs, have been preoccupied in recent years by the practical application of Sharī'a principles amongst the Tatar community.
3 The Tatar population in the former Duchy of Lithuania reached its maximum total during the sixteenth and seventeenth centuries. This preceded a substantial exodus and semi-forced immigration into exile in the Ottoman territories.
4 Borrowings from Arabic, and from other Middle Eastern languages, in Tatar liturgical vocabulary are discussed, with examples, by Dr Shirin Akiner in her 'The vocabulary of a Byelorussian Kitab in the British Museum', *The Journal of Byelorussian Studies*, London, vol. 3, no 1, 1973, pp. 55–84.
5 Personal pilgrimages to the graveyards where families are buried (*zijaretani*) is not only one of the most important religious duties of the Tatars, but the custom has also been extended to include regular visits by families of the deceased to all their extended family relations who have departed. These take place especially during feasts and festivities such as the birthday of the Prophet (*mawlid al-Nabī*) On such occasions, the graves are tended, candles burnt and prayers are said. Tatar cemeteries are well maintained and the gravestone inscriptions may contain extensive quotations from the Qur'ān.

There are numerous examples to be seen in Andrzej Drozd, Marek M. Dzieken and Tadeusz Majda, *Meczety i cmentarz Tatarów polsko-litewskich*, Warsaw, 1999. Some Tatars formerly believed that the soul of the deceased lingered in the vicinity of the grave and the cemetery for an interval of some forty days before its journey to the hereafter.

6 This case has been made by Selim Chazbijewicz in his article, 'Kultura religijna Tatarów polskich', *Rocznik Tatarów Polskich*, Tom.ll, Gdańsk, 1994, pp. 84–5. It was preceded by an article that he wrote specifically about Sufism in Poland. It was published in *Zycie Muzulmanskie* ('The Islamic Life', 'al-Ḥayāh al- Islāmiyyah'), no 9, AH 1409/AD 1988, pp. 30–5, published in Gdańsk. The article bore the title of 'Wplyw Sufizmu (Taṣawwuf) na Zwyczaje muzulmanow w Polsce' (The Influence of Sufism on Muslim customs in Poland). While this article is a neat and comprehensive survey of the beliefs and literary works of the Tatars, it has relatively little to tell about Sufism, per se. On pp. 32 and 33 he comments upon alleged borrowings of Cabbalism from Ḥurūfism, via the Bektāshis. Polish Tatars served in the Janisseries, a likely channel of conversion. On p. 34, he comments on the text of the Tatar *zikr/zikier* and its relationship to the *dhikr* in the Sufi brotherhoods. His comments upon the meal, where bread, water and salt are shared in a form of 'communion', suggest to him Bektāshi influences. This may not have sufficient basis to be accepted, since such a 'communion' is not unknown amongst the Eastern Orthodox Christians.

7 'Religious Tolerance and the Tatar population in the Grand Duchy of Lithuania, the sixteenth to the eighteenth century', *The Journal of the Institute of Muslim Minority Affairs*, London, vol. 9, 1988, p. 129.

8 See A. Muchlinski, 'Zdanie sprawy o Tatarach litewskich (Compte rendu sur les Tatars lithuaniens)', *Teka Wilenska*, vol. IV, 1858, Vilnius, pp. 241–69.

9 The qualifications that were required of a good *imām* have been known for centuries amongst the Tatars. The ideal, at least, is revealed in a paragraph in the British Museum, Kitāb, translated by Dr Shirin Akiner in her 'Oriental Borrowings in the Language of the Byelorussian Tatars', *Slavonic and East European Review*, vol. 56, 1978, p. 241.

'When in a village or a town there should be two learned men, both suitable for the office of imam, then the one who is more learned should be imam; and when they are equal in learning the one who is more God-fearing, who prays, he should be imam; and if they are equal in that too, then the one who is older, he should be imam; and if they are equal in years, he who is of better family should be imam; and if they are equal in that, then the one who is better in looks and bearing and behaviour, he should be imam; and if they are equal in that, then the one the congregation desires, he should be imam; only a slave or serf or a blind man or a bastard or a scoundrel, who lacking learning will think out and say new things and who will go strutting about and those who have their ears pierced for earrings and who shave their beards, all such people are not suitable for the office of imam; and whoever is imam, he should be capable of explaining the Tradition of the Prophet and be able to recite the Koran properly and know all the motions of the prayer (ritual), so that if he should be asked about the prayer he would answer immediately and whoever takes care to avoid greatly sins and prays five times a day.'

10 Dervish Czelebi Hadji Murzicz, Kaji of Dowbucizki is one of the most noted of the early men of learning amongst the Lehistan Tatars whose names have survived. For far more detail about him, his village and its mosque (before it was destroyed) see Andrzej Drozd, Marek M. Dziekan and Tadeusz Majda, 'Meczety i cmentarze Tatarów polsko- litewskitch', *Res Publica Multiethnica*, Warsaw, 1999, pp. 44–6 and plates 262–72.

11 Interest in Sufism extended beyond the 'Orientalists'. A noted example amongst Polish artists was the composer Karol Szymanowski (1882–1937). His third symphony, 'Song of the Night', paid homage to Jalāl al-Dīn al-Rūmī and some of his verse is sung during the course of this symphony.

12 Cambridge edition, published in 1950, p. 569.

13 Alexander G. Seleznev, 'The Northernmost Outpost of Islamic Civilization', *International Institute for the Study of Islam in the Modern World, Newsletter*, no 3, 99, Leiden, p. 33.

14 Edward Tryjarski, 'Les religions des Petchenègues', in *Traditions Religieuses et para-Religieuses des peuples Altaiques, communications présentées au, XIIIe Congrès de la 'Permanent International; Altaistic Conférence'*, Strasbourg, 25–30 juin, 1970, Paris, 1972, p. 140.

15 This Turkic (non-Muslim and Muslim) name for the Almighty is discussed in great detail in Irène Mélikoff's book *Hadji Bektâch, un Mythe et ses Avatars (Genèse et évolution du soufisme populaire en Turquie)*, Brill, Leiden, pp. 13–16, 21, 23–4, 45, 136, 139–40. It is possible that the Lithuanian and Polish Tatars, like the Karaites today, once used this name commonly, as some evidence from the occasional mention of this name in rare written religious texts suggests.

16 One might note that such spirits were not unknown to the pagan Lithuanians at the time of the arrival of the Karaites and Tatars.

17 Pre-Christian Baltic religion is described in M. Gimbutas, *The Balts*, London and New York, 1963 and Stasys Samalvacius, *An Outline of Lithuanian History*, Vilnius, 1995, 'The pre-Christian religion', pp. 15–20.

18 See the article under Khudjand, in the EI (new edition), vol. 5, pp. 45–6, by C.E. Bosworth. The city was called Leninabad in Soviet times. It is located in the present-day republic of Tadzhikistan. A copy of the Dīwān of Kamāl al-Khujandī has been printed in Moscow, see *Kamal Khudzandi, Divaan*, critical edition, by K. Shidfara, Academic Publications, 'Nauka', Moscow, 1975. His text is based upon an Azerbaijanī manuscript, dated AH 878/AD 1473. See Leonard Lewisohn, 'The life and times of Kamal Khujandi', *Journal of Turkish Studies*, Harvard, XVIII, Cambridge, 1994, where, on pages 163 ff, Jāmī's references to the Poet and Sufi in his *Nafaḥāt al-Uns* are quoted and commented upon.

19 Edward G. Browne, *A History of Persian Literature under Tartar Dominion (AD 1265–1502)*, Cambridge, 1920, pp. 328–29, where Browne translated several fragmentary verses which refer to the destructive raid upon Tabriz by Toqtamish.

20 Leonard Lewisohn, op. cit., pp. 166–7.

21 Ramzī, op. cit., vol. 2, p. 48, quoting Ibn 'Arab Shāh.

22 On Khwāja Aḥrār (Ḥaḍrat Īshān), see J. Spencer Trimingham, *The Sufi Orders in Islam*, Oxford, 1911, p. 94 ff.

23 Irène Mélikoff, 'Fazlullah d'Astarabad et l'Essor du Hurufisme en Azerbaydjan, en Anatolie et en Roumelie', 'Mélanges offerts à Louis Bazin

par ses disciples, collègues et amis', *Varia Turcica*, XIX, Paris, 1992, pp. 220–1.
24 Leonard Lewisohn, op. cit., p. 168.
25 On the relationship between the Mongols, their descendants and the Qalandars, see Ahmet T. Karamustafa, *God's Unruly Friends, Dervish Groups in the Islamic Later Middle Period, 1200–1550*, University of Utah Press, Salt Lake City, 1994, pp. 5–8.
26 Following Professor E.G. Browne's translation of the title.
27 See Hamid Algar, 'The Ḥurūfī influence on Bektashism', *Revue des Etudes Islamiques*, 1992, vol. LX, pt 1, p. 41. In his article on Fadlallāh in *Encyclopedia Iranica*, vol. 2, p. 113, Hamid Algar describes the latter as 'one of the ascetics' (*mutaqashshifīn*) and also 'one of the heretics', or heterodox (*mubtada'a*). Aside from his relations with followers of Ḥurūfism, it is likely that Toqtamish could have met others of heterodox belief, for example, followers of the heterodox dervish Sārī Saltuk. He may well have met men who personally knew the latter. The territories of Toqtamish bordered Bessarabia and Babadag. According to Machiel Kiel, *Studies in the Ottoman Architecture of the Balkans*, Variorum, Aldershot and Brookfield, USA, 1990, p. 215, (IX), a *Saltukname* was composed by Koca Kenen Pasha in the early seventeenth century. In it he quoted a text with the title 'Futūhāt Tokhtamish'. Kiel remarks, 'the Khān of the Golden Horde must have been born in 1330–1340 and could easily have spoken with men who had known Sari Saltuk personally'.
28 Leonard Lewisohn, op. cit., p. 173.
29 On this saint, see the views of Selim Chazbijewicz in 'Kultura religijna Tatarów polskich', *Rocznik Tatarów Polskich*, Gdańsk, Tom 11, 1994, pp. 86–7.
30 Photographs that show the mosque in question and the ceremonies which are still held at the tomb of Kontus may be seen in Andrzej Drozd, Marek. M. Dziekan, Tadeusz Majda, op. cit., pp. 52–4 and the accompanying plates in colour.
31 Alexander Dubinski, 'Une légende des Tatars de Pologne', *Hommage à Pertev Naili Boratov*, Paris, 1978, pp. 171–5. This same story is discussed further in Piotr Borawski and Aleksander Dubinski, *Tatarzy Polscy, Dzieje, Obrzedy, Legendy, Tradycje*, Warsaw, 1986, pp. 237–40.
32 Kuntus or Kontos is viewed in Belarus as having been cloaked in attire and with regalia that in their origin are inspired by Sufi sources, whether they were originally in fact present there and were possessed by the historical Kuntus or they were not. Green cloaks, a magic stick, rod or whip, and an ability to fly through space and time are the hallmarks of many dervishes and this folktale may have been affected by Tatar influences from the Crimea and elsewhere in the Ottoman World. Tatar and other pilgrims visit the grave of Auliji Kontusia to this today in Lowczyce (Loūcčycy), namely to 'Mogila świętego Auliji (an Ottoman borrowing) Kontusia', They display rituals and common prayers and circlings of the grave that are to be found in Sufi rituals elsewhere in Islam. Michael Tarelko has specifically discussed the case of Kuntus with me in Minsk in connection with his discovery of documents that are penned in regard to the 'way' of the 'Rijāl al-Ghaib'. In Ḥurūfī manuscript, OR 532 (6), *The Circle of the Rijāl al-Ghayb*, in Cambridge University Library, there is a

tract (pp. 127–32) and within it this term is specified in the Arabic and Persian text, accompanied by quotations from the famous mystic Ibn al-'Arabī, who defines the term as 'The Men of the Verified [muḥaqqaq] World of the Unseen' (see William Chittick, *The Sufi Path of Knowledge*, State University of New York, Albany, 1989, p. 140). We cannot be certain whether the Sufi group in Belarus was Ḥurufī influenced, however, the influence of Ibn al-'Arabi is clearly apparent.

33 Irène Mélikoff, 'Hadji Bektach. un Mythe et ses Avatars', op. cit., pp. 75–82.

34 G.M. Meredith-Owens and Alexander Nadson, 'The Byelorussian Tartars and their writings', *The Journal of Byelorussian Studies*, vol. 11, no 1, Year V, London, 1969, pp. 148–9.

35 Alexandre Bennigsen and S. Enders Wimbush, *Mystics and Commissars, Sufism in the Soviet Union*, Hurst, London, 1985, pp. 9–10.

36 *Oral Epics of Central Asia*, Cambridge, 1969, pp. 297 ff.

37 Chamail (*Chamaily*) are a writen expression of Tatar Islam, in a format that is concise, Cabbalistic and prophylactic, yet principally based upon selected *Sūras* from the Qur'ān. A study, in depth, of one such document may be read in Andrzej Drozd, 'Chamail Sobolewskiego', *Rocznik Tatarów Polskich*, Gdańsk, 1993, pp. 48–61. This Tatar word is derived from the Arabic, *ḥamā'il*, 'suspended prayers, charms, amulets, etc'. Nowadays, small prayer books (*Modlitwa Praktyka i Islamu*) are published and are, in certain respects, the equivalent of certain older forms of Chamail. One that is published by Zycie Muzulmanskie *The Islamic Life*, in Poland, is specifically entitled 'Chamail'. It consists of short prayers, though much of the content is a detailed set of instructions as to how the prayers should be performed, accompanied by illustrations and sketches, indicate the correct posture. A longer Modlitewnik, that is published in type and bound more elaborately for the use of *imāms* rather than for the laity, has been prepared by the Imām of Kruszyniany, Mustafa-Stefan Jasinski. This was published in Białystok in 1986. It contains many more prayers and Qur'ānic *Sūras*, with a special importance being shown to *Sūrat Yā'sīn*, the Pillars of Islam, God's attributes, sins and repentance, ablutions, prayers said at the graveside (*mizar*), prayers during Ramadan, alms given as charity (*sadoge*) and the need for intention (*nijet*), when one celebrates the great feasts (*kurban*). This slender volume ends with an invocation, a laud in praise of Muhammad the Prophet (*pieczec Muhammada Proroka*) and of his successors, the rightly guided Caliphs. This has something of the *ilāhi* – a hymn in praise of the Prophet – and the *ziker/zikier* which is to be found elsewhere amongst Muslims in Eastern Europe. Expressions that are uttered, such as 'hh', 'hh', 'hh', and *'elhadze'*, *'elhadze'*, and *'ja hajju'*, *'ja kajjumu'* suggest the influences of popular Sufism amidst the words that accompany individual Tatar melodies.

38 BM manuscript OR. 13. 020. On the London manuscripts, *Kitāb*, *Chamail* and *Tafsīr*, see G.M. Meredith-Owens and Alexander Nadson, op. cit., pp. 38–54.

39 Me'radz (Ar. *al-Mi'rāj*), the nocturnal ascent of the Prophet Muhammad to Heaven from the furthest mosque (*al-Aqsā*, in Jerusalem) is mentioned by G.M. Meredith-Owens and Alexander Nadson, ibid., p. 162.

40 On Ḥabīb al-Najjār (Chebib Nedzdzar) and *Sūra* 36 (11–26) ibid., p. 163. Also mentioned are other stories from *Tales of the Prophets*, '*Qisas al-Anbiyā*', attributed to Wahb b. Munabbih.
41 On the story of al-Shiblī and al-Nūrī, ibid., p. 174. Both Sufis, together with anecdotes about them, appear in Carl. W. Ernst's *Words of Ecstasy in Sufism*, Albany, 1985.
42 The Belarusian Muslim journal, *Bayram Tatarina Zyauli, Belarus*, no 3, published in Minsk, 1992, pp. 13–21.
43 H. Jankowski, 'A Polish Tatar Ziker', *Acta Orientalia* (Academiae Scientarium Hungaricae), tome XLVlll (3), 1995, Budapest, pp. 40–52.
44 A calligraphic representation of eyebrows, on the one hand those of 'Alī, and, on the other, those of Adam, may be seen in Hamid Algar's article on Ḥurūfism, op. cit., figs 1 and 2.
45 According to Frederick De Jong, in his 'The iconography of Bektashiism: A survey of themes and symbolism in clerical costume, liturgical objects and pictorial art', *Manuscripts of the Middle East*, edited by Francois de Roche, Adem Gacek and Jan Just Witkam, vol. 4, Leiden, 1989, p. 14, 'The letter nūn stands for the stellar constellation of Scorpio (Akrep), symbolizing sexual instinct', in the figure of the Perfect Man. The symbolism here, in relation to the eyebrows, is unclear. Dr Javad Nurbakhsh, in his *Sufi Symbolism*, vol. 1, London, 1984, has much to say in regard to the symbolism of the eyebrows. He quotes Ḥāfiẓ, Attār, Maghribī, and many others. On p. 4, some verses of al-Lāhījī and Kamāl al-Khujandī are included.
46 One of the earliest written articles that discussed Sufi influences in Tatar life and literature was the contribution by Leon Bohdanowicz, Selim Chazbijewicz and Jan Tyzkiewicz, entitled, 'Tradycje mistyki islamsckiej. Pícmíenníctwo religijne magia i. folklor', *Tatarzy Musułmanie w Polsce*, published in Gdańsk in 1997. The most recent, and groundbreaking article was written by Drs Michas (Michael) Tarelka and Irina Sinkova, 'Tekst Sufiyskaga pakhodzhannya z Belaruska – Tatarskaga Khamaila', published in Minsk, in *Aktaliniya Prablemi Palanistiki*, 2005, pp. 29–54. Their research has convincingly proved a marked presence of Sufism in the texts of Belarussian Chamail. Following the recent International Conference in Minsk, titled *Christian-Muslim Dialogue in an era of Globalization*, organised by The Institute for Religious Dialogue and Interconfessional Communications under the Exarchate of the Belarussian Orthodox Church and The International Voluntary Association Saints Methodius and Cyrill Christian Educational Centre (25–28 October 2007), Michael Tarelka has given me more information about this Tatar Sufi movement of the nineteenth (even the late eighteenth) century, Tatars whose other documents have yet to be discovered. His text was found in Gomel in southern Belarus. It is a work written by a Sufi group who called themselves, 'Rijāl al-Ghaib', namely, 'the men of the world of the [divine] absence', or, 'the absence of mind'. This term is unquestionably Sufi see 'Ghaiba' in *The Shorter Encyclopaedia of Islam*, Leiden and London, 1953, p. 110. More information about this term may be found in www.al-baz.com/shaikhabdalqadir. Apart from Sufism, there are Shī'ite aspects to the term 'Rijāl al-Ghaib'. In Ḥurūfī Manuscript *OR 532 (6)* in 'The Circle of the Rijāl at Ghaib' in Cambridge University Library there is a tract (ff 127–133), wherein this term is specified, together with a

166 Islam in the Baltic

reference to the famous mystic Ibn al-'Arabī. By him it is defined as the 'Men of the Verified World of the Unseen' (see William C. Chittick, *The Sufi Path of Knowledge*. State University of New York, Albany, 1989, page 140). We cannot be certain whether this Sufi group in Belarus were Hurūfī influenced, although the influence of Ibn al-'Arabī is clearly apparent.

Chapter 5

1. A. Wheatcroft, Infidels, *The Conflict between Christendom and Islam 638–2002*, Viking, 2003, pp. 233–4.
2. B. Biedronska-Słotowa, *The Orient in Polish Art*, Cracow, 1992, p. 7.
3. W.F. Reddaway, J.H. Penson, O. Halecki, R. Dyboski, *The Cambridge History of Poland, from the Origins to Sobieski (to 1696)*, Cambridge, 1950, p. 569.
4. G. Lederer and I. Takacs, 'Chez les musulmans de Pologne', *La transmission du savoir dans le monde musulman périphérique. Lettre d'information*, Paris, CNRS-EHESS, Programme de Recherches Interdisciplinaires sur le Monde Musulman Périphérique, no 8, January, 1988. An English version appeared as 'Among the Muslims of Poland', *Central Asian Survey*, 9(2), 1990, pp. 119–31.
5. J. Bielawski, *Koran. Z arabskiego i komentarzem*, Warsaw, 1986.
6. G. Lederer, 'Islam in Lithuania', *Central Asian Survey* 14(3), 1995, pp. 425–48.
7. G. Lederer and I. Takac, 'Among the Muslims of Poland', op.cit.
8. K. Armstrong, *History of God*, Heineman, London, 1993, pp. 361–2.
9. G. Lederer, op. cit., p. 443.
10. Andrzej Drozd, Marek M. Dziekan and Tadeusz Majda, *Meczety i Cmentarz Tatarów polsko-litewskich*, Katalog Zabytkow Tatarskich, Tom 11, Res Publica Multiethnica, Warsaw, 1999.
11. F.R. Kreutzwald, *The Kalevipoeg*, translated by Antoine Chalvin, Gallimard, Mesnil-sur-l'Estrée, 2004, page 535.
12. *Q News International*, no 356, May 2004, p. 11.
13. Many facts and reports that appear in this section of my chapter that is concerned with Islam in Latvia are the result of a visit paid to Rīga during October and November, 2006. I wish to express my thanks to the British Academy for enabling me to undertake this research and, in particular, I wish to express my thanks to Mrs Anita Draveniece, head of the department of International Relations, and to Miss Diana Vucāne, International Relations (Starptautiskie Sakari), in the Latvian Academy of Sciences (Latvijas Zinātņu Akadēmija) for giving me such generous help during the fortnight that I spent in their country, including arranging visits and interviews with Muslims and with Latvian specialists, and also visits to institutions and libraries in the City of Rīga.
14. Miss Diana Vucāne has kindly given me the following information from LETA, 1000 GMT, 8 Oct 01: FBIS-SOV – 2001–1008 via World News Connection, regarding the views of the leader of the Latvian Muslims, Musans Macigovs, regarding the attacks on Afghanistan, suggesting that it was a part of a general attack on all Islam, 'he pointed out that criminals are residing in Latvia as well, however, nobody walks in the streets with an automatic rifle to kill them'.

15 Ita Kozakeviča's Society of the National Cultures of Latvia. The society is named after a Latvian lady of Polish descent who was active in the Latvian independence movement during the nearly five decades of the Soviet occupation.
16 Azeri culture is here defined as that of the Republic of Azerbaijan, formerly part of the Soviet Union, and the goal of this society seems to correspond to the general goals of the Azerbaijani community in Tallinn and Estonia, though the latter has taken part in a vigorous campaign to build Tallinn's mosque.
17 In medieval times Baškord, or Bašqurd was amongst the names of the Cumans in the twelfth and thirteenth centuries, whereas Qipčaq (Qipchāq) and Tatar, as personal names, were in vogue during the period of the Mongols of the thirteenth century. On this issue of nomenclature see István Vásáry, *Cumans and Tatars*, Cambridge, 2005, p. 11, notes 35–40.
18 The term 'Uzbek' denotes citizens of the Republic of Uzbekistan in Latvia. The same applies to the Uzbeks in Belarus.
19 'Idel' is derived from the Tatar form of the Arabic name Atīl, Itil, the former capital of the Khazars, on the River Volga. For an ethnic survey of the Volga–Ural Muslims, see Allan J. Frank, *Islamic Historiography and 'Bulghar' Identity among the Tatars and Bashkirs of Russia*, Brill, Leiden, Boston, Köln, 1998, pp. 4–9. Friar William of Rubruck refers to the River Volga and Atīl, and the Baškīrs, in his travels (1253–55): 'After travelling xii days from the Etilia we found a great river which they call Jagac (the River Ural), and it comes from the country of the Pascatir in the north, and falls into this previously-mentioned sea (*i.e.* the Caspian)'. *The Journey of William of Rubruck to the Eastern Parts of the World, 1253–55 as Narrated by Himself*, translated by William Woodville Rockhill, The Hakluyt Society, London, 1930, p. 129. The borders of this geographical region are repeated in *Ebülgâzî Bahadir Han, Khan of Khorezm, 1603–1663, 'Shajare-ye Tork; A General History of the Turks, Moguls and Tatars, Vulgarly called Tartars. Together with a Description of the Countries they Inhabit*, London, printed for J. and J. Knapton, J. Darby, A. Bettesworth, F. Fayram, J. Osborn and T. Longman, J. Pemberton, C. Rivington, F. Clay, J. Batley, and Aaron Ward, 1729–30, pt 1, Ch. X, Section 11, p. 579, 'The *Bashkir Tatars*, as well as those of *Uffa*, inhabit the Province of *Bulgaria*, which makes the Eastern part of the Kingdom of *Casan*; it is situate to the East of the River *Wolga*, and extends on one side from that River to the Mountains of the *Eagles* [*Arall Tag*], and the frontiers of *Siberia*; and on the other side from the Mouth of the River *Kama* in the *Wolga*, almost as far as the Town of *Samara*.'
20 The Azeris are overwhelmingly Shī'ite, though this religious reality is left unmentioned in their leaflet.
21 *Mukhayyam*, in Arabic, a camp for the young and their elders wherein religious instruction forms a part of their activities.
22 Uzbekistan is noted for its hard line against the 'Islamists' and this may well be reflected here.
23 On Midhat-Hadji Satdanov, Imām-Muhtasib and President of 'Idel', see Valters Ščerbinskis, *Ienācēji No Tālienes*, Nordik, Rīga, 1998, pp. 40–1.
24 On the educational role of non-Latvian Muslims, see, Ščerbinskis, ibid., p. 73.
25 Musans Macigovs is regarded as a moderate Muslim leader in Latvia, hence

168   Islam in the Baltic

this comment is not to be regarded as an especially important change of attitude. The Danish cartoon controversy did not spark any major reaction amongst Latvian Muslims.

26 Brīvības 104 is not only the HQ of '*Īmān*' but also the address of the Muslim Consultation Centre in Rīga. The faculty of history in the University of Latvia is housed in Brīvības blv. 32.
27 Dr Rufija Ševirjo/eva is the respected president of the Muslim community in Latvia. She lives in a flat in the suburb of Rīga, Hipokrātu 17–31. She attends conferences and she frequently travels to Russia to visit Moscow and Kazan. One of her dearest wishes, which she discussed with the author, is to hold a 'Conference on Islam in the Baltic Sea Countries'. Her reasons include the steady growth of Muslims in these countries which is unmatched, in her view, by the existing organisational structures to face such issues as: a) Islamophobia; b) Extremism and terrorism; c) The need to be educated in both Islam and in one secular subject; d) The evaluation of leadership within Islam. It is her wish to include invited guests from the United Kingdom, Belarus, Poland and Russia as well as the Baltic States. The theme of such a conference would be 'Islam in the Baltic Region: its Past, Present and Future'. The conference would concentrate on how the Islamic movements should organise themselves, how to study their problems, to define the conditions and factors that influence their problems and a discussion for a practical coalition for true co-operations. Her approach is essentially above sectarian divisions and merely political goals.
28 'Antisemītisms un Islamofobija Latvijā – pagātne, aktuālā situācija, risinājumi', published by The Latvian Bible Association (Latvijas Bībeles biedrība), Rīga, 2006. An English summary may be read at the conclusion of each lecture.
29 Uldis Bērziņš is Latvia's widely regarded leading poet. He is also an Orientalist with a knowledge of Arabic and Turkish, and with a deep interest in Islamic studies.
30 Uldis Bērziņš had been commissioned to publish the first translation of the Qur'ān from Arabic into Latvian. A translation of the Qur'ān into Estonian has been published recently according to information conveyed to me by Dr Anita Draveniece.
31 Professor M.A.S. 'Abdel-Haleem, *Qur'ān*, Oxford World's Classics, 2004/5, p. 238, note *a*.
32 Ali Abi Issa, '*Komentarz fragmentu LXX Sury STOPNIE w. 19–35*' (*Sūra 70, The Ways of Ascent (al-Ma'ārij), vv. 19–35*), *Journal of Islamic Affairs, Świat Islamu*, no 5, August, 1995, p. 3.
33 Dr Valters Ščerbinskis kindly gave me up-to-date information in regard to the Muslim and other minority communities in Latvia during an interview in his office in the Latvia State Historical Archive, Slokas Street, Rīga, 16. His published work, in Latvian with an English summary, entitled *Ienācīje No Tālienes, Austrumu un Dienvidu tautu pārstāvji Latvijā no 19. gadsimta beigām līdz mūsdienām*, is a pioneer study of the arrival of emigrants and families from the East and from the Caucasian region (from Armenia and Georgia in particular) dating from the nineteenth century up to the years of Latvian independence. It is currently the standard published source of information and was published in 1998, by Nordik, Rīga, although, to my

Notes and references 169

knowledge, the work is no longer in print. Subsequent to its publication, Ščerbinskis has been studying the most recent developments in this field.

34 The arrival of emigrants from former Central Asian, Caucasian and European Tatar regions of the ex-Soviet Union is a matter that has concerned all the Baltic States and both Poland and Belarus. Similarly, in the Russian Oblast of Kaliningrad, formerly Königsberg, East Prussia, with a current population 78 per cent of whom are Russian, there are found Tatars from Kazan, from the Baškīr and from the Caucasus. Relations between Orthodox Christian clergy, Muslims and Jews have greatly benefited from the interfaith conferences that have been held in Kaliningrad in recent years in which all three religious communities have been represented. In this connection one should also not forget the important Tatar community to be found today in St Petersburg. For a recent update on the situation of Russia's Muslims in the main regions with Muslim populations (including Tatarstan) see 'Russia's Muslims, a benign growth', *The Economist*, London, 7 April 7 2007, pp. 39–40. Islamophobia is a factor within Latvian society, hence, the recent discussions and the conferences which have been held. In the Current Affairs section of *The Baltic Guide in English about Latvia* published in Rīga, October, 2006, p. 15, it was noted that: 'One third of Latvia's population do not want homosexuals as their neighbours; however, more people would prefer not to live next door to alcoholics, a survey carried out by the organisation Dialogi.lv shows. The survey on tolerance indicates that 84.1% of people do not want to see drug addicts as their neighbours. 71.6% would not like to live next door to alcoholics and 45.2% would not like to be neighbours of people with criminal records. As many as 38.8% of those polled don't want Gypsies (Roma) as their neighbours, 35.3% would not like to live next to gay people and 21.7% wouldn't like to live next to Muslims. Most respondents would like to introduce restriction for some groups of people. As many as 32.6% of respondents believe that the right to declare opinions in public should be restricted, while 5.2% of people said that gays should have restricted voting rights.'

35 On Hasan Haretdinov-Konikov, Abdula Husnetdinov and Š. Eriss (Husnetdinov) and other leading Tatar religious leaders, see Ščerbinskis, op. cit., pp. 16, 17, 28, 62, 66–7.

36 Ibid, p. 16, where a photograph of Imām Šakirs Husnetdinovs is reproduced.

37 The figures for 1943, as shown by Ščerbinskis, ibid., p. 46, indicates forty-eight Tatars and sixty-four Turks.

38 By 1989, this figure had grown to 121 Avars, 2,765 Azerbaijanis, 629 Baškīrs, 158 Chechens, 189 Kirghiz, 348 Lezgins, 343 Tajiks, 4828 Kazan Tatars, 60 Crimean Tatars, 228 Turkmenians, and 925 Uzbeks, see, Ščerbinskis, ibid., p. 47.

39 Ibid., p. 75.

40 According to the Latvian *Human Development Report*, Chapter 2, 'The Development of a Multi-Ethnic Society', p. 3 of 9.

41 On future prospects and the promotion of integration, see, ibid., pp. 8–9.

42 On Islam in Finland, with a specific reference to the rôle played by the Finnish Tatars, see Jørgen Nielsen, *Muslims in Western Europe*, Edinburgh University Press, third edition, 2004, p. 88.

43 F.W. Hasluck, *Christianity and Islam under the Sultans*, Oxford, 1929, vol. II, pp. 430 and 577.

44 Recent research in Bulgaria has discovered an Ottoman mosque complex, dating between the sixteenth and eighteenth centuries, in the vicinity of Kaliakra.
45 I am most grateful to Dr, and Assistant Professor, Jonas Otterbeck, International Migration and Ethnic Relations (IMER) in Malmö University, and to Professor Åker Sanders of the University of Göteborg, Sweden, for drawing my attention to this information. Professor Otterbeck's article 'The Baltic Tatars – the First Muslim Group in Modern Sweden', published in *Cultural Encounters in East Central Europe*, edited by Karin Junefelt, Martin Peterson, and co-edited by Lise-Lotte Wallenius with English language supervisor Jan Teeland, printed by by FRN, Forskningsrådsnämnden, Swedish Council for Planning and Coordination of Research, Uppsala, 1998, pp. 145–53, is the first study of this subject in English. The article contains useful references and bibliography. Professor Otterbeck has also published an article 'What is Reasonable to Demand? Islam in Swedish Textbooks', *Journal of Ethnic and Migration Studies* (Routledge), vol. 31, no 4, July, 2005, pp. 795–812. He has also contributed to *The Legal Treatment of Islamic Minorities in Europe*, edited by Roberta Aluffi B.–P. and Giovanna Zincone, Peeters, Leuven, 2004, pp. 233–54, on the subject of 'The Legal Status of Islamic Minorities in Sweden'.
46 On the subject of Sweden's Muslims and organisations, see Anne Sofie Roald, 'From "People's Home" to "Multiculturalism": Muslims in Sweden', in *Muslims in the West, From Sojourners to Citizens*, edited by Yvonne Yazbeck Haddad, Oxford, 2002, pp. 101–20. Also see Jørgen Nielsen, op. cit., pp. 82–6. See also Göran Larsson, the Department of Religious Studies and Theology, Göteborg University, 'Muslims' in *Swedish Media and Academia*, ISIM Review 18/Autumn, 2006, International Institute for the Study of Islam in the Modern World, Leiden, pp. 38–9. A list of Muslim organisations in Sweden (*Muslimska organisationer i Sverige*) may be found in Jonas Otterbeck, *Islam, muslimer och den svenska skolan*, Studentlitteratur, Lund, 2000, 7 Appendix, pp. 135–6. See also Gören Larssen, 'Muslims' in *Swedish Media and Academia*, ISIM Review, International Institute for the Study of Islam in the Modern World, Leiden, no 18, Autumn 2006, pp. 38–9 and his *Islam och Muslimer i Sverige: En kommenterad bibliografi*, Göteborg and Stockholm Makadam Förlag, 2004.
47 Jonas Otterbeck, op. cit., pp. 147–9.
48 Ibid, pp 151–2.
49 Bazaar Vest is located within the district of Gellerup in Århus.
50 Geographically, Århus is situated on the coast of the Kattegat and not in the Baltic Sea like Copenhagen. However, in view of its importance as Denmark's second city, and its considerable Muslim population, it is fully representative of Denmark's current problems of integration.
51 Marianne C. Qvortrup Fibiger (ed.) *Religiøs Mangfoldighed, En Kortlægning af Religion og Spiritualitet i Århus*, Forfatterne og Systime A/S, Århus, 2004, pp. 175–234.
52 L. Kühle, 'Islam i Århus', in *Religious Multiplicity* (*Religiøs mangfoldighed*), edited by Marianne C. Qvortrup Fibiger, Centre and Department for Multi-Religious Studies within the Theological Faculty of Århus University. Lene Kühle is employed in the Afdeling for Religionsvidenskab, in the Theology

Faculty. Her specialities include the sociology of religion, the relationships between religion and state and the religious minorities in Denmark. I am very grateful to Professor Qvortrup Fibiger and her colleagues for receiving me and furnishing me with this information during a visit paid to the Faculty of Theology in Århus University.
53 Marianne C. Qvortrup Fibiger and Lene Küle, op. cit., pp. 188–93. The addresses of the associations are listed in each section.
54 Ibid., pp. 194–8.
55 Ibid., pp. 199–203.
56 Ibid., pp. 203–5.
57 Ibid., pp. 206–10.
58 Ibid., pp. 210–15.
59 Ibid., pp. 215–19.
60 On Uways al-Qaranī see Alexandre Popović et Gilles Veinstein, *Les Voies d'Allah*, Fayard, Paris, 1996, pp. 30–2.
61 Fibiger and Kühle, op. cit., pp. 220–5.
62 Ibid., pp. 225–30.
63 Ibid., pp. 231–4.
64 Ibid., p. 179.
65 *The Dialogue of Christians and Muslims in Poland*, DOM Foundation.
66 M.A.S. Abdel Haleem, *The Qur'an*, Oxford World Classics, 2004, p. 63.
67 Ibid., pp. 338–9.
68 Professors Andrey Danilov and Grigori Dovgyuallo are joint authors of the 'Bridges of Europe' project in Belarus.
69 From the Orthodox viewpoint dialogue is helped by the traditional view that Islam is an 'Arianism', a Christian heresy, or, 'Falsorum Christianorum' as defined by Michalonis Litvani (sixteenth and seventeenth centuries) rather than a distinct religion. See the Orthodox position as exolained by John Garvey in his *Seeds of the Word, Orthodox Thinking on Other Religions*, St Vladimir's Seminary Press, New York, 2005, pp. 88–97 and 117–19.

Conclusion

1 For a fuller introduction to Professor Seraya Szapszal and his contribution to Oriental studies, especially to Turkish, Persian and Karaite studies, see my article, 'Karaite origins in Lithuania and in Poland, according to Professor Seraja Shapshala', in *Sifting Sands, Reading Signs, Studies in Honour of Professor Géza Fehérvári*, edited by Patricia L. Baker and Barbara Brend, Furnace Publishing, London, 2006, pp. 121–31. See pp. 122–4.
2 Ibid., pp. 123–4.
3 An article on the subject of 'In Minsk, the mosque under construction' (*V Miintske stroyitstaya Mečet*) with photographs showing the old mosque and the newly designed mosque to replace it appeared in the Belarusian newspaper *Večerniy Miinsk* on 27 February 2004. Photos of the destroyed mosque may be seen in Andrzej Drozd, Marek. M. Dziekan and Tadeusz Majda, *Meczety i Cmentarze Tatarow Polsko-Litewskich*, Res Publica Multiethnica, Warsaw, 1999, plates 301–3 and pp. 74–5.
4 The Mufti's appeal included the number of the bank account of the Muslim Religious Union in Belarus. It was signed by Ismail Alexandrovich, the

172 Islam in the Baltic

chairman of the board (Mufti) of the Muslim Religious Union of the Republic of Belarus and it was dated August 2002.
5 Zigmas Zinkevičius, Aleksijeus Luchtanas and Gintautas Česnys, *Where We Come From, The Origin of the Lithuanian People*, Science and Encyclopaedia Publishing Institute, Vilnius, 2005, pp. 29, 68, 69.
6 Stasys Samalavičius, *An Outline of Lithuanian History*, Diemedis, Vilnius, 1995, p. 20.
7 Anne Applebaum, *Between East and West, Across the Borderlands of Europe*, Papermac, Macmillan Publishers Ltd, London and Basingstoke, 1995, Introduction xiii. Anne Applebaum's book is now out of print. It is to be found in very few libraries in the United Kingdom. However, it is an extremely valuable description of the entire region of Belarus, Lithuania and Poland, in the 1990s, and it sheds much light on the societies amongst whom the Tatars were still living at that time. The book also contains a useful list of sources, between pages 309 and 311. Ten years have seen remarkable transformations in many parts of these regions.
8 Ibid., Introduction, xii–xiii.
9 Ibid., pp. 77–8.

Appendix

1 The Department of Rarities of Latvia's National Library is situated in 6/8 Jēkaba Iela in Old Rīga. I am most grateful to the librarian, Ināra Klekere, for granting me permission and assistance in examining this book and in arranging for me to have photocopies made of selected pages from this work.
2 'The Exordium', the opening chapter in the Qur'ān.
3 Isrāfīl. On the day of the Resurrection, the archangel will stand upon the holy rock in Jerusalem and he shall blow the trumpet, signalling thereby the resurrection of the dead.
4 'Azra'īl as vocalised in the text, more correctly 'Izra'īl, the 'Angel of Death' in Islam.
5 The prostration before Ādam by the angels is referred to in the Qur'ān in several passages (*Sūrat* 2, verse 36, *Sūrat* 7, verse 12, *Sūrat* 17, verse 60). Satan (*Iblīs*), alone amongst the angels, disobeyed. He was cast out of Heaven and was instrumental in bringing about Ādam's fall.
6 This passage is very corrupt indeed in the text. Āmina, the mother of Muhammad, appears to be intended. This identification is supported by the fact that the Prophet himself is the following person in our text for whom prayers and blessings are requested. The text follows the substance of the Āmina 'legend' which Jan Knappert has outlined in his *Islamic Legends, Histories of the Heroes, Saints and Prophets of Islam*, vol. 1, E.J. Brill, Leiden, 1985, pp. 186–7.
7 Hābīl is not mentioned by name in the Qur'ān.
8 Shīth, Shatt, in the text, hence 'Seth' is hypothetical, though very plausible. Referred to in the Bible, in Genesis 5, verse 3, and the Gospel of St Luke 3, verse 38, he was praised in the Muslim tradition amongst the Moriscos. Eve, it was believed, begot Seth in whom she saw the light of the Prophet Muhammad (*al-Nūr al-Muhammadī*) whilst still in her womb. See Anwar

G. Chejne, *Islam and the West: the Moriscos*, State University of New York Press, Albany, 1983, pp. 98–9; and *The Shorter Encyclopaedia of Islam*, Brill, Leiden, 1953, p. 544.

9 The Prophet Idrīs is identified with the Biblical Enoch, see Knappert, op. cit., pp. 56–9.

10 The South Arabian Prophet who, according to the Qur'ān, *Sūra* 11, which bears his name, preached to the pagan 'Ādites. He is also identified with the Biblical 'Ābir, (Eber, the ancestor of the Hebrews).

11 Sāliḥ was the prophet sent by God to preach to the pagan Thamūdites, see Qur'ān, *Sūra* 7, verse 73, and *Sūra* 17, verse 59, and M.A.S. Abdel Haleem, *The Qur'an, A New Translation*, Oxford World Classics, 2004, pp. 99–100.

12 This person is variably called al-Khaḍir, or al-Khiḍr, Khwāja Khiḍr, Khiẓr, and other variants of this name. He is universally known throughout the Muslim World as the 'Green Man', an inspirer of Sūfīs, and the advisor to Dhū'l-Qarnayn, see below. He is in particular associated with events described in *Sūra* 18, vv. 83 ff, in the Qur'ān. See the article on him in *The Shorter Encyclopaedia of Islam*, op. cit., pp. 232–5.

13 Dhū'l-Qarnayn. Some Muslims believe that Alexander the Great is intended by the term the 'lord of the two horns'. On the other hand, stories are found of a number of noted pre-Islamic rulers and princes of the Yemen who bore this title and tales of their exploits were circulating widely in Arabia during and before the time of the Prophet Muhammad. It is clear from the note of M.A.S. Abdel Haleem, op. cit., pp. 188–89, that the balance of argument today is seen to be in favour of the former amongst a majority of Muslims. Edward William Lane, in his *Selections from the Kur-an, commonly called in England, The Koran*, Madden and Co, London, 1883, that, in his day (near in date to the Rīga manuscript), page 138, suggests that the chronology of this character, around the end of the nineteenth century, was more ambiguous and open to varied interpretations.

14 Shu'ayb. A messenger who was an inspiration to the Propher Muhammad, see M.A.S. Abdel Haleem, *The Qur'ān*, op. cit., pp. 100–1.

15 Shiqq, although here in the text spelt Shikk. Shiqq and Satīh were two diviners who flourished before Islam, see Nabih Amin Faris, *The Antiquities of South Arabia*, Princeton, 1938, pp. 42–3, 69.

16 Seraya Szapszal's Karaim Collection, Library of the National Museum of Lithuania, compiled by Žygintas Būčys, 2003, in particular pp. 127–33, Tartar-Slavic manuscripts.

17 See in particular, Shirin Akiner, 'The Vocabulary of a Byelorussian Kitab in the British Museum', *The Journal of Byelorussian Studies*, 1973, 3(1), pp. 55–84 and 'Oriental Borrowings in the Language of the Byelorussian Tatars', *Slavonic and East European Review*, 1978, 56(2), pp. 224–41, and, Meredith-Owens and A.G.M. Nadson, 'The Byelorussian Tatars and their Writings', *The Journal of Byelorussian Studies*, 1970, 2(2), pp. 141–76.

18 On the whole subject of the influence of Christian literature, especially apocryphal, on Tatar literature see Andrzej Drozd, Marek M. Dziekan and Tadeusz Majda, *Piśmiennictwo i muhiry Tatarów polsko-litewskich*, Tom III, Res Publica Multiethnica, Warszawa, 2000, pp. 30–3 and Bibliography,

p. 81. In particular the following articles by Andrzej Drozd: a) 'Starpolski apokryf w muzułmańsckich księgach, (Tatarska adaptacja Historyji barzo cudnej o stworzeniu nieba i ziemie Krzystofa Pussmana)', *Poznánskie Studia Polonistyczne*, Serie Literacka, 1996, 3(23), pp. 95–134. b) 'Wpływy chrześcijańskie na literaturę Tatarów w dawnej Rzeczpospolitej. Między antigonizmem a symbiozą', *Pamietnik Literacki*, 1997, 88(3), pp. 3–34.

Bibliography

Bukharaev, Ravil. *Islam in Russia, The Four Seasons*, Curzon Press, Richmond, Surrey, 2000.
Chazbijewicz, Selim. *Tatarzy Krymscy, Walka o Naród i Wolną Ojczyznę*, LIKON, Poznań-Września, 2001.
Jankowski, Henryk. 'Islamic components in the art of Lithuanian–Polish–Belarusian Tatars', *Collectanea Eurasiatica Cracoviensia*, Krakow, 2003, pp. 71–92.
Masteika, Romas. *Zalgirio musis*, RaMastas, Vilnius, 1999.
Norris, Harry Thirlwall. 'Islam and Qur'anic Studies in the Baltic Region: The contribution of the Baltic Tatars amid the growing inter-ethnic Muslim communities of Belarus, Estonia, Latvia, Lithuania and Poland', *Journal of Qur'anic Studies*, Centre of Islamic Studies, School of Oriental and African Studies, University of London, VII(1), 2005, pp. 113–23.
von Kügelgen, Anke, Michael Kemper and Allan. J. Frank. *Muslim Culture in Russia and Central Asia from the 18th to the early 20th Centuries*, Vol. 2: *Inter-Regional and Inter-Ethnic Relations*, Islamkundische Untersuchungenband 216, Klaus Schwarz Verlag, Berlin, 1998.
Zajaczowski, Ananiasz. *La Chronique des Steppes Kiptchak, Tevârîh-i Dešt-i Qipĉâq du XVIIe siècle*, Edition Critique, Warsaw, 1966.

Belarus

Akiner, Shirin. 'The Vocabulary of a Byelorussian Kitâb in the British Museum', *The Journal of Byelorussian Studies* (London), 3(1), 1973, pp. 55–84.
Akiner, Shirin. 'Oriental borrowings in the language of the Byelorussian Tatars', *Slavonic and East European Review* (London), 56(2), April, 1978, pp. 224–40.
Dumin, C.U. and I.B. Kanapatski. *Belarutskiyya Tatari, Minulae i Suchasnastch*, Minsk, 1993.
 This is arguably the most authentic and comprehensive description of the religious life today, amongst the Muslim 'Lithuanian' Tatars in present-day

176   Islam in the Baltic

Belarus written by noted Tatar authorities in Belarus. Also, see, below, under I.B. Kanapatski and A.I. Smolik.

Kanapatski, I.B. and A.I. Smolik. *Gistorija i Kultura Balaruskikh Tatar*, Minsk, 2000.

This is a more recent description on the same subject.

Lakomka, A.I. *Berag Bandravannyaŷ tsi agkulb u Belarusi myachztsi*, Minsk, 1994.

This book describes Belarus mosques in the context of mosque architecture in the World of Islam. There are rare photographs of early mosques in Belarus that have now vanished.

Owens, Meredith and Alexander Nadson. 'The Byelorussian Tatars and their writings', *The Journal of Byelorussian Studies* (London), 2(2), 1970, pp. 141–76.

Bayram (al-Kitābah), 2000 bipusk 1–2, Minsk, 2000.

A publication from the Muslim community.

Belarusian Tatar Manuscripts of the end of the 17th up to the beginning of the 20th centuries from the Collection of the Yakub Kolas Central Science Library of the National Academy of Sciences of Belarus, American Council of Learned Societies, Minsk, 2003.

A valuable catalogue of Belarusian Islamic manuscripts. The work contains a bibliography, illustrations and an English Catalogue and a Foreword which outlines the history of the composition of these Islamic manuscripts the earliest of which dates back to the eighteenth century.

Islām i Umma (abshchina) Tatar- Musulman Belarusi, Litvi i Polshchi na Myaži Tisyachagoddzyay, Jam'iyyat al-da'wa al-Islāmiyya al-'Ālamiyya, Minsk, 2001.

A collection of essays published by the Muslim community.

Latvia

Ščerbinskis, Valters. *Ienācēji no Tālienes, Austrumu un Dienvidu tautu pārstāvji Latvijā no 19. gadsimta beigām lidz mūsdienām*, Nordik, Rīga, 1998.

This is to date the only publication that gives the history of the Latvian Muslim community. There is an English summary of its content.

'*Antesemītisms un islamofobia Latvijā – pagātne , aktuālā, situācija, risinājumi*', Latvijas Bībeles biedrība, Rīga, 2006.

A conference that took place on the 5 April 2005 in Rīga. ISBN 9984–564–84–3.

A series of papers in which Islamophobia figures centrally in their content. The title of the conference, in English, was 'Facing Islamophobia and Anti-Semitism', the editor-in-chief was Valdis Tēruadkalns. Uldis Bēržiņš contributed a paper on 'Dažas replicas par iecietību un par Korānu', 'Some remarks about tolerance in the Koran', pp. 28–38.

Lithuania

Bairašauskaitė, Tamara. '*Lietuvos Totoriai XIX amžiuje*', Lietuvos Istorija Institutas, Vilnius, Mintis, 1996. This thesis is a pioneer study of the Lithuanian Tatars in the nineteenth century and contains a summary, in English pp. 298–304.

Bohdanowicz, Arslane. La Horde d'Or, La Pologne et la Lithuanie (1242–1430), *Revue Internationale d'Histoire Politique et Constitutionelle* (Paris), 1955, tome X, pp. 168–200.

Borawski, Piotr. 'Religious Tolerance and the Tatar population in the Grand Duchy of Lithuania: 16th to 18th Century', *Journal of the Institute of Muslim Minority Affairs* (London), 9(1), 1988, pp. 119–33.

Lederer, Gyorgy. 'Islam in Lithuania', *Central Asian Survey*, 14(3), 1995, pp. 425–48.

Litvani, Michalonis. (ed. A.L. Khoroshkevich) *De Moribus Tartarorum Litvanorum et Moschorum, Fragmina X Multiplici Historia Referta*, Miikhalon Liitviin, Provach Tatar Litovtsev i Moskvityan, reprint, Moscow, 1994.

Loewe, Karl von. *The Lithuanian Statute of 1529*, Leiden, E.J. Brill, 1976.

Miškineienė, Galina. *Seniausi Lietuvos Totorių Rankraščiai, Grafika, Transliteracija, Vertimas, Tekstų strukūra ir turinys*, Vilnius University, 2001. An important recent study. The text is in Lithuanian, and in Russian, on the format and the content of Tatar manuscripts, with selected examples of transcribed text.

Potasenko, Grigorijus (ed.). *The Peoples of the Grand Duchy of Lithuania*, Aidai, Vilnius, 2002.

In many respects, this is the most recommendable book in print, in English, that introduces the history of the Karaims and Tatars, in Lithuania, and in the sister countries which once formed a part of the Grand Duchy of Lithuania. Jurgita Siauciunaite-Verbickiene has contributed articles on the Jews, the Karaims and the Tatars, but there are also very well written articles on the Ruthenians, the Roma, the Russian Old Believers and on multiculturalism in general, thus providing a wide context for the study of these minorities in Lithuania, past and present.

Tyszkiewicz, Jan. *Tatarzy na Litwie i w Polsce, Studia z dziejǿ XIII–XVIII w*, Państwowe Wydawnictwo Naukowe, Warsaw, 1989.

A very distinguished history of the Tatars but unfortunately without an English summary.

Z.M. 'Les Musulmans de Lithuanie', *Revue du Monde Musulman*, vol. XI, June, 1910, no XI, pp. 287–91.

The Lithuanian Tatars in the Nineteenth Century, Humanities, 05 H History Lithuanian Institute of History, Vytautas Magnus University, Vilnius, 1998. This is a relatively short, 45-page English summary of much of the content of the above work. The content is expanded and it is presented in far greater detail.

Politische Integration und religiöse Eigenständigkeit der litauischen Tataren im 19. Jahrhundert.
See, *Muslim Culture in Russia and Central Asia from the 18th to the early 20th Centuries*, under von Kügelgen, Kemper and Frank, above, pp. 313-34.
Z Historii Tatarów Polskich 1794-1944, Zbiór szkiców z aneksami źródłowymi, Pułtusk, 1998.

Poland

Bohdan, Baranowski. *Polska a Tatarszczyzna w Latach 1624-1629*, Łódź, 1948. This book has a French summary pp. 119-30. This book is informative about the relationship between the Polish Tatars and those in the Crimea.

Bohdanowicz, Arslane, 'La Horde d'Or, la Pologne et la Lithuanie (1242-1430), *Revue Internationale d'Histoire Politique et Constitutionelle* (Paris), 1955, Tome V, pp. 168-200.

Bohdanowicz, L. 'The Muslims in Poland. Their Origin, History and Cultural Life', *The Journal of the Royal Asiatic Society* (London), October, 1942.

Borawski, P. and A. Dubiński. *Tatarzy Polscy. Dzieje, Obrzędy, Legendy, Tradycje*, Warsaw, 1986.
A comprehensive study of Tatar culture in Poland including particularly interesting chapters on heraldry and coats of arms, legends of the Tatars and the Tatar language. Dr Dubiński was an Ottomanist in Warsaw University.

Borawski, P. *Tatarzy w Dawnej Rzeczypospolitej*, Warsaw, 1986.
The Polish Tatars in the former Republic, an important military history.

Chazbijewicz, S. 'Wplyw Sufizmu (taşawwuf) na zwyczaje muzulmanow w Polsce', *Zycie Muzulmanskie*, 1988, no 9, pp. 30-5.
The influence and evidence for the presence of Sufism in the faith and practice of the Polish Tatars. The only study on this subject to date.

Drotlew, Zula Janowicz-Czainska. 'Przez lasy Syberii do Wielkiej Brytanii', *Rosznik Tatarow Polskich* (offprint from *The Tatar Annual*), Tom VII, Gdańsk, 2001.
The journal of a Polish Tatar's exile. It describes the tribulations of her exile which took her from Eastern Europe to Great Britain during, and, again after, the Second World War.

Drozd, Andrzej. 'Tatarska wersja piesni-legendy o Sw Hiobie' (The Tatar version of the song legend of St Job, based upon Polish anonymous hagiographic legend dating to the 15th century), *Poznanskie Studia Polonistyerne Serie Literacka*, Tom II (XXII), Poznań, 1995, pp. 163-95.

Drozd, Andrej, Marek. M. Dzieken and Tadeusz Majda. 'Meczety i cmentarze Tatarów polsko-litewskich', *Katalog Zabytkow Tatarskich*, Tom II, Warsaw, 1999.
This unique, superbly illustrated and documented survey of Tatar historical monuments, mosques, cemeteries, gravestones and mosque furniture is probably the best introduction to the religious life of the Tatar communities in Belarus, Lithuania and Poland, which is now in print. The text is in Polish,

but there are summaries, in English, of the monuments that are shown in the plates.

Drozd, Andrej, Marek. M. Dzieken and Tadeusz Majda 'Piśmiennictwo i muhiry Tatarów polsko-litewskich', *Katalog Zabytków Tatarskich*, Tom III, Warsaw, 2000.

This is a sequel to the above work and uniquely valuable in its coverage of Tatar manuscripts of all kinds, religious pictures and paintings, amulets and talismans in collections which are to be found in Belarus, Lithuania, Poland and the British Library. The work is lavishly interested with black and white photographs, and many in colour of these works of art.

Konopacki, Maciej. *Les Musulmans en Pologne*, Librarie Orientaliste, Paul Geuthner, Paris, 1968.

Kryczyński, Leon Najman Mirza. *Bibliografja do Historiji Tatarów Polskich, Zycie Polityczne Spoleczne i Kulturalne*, Warsaw, 1935, Section XIII, pp. 44–54.

Kryczyński Stanisław, Tatarzy Litewscy, 'Próba Monografii Historyczno-Etnograficicznej, (Les Tatares Lithuaniens. Esquisse d'une Monographie Historique et Ethnographique) Wydanie II', reprinted from *Rocznik Tatarski, Tatar Yili – Annuaire Tatare*, Tom III, Warszawa/Warsaw, 1938 and Gdańsk, 2000.

This monumental work is a classic. It is an essential source for all who wish to understand the life, culture, religion, language, literature and the social structure of Tatar society in Poland and in Lithuania.

Łapicz, Czeslaw. *Kitab Tatarów Litewsko-Polskich (Paleografia. Grafia. Język)*, Toruń, 1986.

This is a major linguistic, paleographical, and literary study of Tatar manuscripts, especially the Kitāb. A short English summary of the contents is found pp. 234–6.

Lederer, Gyorgy and Ibloya Takacz. 'Amongst the Muslims of Poland', *Central Asian Survey*, 14(3), 1995, pp. 425–48.

Miśkiewicz, Ali. *Tatarzy Polscy, 1918–1939, Życie Społeczno-Kulturalne i Religijne, Państowe Wydawnictwo Naukowe*, Warsaw, 1990.

A most informative book on the Tatars during the Second World War.

Reychman, Jan. 'Zabytki Islamu w Polsce' (Monuments of Islam in Poland), *Euchemer* (Warsaw), 5(6), 1958.

Rowell, Stephen C. *A History of Lithuania*, Reda Griskaite, Gediminas Rudis, 2002.

Sokólska, Joanna, Lenice Henryk, Ali Miśkiewicz and Sacuik Ryszard. *Śladami Tatarów Polskich*, Supraśi, Białystok, 1994.

A little book on the Polish Tatars with superb colour photographs of homesteads, mosques, tombstones, astrological maps, and landscapes. The book has a summary in English on pages 70–5 and in Arabic, pages 76–7, Tatār fī Būlandā.

Steinbach, L. 'The Muhammadans in Poland', *Islamic Culture* (Hyderabad, Deccan), XII(4), Oct., 1942, pp. 371–9.

Talko-Hryyncewicz, *Muślimowie Czyli Zwani Tatarzy Litewscy*, Bibljoteczka 'Orbis', Kraków, 1924.
This is a very rare book and one of the earliest about the Baltic Tatars.

Warminska, Katarzyna, *Tatarzy Polscy Tożsamość, Religijna i Etniczna*, Universitas, Cracow, 1999.
This is amongst the most recent academic studies of the Polish Tatars to be published in Poland. The viewpoint is that of an ethnologist and a sociologist who is especially concerned with Tatar ethnicity and its relationship to the Muslim faith from the time of the first arrival of the Tatars, their recent history, and the current situation. It is unfortunate that, as yet, there is no English translation of this work that would be of a wide interest to anthropologists who are studying ethnicity and the Muslim faith in parts of Eastern Europe, Africa and Asia.

Wisniewskie, J. 'Osadnictwo Tatarskie w Sokólskiem i na Póolnocnyma Podlosin' (Tatar settlements in the Sokolka region and in northern Podlosie)', *Rocznik Białostocki* (Warsaw), Tome XVI, 1989 and 1991, pp. 293–324.
Tatar settlements in the Sokólka region and in northern Podlasie. This lengthy survey has an English summary in pages 403–5.

Woronowicz, 'Alī ('Alī Ismā'īl Furūnufitsh), *Al-Islām fī Būluniyā* (Islam in Poland), Cairo, 1354/1936.

Zakrzewski, Andrzej B. 'Assimilation of Tatars within the Polish Commonwealth 16th–18th centuries', *Acta Poloniae Historica 55 Orientalistycznej*, no 2, 1975, pp. 85–106.

'Dziejow Kolonizacji Tatarskiej Wielkim Ksiestwie Litewskim w Polsce (XIV–XVll w)', Przeglad Orientalistyczny (Warsaw), 4(104), 1977, pp. 291–304.

'Kultura religijna Tatarow Polskich', Zwiazek Tatarow Polskich, *Rocznik Tatarów Polskich*, Gdańsk, Tome II, 1994, pp. 66–88.

'Muzulmanie w Polsce', *Zycie Muzulmanskie* (special issue), 1990, pp. 14–23. English version, ibid., pp. 33–41.

'The Polish Tatars', lecture delivered to the Royal Anthropological Institute, Dec. 1943, published in *Man*, 1944, (96), pp. 116–21.

'Rekopis Tatarow polsko-litewskich w zbiorach Biblioteki Gdańskiej, PAN', *D'Oriana*, 3, 1996, pp. 18–27.

Tatarzy Krymscy, walka o narod i wolna ojczyzne, a supplement to *Rocznika Tatarów Polskich*, The Tatar Annual, 2001 (ISBN 83–916144–1–7,Oficyna Wydawnicza Likon,Poznan-Wrzesnia).
This is a concise survey by a leading Polish Tatar historian about the cultural and political history of the Crimean Tatars, their persecution and deportation under the Soviets and their current resettlement in their former homeland. His study contains a 'pan-Tatar view' of this tragedy.

'Trzy Redakeje jezykowe Muzulmanskiej Legendy w Pismienn – ictwi Tatarów Litewsko-Polskich', *Acta Balta-Slavica*, XX, 1989, pp. 155–68.

See *Encyclopaedia of Islam* (new edition), E.J. Brill, Leiden (1960, in progress), under 'Leh' by Abrahamowicz, Z. pp. 719–23, and 'Lipka', under Abrahamowicz Z. and Reychman, J. pp. 765–767.

Finland

Nielsen, Jørgen. *Muslims in Western Europe*, The New Edinburgh Islamic Surveys, Edinburgh University Press, 2004, pp. 88 and 184–5.

Sweden

Otterbeck, Jonas. 'The Baltic Tatars – The First Muslim Group in Modern Sweden', *Cultural Encounters in East Central Europe*, eds Karin Junefelt and Martin Peterson, FRN Forskningsrådsnämnden, Uppsala, 1998, pp. 145–53.

Karaims

El-Kodsi, Mourad. *The Karaite Communities in Poland, Lithuania, Russia and Crimea*, Wilprint Inc, Lyons, New York, 1993.
Harviainen, Tapani. 'Karaims in Lithuania', *Tiltas*, Journal of the British Lithuanian Society, Vol 9. No. 1, February 2008, pp. 23–25.
Hirschfeld, Hartwig. *Judah Hallevi's Kitāb al-Khazarī*, London, 1931.
Nemoy, Leon. (ed.) *Kitāb al-Anwār wa'l-marāqib, Code of Karaite Law*, Alexander Kohut Memorial Foundation, New York, 1939.
Szyszman,. S. *Les Karaites d'Europe*, Uppsala and Stockholm, 1989.
Zajaczowski, A. *Karaims in Poland, History, Language, Folklore, Science*, Warsaw and La Haye, Paris, 1961.
Karaite Anthology, Excerpts from the Early Literature, New Haven, Yale University Press, London and Oxford, 1952.
Two articles on Karaism, by Leon Nemoy and A. Zajaczowski are to be read in *The Encyclopaedia of Islam*, 2nd edition, pp. 603–9.

Glossary

Bayram A term that is primarily used for both the two main feasts in the Muslim calendar, each called *Kurban. Bayram*, the 'great' feast of *'Īd al-Aḍhā*, during the pilgrimage month, and the 'little' feast of *'Īd al-Fiṭr*, at the end of the fast month of *Ramaḍān*. This term has long been in use amongst the Lithuanian Tatars. Gatherings to celebrate the feasts take place in Kaunas, Bohoniki, Nowogrudok, Gdańsk and elsewhere throughout the Tatar world. According to the *Fundamentals of Islam*, a work popular amongst Tatars in the United States, prepared by Niaz Maksoudoff and published by The American Mohammedan Society, 104 Powers St, Brooklyn (April 1947), page 19: 'There are two yearly "ID" prayers. One is called "IDFITR" which comes after the thirty day fasting in the month of Ramadan and falls on the first day of "Shawal". The other is "IDUZHA" which falls on the tenth day of Thulhija, during the time of pilgrimage to Mecca. On this occasion Moslems offer sacrifice by killing a sheep, cow or camel, according to their means. One–third of the meat is distributed to the poor and one-third to friends.'

Chamail (Polish Chamaiły) This word is also occasionally spelt 'Hamail'. It has become a major form of literature of the Lithuanian Tatars throughout Eastern Europe and in parts of Asia. *Chamail/ Hamail* is a plural form. It is derived from the Arabic word *ḥamīla/ ḥamā'il*, which, to quote Lane's *Lexicon*, Book One, London, 1863, page 650, meant a 'suspended thong (or cord, or shoulder belt) by which the wearer hangs it around his neck', namely, in this instance, a protective charm or amulet, although, amongst the Tatars, *Chamail* covers a far more extensive vocabulary, ranging from amulets to prophylactic formulae and 'pocket' books of prayer in the form of breviaries. Other *Chamails* are of some antiquity. They are of a large size and bound in book format. Some are even printed. They include the Muslim calendar, the interpretation of dreams, the explanation for unlucky days (*niechsiove*), and sundry magical recipes used in healing. Such prayers are called *nuski*. Pieces of paper are used to treat ailments of the eyes. Older *Chamails* are handwritten manuscripts, composed in a mixture of Arabic (invariably with quotations from the Qur'ān and entire *Sūras* thereof, which are used for prophylactic purposes). Byelorussian, Polish and a vocabulary of Turkic and Persian loan words abound. *Chamails* may be divided into two special categories:

a **Fawdjeyski** (see **Faw**, below). These are employed by *fawdjeys*, that is to say healers, fortune-tellers, rainmakers and others who are regarded as possessors of Shamanistic powers, men who are able to predict the future and cure the sick. They are especially concerned with problems of mental health, female infertility, the prediction of events and forecasts in regard to the weather.

b **Mollinski** (**Modlitwa**) which are used by *imāms* (see below). They contain detailed descriptions of religious ceremonies during public prayers and Muslim religious ceremonies during the course of the lunar calendar. Some have sermons (*khuṭbas*) and prayers for healing and for divine punishment. At one time, it was widely believed amongst the Muslim Tatars that such prayers had the power to kill, or to make the victim mad. Such punishment was brough about through the reading of a prayer, termed '*karshiinnaya duaya*'. This was usually said in a cemetery, amongst the graves, before the time of the noon prayer. If the prayer was recited in full, then either death, or insanity, would befall the victim. The recital of half would result in his unhappiness. For healing purposes, the prayers ('*odpievanie*', 'singing', or in Belarus, '*odkurenie*', 'smoking out') were usually recited over the patient. At the same time, such prayers were burnt and the fumes were inhaled. A popular healing technique was the employment of loose sheets with Arabic prayers written upon them (*nuski*).

Such *Chamails*, and similar charms, were used in order to restrain the Tatars from using magic themselves, without the sanction of the Muslim faith. The use of unlawful magic was believed to bring grave harm to the offspring of those who sinned in this way. *Chamail* of a high literary order have been studied by Andrzaj Drozd, the leading Polish expert, and published in articles in Poland. *Chamails* are also discussed, at some length, by G.M. Meredith-Owens and Alexander Nadson, in their 'The Byelorussian Tartars and their Writings',

The Journal of Byelorussian Studies, vol. 11, no. 1, year V, 1969 and vol. 11, no. 2, London, 1970, pp. 307–13. There is likewise an introduction to *Chamails*, their format, choice of language and manuscript format in, Andrzej Drozd, 'Chamail Sobolewskiego', in *Rocznik Tatarow Polskich*, Gdańsk, 1993, pp. 48–62 and in Piotr Borawski and Aleksander Dubinski, *Tatarzy Polscy Dzieje Obrzedy, Legendy, Tradycje*, Warsaw, 1986, pp. 248–54.

Cuman This name is commonly found in Greek and Latin sources for the Turkish people, or peoples, who are referred to, in Oriental and Russian sources, as Qipchāqs (Kipchaks) or as the Polovtsi. They formed the most westerly grouping of Turkic peoples and their borders extended from the Danube to the middle of Kazakhstan, as we know it today. The Cuman steppe is to be identified with the Dašt-i Qipchāq and part of the Crimea, although the precise relationship between Cuman and Qipchāq has yet to be clearly understood. The Cumans dominated the Crimean Peninsula from around AD 1030. The Cumans also played a major role in Russian and Hungarian medieval history. A Cuman warrior is portrayed in a Slovak church mural which was painted in AD 1370. For a general description of their identity and historical role, see *The Cambridge History of Early Inner Asia*, edited by Denis Sinor, Cambridge University Press. 1990, pp. 277–84 and also István Vásáry, *Cumans and Tatars, Oriental Military in the pre-Ottoman Balkans, 1185–1365*, Cambridge, 2005.

Dervish An Arabic and Persian term, denoting 'poor', or 'indigent' (*faqīr*) and is generally used to describe a Sufi ascetic. The life and status of the dervish, in Muslim society, is discussed in detail in Ahmet T. Karamustafa, *Gods Unruly Friends*, Salt Lake City, 1994. Stanislaw Kryczynski, in his authoritative study *Tatarzy Litewscy*, Warsaw 1938 and Gdańsk, 2000, p. 179, makes it clear that where this name is attached to Polish and Lithuanian Tatars, usually as '*Czelebi*' its meaning is understood as one who is devoted to 'contemplative mysticism', and it is not merely an honorific title. Where '*Czelebi*' is found associated with dervish (p. 180), the title indicates a writer, man of letters, poet, calligrapher, or scholar, and it not merely a formal term of respect

Dievas The Lithuanian word for the Deity and hence it is applied, in general, to a Supreme God. In pagan times '*dievaitis*' denoted 'a god' and '*dievaite*' denoted a 'goddess'. However, Stasys Samalavicius has pointed out, in his *An Outline of Lithuanian History*, Vilnius, 1995, pp. 17–19, that Dievas, indicating a supreme deity, may also have been known at that time. 'Some historians are of the opinion that although in pre-Christian times Lithuanians worshipped numerous gods, one of them was the eldest. He was considered to be the omnipotent master of the universe, ruling everything in heaven and on earth. He was at first called simply *Dievas*, with the meaning of 'God'. But, with time, different names came to be used to call the eldest heathen god. So, in one part of Lithuania, he was called *Praamzius*, in another *Prakurimas*, still in other regions the eldest god was known by the name of *Ukopirmas*. All the universe was in his power: the heaven, the air, water and land alike. All other gods as well as other living beings had to obey him'.

The concept of *Dievas* as a 'High God', whose identity underpinned the forms of the deity which manifested itself in 'paganism' in all of the Christian churches and sects, in Judaism in all its forms (both Rabbinical and Karaim) and in Islam, is one of the chief reasons for the amazing tolerance in the Lithuanian Dukedom. As Alfredas Bumblauskas has remarked (in *The Peoples of the Grand Duchy of Lithuania*, p. 40): 'In the context of the East–West dichotomy, Vilnius is a unique phenomenon as well. At one time it was the capital of the last pagan country in Europe, and the last city to be Christianised. It was the easternmost and outermost city of Central Europe and the Western world in general. More, it was the only European capital on the borderland of two civilisations, Latin and Byzantine. Indeed, in what other city do we find such Gothic and Baroque Orthodox churches? So, Vilnius is not only a city of Central Europe: it is also a centre of Eastern European culture. Besides, we should not forget the role Vilnius has played in Jewish culture. All this shows Vilnius as a place in which civilisations met and interacted and where ten different religions competed. It was a city of Roman Catholics, Eastern Orthodox Christians, Uniates, Old Believers, Lutherans, Calvinists, Antitrinitarians, Karaims, Muslims and Jews ... If so, then can we call Vilnius a "Jerusalem of the North" not only because of its exceptional role in Jewish culture, but also because there is no other place on earth where we can observe, up to the 20th century, such a diversity of denominations and ethnic groups living next to each other? Moreover, Vilnius is not a mosaic of civilisations, but a creative amalgam of them.'

The god *Dievas* has resurfaced in the neo-paganism which is active in the Baltic states, for example the Dievturiba, in Latvia, 'the keepers of the god Dievs'. Neo-paganism is most active in Lithuania. It has most followers in that country as well as

186 Islam in the Baltic

amongst Lithuanians in Canada and in the United States and it has a number of Internet websites. Called the Romuva movement, it derives its name from a pagan site called Chernahovsk (in Russian Kaliningrad Oblast) where there was once a major pagan temple which attracted worshippers amongst the ancient Prussians, Latvians and Lithuanians. This movement was founded in 1967. In 1971 it was banned by the Soviet regime and it was revived by the 'Society for Ethnic Lithuanian Culture' in 1988. Both Dievturiba and Romuva are closely connected as part of the 'pan neo-pagan' Baltic movement. *Dievs/Dievas* indicates 'serenity' and the aims of these movements is self-knowledge and awareness of the division of the universe into the living, the dead and the 'Divine Heights'. The holy oak symbolises the movement and the old pagan deities of *Dievas*, Mother goddess, Laima and Zcmyna are central to the faith, at least symbolically. These neo-pagan Baltic religious movements have incorporated many ideas from the New Age cults and show toleration for other faiths in the modern world. Each seeks to cooperate with them. Poland also has a pagan revival although there the 'gods', and their attributes, are derived from the ancient pagan Slav religions.

Fātiḥa The first *Sūra*, in the Qur'ān, *al-Fātiḥa*. It is recited on countless occasions by the Tatars. In early manuscripts of *Chamail* and *Kitābs* it is invariably written in Arabic, fully vocalised, or at least in Arabic script, despite numerous spelling mistakes. Comments and Commentaries in Byelorussian abound.

Examples of finely written Tatar Qu'rāns which date back to the seventeenth and the eighteenth centures are rare, however. Amongst the oldest texts, a commentary (*tefsīr*) in the Byelorussian language is preserved in the British Library in London. Dr Andrzej Drozd has described this manuscript and has assessed its value both as a written text and in translation in two articles, first in 'Rekopisy tatarskie w zbiorach londynskich', *Roznik Tatarow Polskich*, T. II, 1994, and, second, in his article 'Starpolski przeklad Koranu', *Swiat Islamu*, no 1 March–April, 1995, pp. 4–5.

In modern times, a variety of transcribed forms of the sacred text are to be found in publications and on epitaphs. Most make little attempt at a close transcription of the written text, but rather follow the common forms of the pronunciation of the Scriptures (*tadjwidy*), (see below) in mosques in Poland, Lithuania and Belarus. The following example is taken from a prayer book (*Kitāb-us-Ṣalāt*), a *Modlitewnik*, prepared by the *Imam* of Kruszyniany, Mustafa Stefan

Jasinski, typed and bound for sale and distribution in Bialystok, in 1986, page 78:

Bismillahir-rahmanir-rehim Elhamdu lillahi rebbil-aleminer rehminer-rehim, maliki jaw'middin ijjakie nau'budu wa ijjakie nesteyin.ihdynes-syratal-mustekimie syratal-mustekimi. Syratal-lazine en-amte alejhim gajril-megdubinalejhim we led-dalin. Amin.

A rather different text is to be found in the cemetery of the mosque of Nemėžis, in Lithuania. This is inscribed upon the gravestone of Merjemy and Jakuba Jakubowskich, who died in 1979 and 1996, respectively. The inscription also contains *Sūrat al-Ikhlāṣ*. Andrzej Drozd, Marek Dziekan and Tadeusz Majda, in *Meczety, Cmentarze Tatarów Polsko-Litewskich*, Warsaw, 1999, have published the following text, on page 43:

Bismillahi rechmani rachymi Elcham dulilahi rebilaleminie Erachmani rachymi, Maliki jeumidini ijakie nubudu wieijakie Niescieyin ihdyniessyratel mustiekymie
Syratel lezinie enamte elejhim gajryl miegdubi elejhim wieladalinie.

Other written copies of the Qur'ān, without a *tefsīr*, date back to the seventeenth and eighteenth centuries among the Lithuanian and Polish Tatars. An earlier date than this, though probable, has far less evidence to indicate its format and its distribution. The Muftiate in Vilnius is now in the process of translating the Qur'ān into Lithuanian for the first time. In Rīga, the poet, Uldis Bērziņš is currently translating the Qur'ān into Latvian for the first time.

Faw Fortune-telling amongst the Lithuanian Tatars. The word is derived from the Arabic, '*fa'l*', denoting an auspicious omen. Amongst the Tatars, fortune-telling was based on the belief that every letter of the Arabic alphabet was given a specific numerical value and that several letters had correspondents in the widely believed and consulted astrological tables. They also corresponded to Cabbalistic borrowings from *Ḥurūfism* (see *Ḥurūfī*, below) and other Middle Eastern systems. The Arabic alphabet consists of twenty-eight letters. Each letter had a consecutive number ascribed to it. The derived number which was the sum of the numerical value of the numbers provided a basis for foretelling the future. If the sum total exceeded twenty-eight, then twelve was subtracted. The resultant figure indicated a planet and its constellation and from these the future might be foretold and predicted. Seven planets were to be found in the astrological tables. Each day of the week was assigned to a planet. In certain tables twelve planets were mentioned. To each of them one month was assigned. Two spirits goverened each planet. One of these was an evil spirit, called '*fiereys*', the other, which was good and helpful to man was called '*spornik*'. Dualist elements were undoubtedly present in these beliefs. The '*fawdjeys*', the fortune-tellers, were also healers and rainmakers. '*Fawdjey*' is derived from the Arabic *fa'ala* and *fa'l* and *dji* is a Byelorussian version of the Turkish suffix-'*dji*'. On the arts of the '*fawdjeys*', see the entry on *Chamail* (above).

Ḥurūfī 'Ḥurūfism' expresses a distinct and eclectic view of man's place in the universe. Its philosophy, theology and Cabbalisim draw upon both Sufi and Ismāʻīlī sources, as formulated by the 'man-god' Fadlallāh al-Astārābādī (martyred in AH 796/AD 1394, by the order of Tīmur's son, Mīranshāh). Unlike Turkey and some Balkans lands where 'Alawi, heterodox, Bektashi and Baba'i communities are to be found, the Tatars of Lehistan (like those in Russia) have eschewed the gnostic teachings of Fadlallāh and his disciple, Nasīmī. However, it is arguable, that some aspects of popular Ḥurūfism Cabbalism may have been absorbed into Tatar Islam in Belarus, Lithuania and Poland. These are:

a   Numerology and symbolism. This is to be found occasionally, for example, in Tatar Qur'āns, and in their commentaries.
b   Magical symbols. These are depicted in manuscripts and in objects of ritual.

A 'communion' of bread, water and salt (possibly borrowed from the Bektashis, who were the heirs of *Ḥurūfism* in Ottoman times). These appear are placed on the table when celebrations are held for the newly born, at weddings, prayer meetings in house groups and prayers said following a decease. Selim Chazbiewicz advocates this opinion. On the other hand, an offering of bread and salt is very common in Orthodox communities in Slav countries. For example, the wife of the Orthodox priest of a village near Kyiv, offered a party, to which the author belonged, both bread and salt as an offering of friendship at the door of the Orthodox Church. Greater research on its origins is needed.

The strict Orthodoxy of Tatar Islam, in Europe, has constantly opposed such heterodoxy and such 'heretical' influences akin to *Ḥurūfism*, Cabbalism may have come to them through Catholicism and Orthodoxy. Cabbalism is known to have existed amongst the Jewish communities in Poland and Lithuania and Belarus. Cabbalism is alien to the Karaims.

Imām The leader in prayer in mosque worship and the building's custodian. This has been the practice amongst the Lithuanian Tatars since the earliest records were kept. *Imāms* were the leaders of the Tatar communes, known as *djemat*, and they chaired their regular meetings. They were themselves elected by the *djemats*. Piotr Borawski (*Journal of the Institute of Muslim Minority Affairs*, 9(1), January 1988, p. 128) has quoted the record of the electing of the *imām* of Lowczyce (Belarus), in 1783: 'We, standard-keepers collators and the whole *Djemat* (*sic*) of Lowczyce land of the Novogrod Voivodship as signed below, announce to all and sundry that, together with the entire *Djemat*, we unanimously elect Achmet Assowicz to be our present *imām* and, in accordance with our faith, we oblige him to fulfil all his duties before the *Djemat*, just as we are obliged to fulfil our duties towards him, to pay the fees and duties of endowment (*vakuf*) as was the case in the days of our ancestors. We place those sums at his disposal, however, as imām, he should remember well that it is his duty to take care of the same and in no way to decrease the value thereof. Written on the 4th of June, in Lowczyce, Major of the Polish Crown army, the Tatar standard-keeper of the Novogrod Voivodship Alexander Ulan.'

The ideal Tatar *imām* is admirably revealed in a paragraph in the *Kitāb* which is in the British Library. It has been translated by Dr Shirin Akiner and published in her 'Oriental Borrowings in the language of the Byelorussian Tatars', *Slavonic and East European Review,* vol. 56, 1978, p. 41):

When in a village or a town there should be two learned men, both suitable for the office of imam, then the one who is more learned should be imam, and when they are equal in learning the one who is more God fearing, who prays, he should be imam; and if they are equal in that too, then the one who is older, he should be imam; and if they are equal in years, he who is of a better family should be imam; and if they are equal in that, then the one who is better in looks and bearing and behaviour, he should be imam; and if they are equal in that, then the one the congregation desires, he should be imam; only a slave or serf or a blind man or a bastard or a scoundrel, who is lacking learning will think out and say new things and who will go strutting about and those who have their ears pierced for earrings and who shave their beards, all such people are not suitable for the office of imam, and whoever is imam, he should be capable of explaining the Traditions of the Prophet and be able to recite the Koran properly and know all the motions of the prayer ritual, so that if he should be asked about the prayer he would answer immediately and whoever takes care to avoid great sins and prays five times a day.

In several mosques, the wife of the *imām* leads the prayer of the womenfolk. They occupy a balcony, or a side room, which is reserved for womenfolk and which has a window looking into the prayer hall of the mosque. However, the *imām* has many other pastoral duties in Poland and in Lithuania. He will lead house meetings, where the Qur'ān is read, prayers said and hymns sung (*ilahis* and *zikers*). Tatar *imāms* are strictly orthodox Hanafis and are strongly opposed to the 'heretical' (in their view) Ahmadiyya sect, which has a following in Poland. In past times, many *imāms* who were proficient in Arabic came from the Crimea and from other Ottoman domains and, at a later date, *imāms* from Poland were trained in Sarajevo and in Istanbul. Others went to Russia, Kazan in particular, to Central Asia and to parts of the Arab World, especially Cairo, Damascus, Mecca and Medina and to Morocco. In recent years, *imāms* from Bosnia and from the Arab Middle East, and even Chechens, have made a contribution to the instruction of Muslims, whether Tatar, or non-Tatar, in Poland. Because of diplomatic connections it has been easier for Tatar *imāms* in Lithuania to be trained in Istanbul. *Imāms*, as well as *hodjis* have played an important role in teaching Tatar children the Qur'ān up to the age of seven after which a celebration is held and a copy of the Qur'ān tied to the child's head. This ceremony is known as *lahi*. Circumcision ceremonies (*sunniet*) also took place at the age of seven and *imams* play a leading part in the burial of believers in cemeteries (*mizars*) (see below) and at weddings where, by tradition, the couple who are to be married, stand upon a thick felt rug (symbolic of wealth and fertility) before the *imām*, who leads the ritual and ceremonies. The preaching of sermons is a part of his duties. It is said that this wedding custom, like many others, harks back to the age of the Golden Horde. An *imām* was obliged to act as a registrar and to keep books of births, marriages and deaths. The earliest of such records dates from 1556.

The legal status of *imāms* was on a level with the average Tatar landowner. They also served as military chaplains. In 1792, soldiers in Tatar regiments swore on the *Qur'ān* to their *imāms* that they would defend the king, the homeland and the constitution. The *imām*'s signature was conspicuous on every document written by the Tatars between the sixteenth and eighteenth centuries. Dervish Czelebi was appointed *Kaji*, the highest religious authority in the Lithuanian Duchy in 1586. At the same time he was the *imām* of Dowbuciszki.

Gifted *imāms* lead the singing of *tekbirs* and *zikers*. These prayers and invocations are set to melodies which are unique in the entire World of Islam. Some of the melodies, which are still heard today, were originally melodies which were sung in the Dašht-i Qipchāq. Minarets are not used for the call to prayer in the traditional Lithuanian wooden mosques. The high minaret in the mosque in Gdańsk is a very recent structure, so is that of the Kaunas mosque and the former mosque in Minsk. The earlier minaret in Iwye in Belarus is ornamental. The entire mosque service, including the call to prayer, is said and sung within the chapel mosque in which candles were lit although some *imams* today frown on this practice

In his *Talfīq al-Akhbār*, Muhammad Murād Ramzī lists eminent scholars and trainee *imāms* of humble origin who travelled frequently from Russia to Central Asia, to the Caucasus and to the Middle East in order to further their education and training. Many of these novices came from a humble background and were not from Tatarstan and the region of Kazan. Many of them returned as *Qāḍis* and they founded *madrasas* in poorly served localities. Subjects such as *Qur'ān* reading and recitation (*tajwīd*), jurisprudence (*fiqh*) and poetry (*shi'r*) were taught. A number of the *imāms* were themselves poets. They had mastered figurative speech, metaphor and trope (*majāz*), double-hemistiched verse (*mathnawī*) and Sufi liturgical practices which were held in assemblies (*samā'*). There were also centres for *imāms* in Russia itself, including Astrakhan and Aq-Kirman, near Odessa, which was a location especially sought by *imāms* from Belarus, Lithuania and Poland. Others came from Ufa and from Siberia. *Imāms* were also trained in *madrasas*. For example, five of these were in Orenburg, two were in Ufa, two in Kargaly and others in the Crimea and the Caucasus. Three were in Kazan.

Karaims (or **Karaite(s)**)   The Karaims, share a tradition with the Tatars that they were brought by Vytautas the Great from the Crimea to Lithuania. They arrived, as captives of war and as privileged settlers of the future, during the eventful years of 1397 and 1398, though Simon Szyszman, a highly respected authority on Karaim communities in Europe and the Levant, was of the opinion that at least a few of them may have been present in the Duchy some while before those historical dates. As is the case amongst the Tatars, Vytautas Magnus is regarded as the 'father figure' of the community and his portrait may be seen in a prominent place in the house of almost every Karaite family. However, other important figures in Lithuanian history were responsible for their privileges. In 1441, Kazimieras Jogailaitis the Grand Duke, granted the Magdeburg Law to the Trakai Karaims. This guaranteed self-government for their community which they were to enjoy until the end of the eighteenth century. Their community was headed by the '*vaitas*' that embodied powers both legal and administrative and was subject directly to the Grand Duke. After 1850, they became subject to the religious board of the Crimean Karaims which had been established as early as 1837. In 1863, following an order issued by the Tsar, they were made equal to the local residents of the Russian Empire.

According to Jurgita Siauciunaite-Verbickiene, the name of Karaim, referring to a religion, appears for the first time in the documents of the Grand Duchy in 1506. It is to be found in a petition to the Grand Duke by 'all the Jews of Łutsk, both Rabbinical and Karaims', thus leaving the question of identity as one to be answered in the centuries which were to follow. Since that time, Trakai became the Karaite 'capital', though Čufut-Kalé, in the Crimea, holds the key to their earliest history. This holy location contains the ancient Karaite cemetery of ' Balti Tiimez'. A pilgrimage takes place there. It brings Karaims together from the whole world to 'Balti Tiimez', the site where Karaite princely heroes Uzun, Kirk, Alani and other heroes defended Kirk Er (*Čufut Kalé*).

The small community of Karaims, in Lithuania, means that their physical survival, as well as linguistic survival, is a grave national concern. Spouses of differing nationalities reveal the following statistics: Lithuanian, 52 per cent, Polish 5 per cent, Russian 35 per cent and Ukrainian 5 per cent. Others account for 3 per cent. Following a questionnaire, 'Which faith do you practise?', 86 per cent of Lithuanian Karaims declared that they believed in their faith, 13 per cent were non-believers and about 1 per cent practised other faiths. Some 44 per cent of married, divorced widows and widowers indicated that they had been married by a priest.

In 1989 the number of Tatars in Lithuania was 5,135; during the new independence, however, approximately 2,000 Tatars have left their native country as part of the recent migration of peoples to the West.

Kenesa (variant, **kenessa** and **kieniesa**, in Lithuanian **kinese**, Arabic **kanīs(a)**) This is the term which appears in Arabic documents which relate to the former *kenesa* in Damascus which was later sold to the Melkite Catholics, for their use as a church. 'Synagogue', 'temple', or 'church' have been used to describe the house of prayer wherein the Karaims hold their weekly services. Once, *keneses* could be found widely distributed in many areas of Eastern Europe, including Russia, where Karaite communities of varied size existed. Other *kenesas* were to be found, and to this day exist, in major cities of the Middle East, such as Cairo, Jerusalem (in the Old City) and in Damascus, and in other parts of the Ottoman Empire. According to Professor Seraja Szapszal, the *kenesa* in Istanbul was located in the vicinity of Ainaly Kavak Zadesi, in Chaskoi on the Golden Horn. Karaite religious structures and cemeteries were also conspicuous in the Crimean peninsula, where, before the Second World War, the majority of the Karaims in the Soviet Union were concentrated, but especially in Feodosiya, Yevpatoriya, Bakhshiserai (*Čufut-Kalé*) and Staryi Krym (*Solkha*t)(to quote Tapani Harviainen, University of Helsinki). There are two active *kenesas* in Lithuania. That in Vilnius is an 'Oriental type' structure in a style not dissimilar to that of the former mosque in Minsk. It was consecrated in 1923. The Trakai *kenesa* is a historical and a national monument. According to the authority Michael Zajaczkowski the existing *kenesa*, in Trakai, was rebuilt during the sixteenth, eighteenth and nineteenth centuries, although it stands on the site of a fifteenth-century building. It was reconstructed in 1911, although work on it was disrupted during the First World War. The *kenesas* in Birzai, Naujamiestis and Panevezys were built in the seventeeth and eighteenth centuries.

According to Ananiasz Zajaczkowski, the first Karaite prayer books, which are to be found in varied editions in the *kenesas*, were printed in Venice in the middle of the sixteenth century. Collective prayer, which takes place in the *kenesa*, under the direction of a celebrator, is joined by the choir, by the whole 'commune', by the *djimat* (the same term as is used by the Muslim Tatars, in Arabic, *jamā'a*). The House of God is entered in reverence, women covering their heads, as is the case in Tatar mosques. The prayer is said slowly and with intention (*niyet/nijjet*). This latter word is also of great importance to the Muslim Tatars as well (see below). When praying, the Karaites turn their faces in the direction of Jerusalem. Hence, the altar of the *kenesa* is turned in a manner akin to the southward orientation of the *qibla*, which faces Mecca in the Muslim faith. The whole question of the *qibla* and its importance is discussed by the tenth-century Karaite scholar, al-Qarqasānī, in his major Arabic work, *The Book of Lights and Watch Towers* (*Kitāb al-Anwār wa'l-Marāqib*), Chapter 18.

There was also a Tatar community in Trakai at one time. Its mosque was destroyed but the community has left its name in the town. The lake which divides the Karaite town from the Island Castle, the residence of the Grand Dukes, is called Lake Totoriskiu. The Trakai *kenesa* must be seen as part of a whole district still occupied by Karaite families. According to Gabrielius Alijunas ('the people from the peninsula', *Lithuania in the World*, no 4, 1997, Vilnius, p. 12):

Karaimu Street winds along the length of the town, which is squeezed between lakes Galve and Totoriskes. The name of the street is no coincidence. Historic ties have linked Lithuania and Karaims for 600 years, and Trakai has always been the Karaims' administrative and religious centre.'

Not only the name of the street retains the memory of Karaims in Trakai. The eye is drawn by their houses (with three windows overlooking the street, and consisting of four parts: a porch, kitchen, female and male sections), by the house of prayer, the *kenesa*, and by the exhibition of artefacts in the museum of the castle. [Trakai now has its own Karaite museum in the town where valuable religious objects are displayed.]

Khaqan (also **Hakhan** and **Hakham**)   The supreme spiritual head of the Karaites whose scholarly credentials were viewed with greatest regard by his community. He was perceived as one who corresponded in status and authority with the *Muftī*, in al-Islām, one who has the authority to issue a formal legal opinion to a question submitted to him by a judge or by a private individual. The office of *Khaqan* was re-established in Lithuania in 1936.

Kitāb. Within Tatar literature the comprehensive written expression of Islamic thought amongst the Tatars. The *Kitāb* attained the peak of its artistic, reflective and individual expression between the seventeenth and early nineteenth centuries. These, often substantial manuscript works, are to be found in libraries and museums and in private collections, in Russia, Poland, Lithuania, Belarus, the United Kingdom and elsewhere, where collections of Tatar manuscripts have been stored. *Kitābs* have been extensively studied by Drs Shirin Akiner, Andrzej Drozd, Marek Dziekan, Alexander Dubinski, Professor Czelaw Łapicz, Dr G.M. Meredith-Owens and Rev. Alexander Nadson (the Frances Skaryna, Byelorussian Library in Woodside Park, London), and by other scholars and Orientalists, particularly by those who are specialists in the evolution and dialectical forms of the Tatar language and its interrelationship with other languages in Eastern Europe and in Central Asia. The *Kitābs* themselves embrace commandments given to the Muslim Tatars in respect to their daily lives as Muslims, in non-Muslim societies, and the precepts which they should abide by in their lives. There are explanations for religious ceremonies throughout the lunar calendar and the seasonal rituals. Many folios are concerned with the history of the Biblical prophets, together with genealogies and diagrams which indicate their relationship, one patriarch with the other. The *Kitābs* offer a valuable insight into past dialogue between Islam and Christianity, in all its forms, when the two faiths were in constant daily contact. The biography (*Sīra*) of the Prophet figures centrally in the content, likewise the popular narratives (*qiṣaṣ*) in regard to Biblical and Qur'ānic personalities. There are citations from apocryphal works, stories about certain Sufis and their wisdom, parables, legends, satirical poems and magical and Cabbalistic formulae. The texts in the *Kitābs* are composed in various languages, in Byelorussian, Polish, Russian and in Arabic and Turkish. Tatar palaeography and adaptation of the Arabic alphabet is to be found throughout these works.

Jurgita Šiaučiūnaité-Verbickiené, in her chapter 'The Tatars' (in *The Peoples of the Grand Duchy of Lithuania*, Vilnius, 2002, p. 80), comments upon the prevalence of Christian, particularly Biblical, motives in *Kitābs* . On the basis of most recent research, she notes that the most cited Bible translation is that of the Antitrinitarian, Szymon Budny (1572) and that it was through this translation that the Tatars were able to dispute in their writings, so did the Karaim, Isaac of Trakai, in his Consolidation of Faith.

A comprehensive description of the content of the *Kitāb* which is held by the British Museum (OR. 13, 020) is to be read in G.M. Meredith-Owens and Alexander Nadson's 'The Byelorussian Tatars and their Writings', *The Journal of Byelorussian Studies*, vol. II., no 1, Year V, London, 1969.

Two recent studies, in Polish, on the content of *Kitābs*, particularly the Jewish and Christian content which is derived from the Bible, from legendary and hagiographical material, hagiographical sources and from Muslim 'Tales of the Prophets', *Qiṣaṣ al-Anbiyā'* are to be read in Cz. Łapicz, 'Trzy redakeje jezykowe muzulmanskiej legendy w pismiennictwie Tatarów litewsko-polskich, tamze', *Acto Baltico-Slavica*, t.XX, 1991 pp. 155–68, and 'Zwartosc tresciowa kitabu Tatarów litewsko-polskich, ibid., pp. 169–91.

Leh/Lehistan   The Ottoman name for Poland and the Poles (*Lech*). The term, *Leh vilayeti* and the Polish language, *Lehlu*, were also to be found, likewise *Lehistan* and the Polish people, *Ahl-i Lehistan*. In the sixteenth century, the Crimean Tatars, who have always had a close relationship with the Lithuanian Tatars, used the expressions, *Lakh* and *Koral*, 'the kingdom'.

Lipqa and **Libqa**   This was a specific name once given to the Lithuanian and Polish Tatars and it was the old Crimean Tatar name for the Lithuanians until the nineteenth century. On the issue of Tatar nomenclature, Professor Tamara Bairašauskaité has, in her *Lietuvos Totoriai X1X amziuje'*, Vilnius, 1996, pp. 13–4, made the following observations:

The term Lithuanian Tatars is still a debatable issue in the historiography. Many authors have doubt as to the historical, scientific and professional preciseness of this term. In J. Sobczak's opinion the inaccuracy appeared while using the synonyms based on the geographical factor: Lithuanian Tatars, Polish Tatars, Polish and Lithuanian Tatars. He also rejects the definition of Muslims, or Lipka. The researcher reminds that the forms used in the historical sources of the fifteenth–eighteenth centuries were: the Tatars of GDL, Sovereign's Tatars, the Tatars of Radziwill, Tatars-Cossacks, Tatars landowners etc. Therefore, he recommends that one strictly follow the language of historical sources of each period.

The supporters of the modern use of the term do not deny the principle of historicity and recognize the validity of the term Lithuanian Tatars when applied to the 19th century, i.e., the period when this term came into an official use, seeking to distinguish between the Tatars inhabiting the territories annexed to Russia and the ones living in the Crimea, Kazan, Siberia and other parts of the empire. This is the term used in the scientific literature and state documents. However, sometimes we encounter the terms the 'Tatars of the Western land' or the 'Tatars of the Western provinces'. Nevertheless, some historians disagree that the term Lithuanian Tatars may be used, referring to the history of modern times. The authors who prefer the terms Polish Tatars or Polish and Lithuanian Tatars (Polish–Lithuanian Commonwealth Tatars) motivate their choice by the necessity to take into consideration the assimilation of Tatars in either nation (or state). In the opinion of S. Chazbijewicz and A. Miskiewicz we cannot speak about the Lithuanian character of Tatars in the inter-war period when most of them yielded to the influence of Polish culture. They recognize the term Lithuanian Tatars only in relation to those Tatars who live in the ethnographic Lithuania. Similar ideas are shared by S. Dumin and I. Kanapackij who divided the modern Tatars into 'national groups'. From the point of view of language, culture and genealogical traditions they are attributed to Slavs (Belarusians, Poles), of territory and state – to Belarusian Tatars – both in the Middle Ages and in modern times.

As far back as 1833, M. Kazimirski and M. Amedé Jaubert made the following comment in regard to the 'Lithuanian Tatars' in 'Précis de l'histoire des Khans de Crimée, depuis l'an 880 jusqu'à l'an 1198 de l'hègire, *Journal Asiatique*, vol. X11, pp. 357–8:

We believe it necessary to add, here, a few details about the Tatar families, established in Poland, in the Lithuanian provinces, at the beginning of the 15th century. At the end of the 14th century, Witold, the grand Duke of Lithuania, resisted the invasions of the Tatar hordes which had surrendered to the sceptre of Tamerlaine and he fought them, often with great success and he transported the prisoners of war into Lithuania. The number of these Tatars subsequently increased in number through frequent emigrations of several families who left their homes, torched due to discord and by civil warfare. Once they were established in Lithuania, they enjoyed equal rights there as the local peoples did and they were admitted to have political rights by virtue of letters recognizing noble status which was accorded to several amongst them. Soon, in 1410, one saw them in the ranks of the Polish army in the bloody battle that was fought against the Teutonic Knights, at Grunewald. These Tatar families have preserved their customs and their religion right up to our days, though the text of the Qur'ān not being as familiar to them as was formerly the case, has been explained by them, and they have added commentaries, employing the Polish language.

The authors then quote a passage in Ottoman Turkish which not only explains this but also why the Lithuanians respected them more than other 'infidels'.

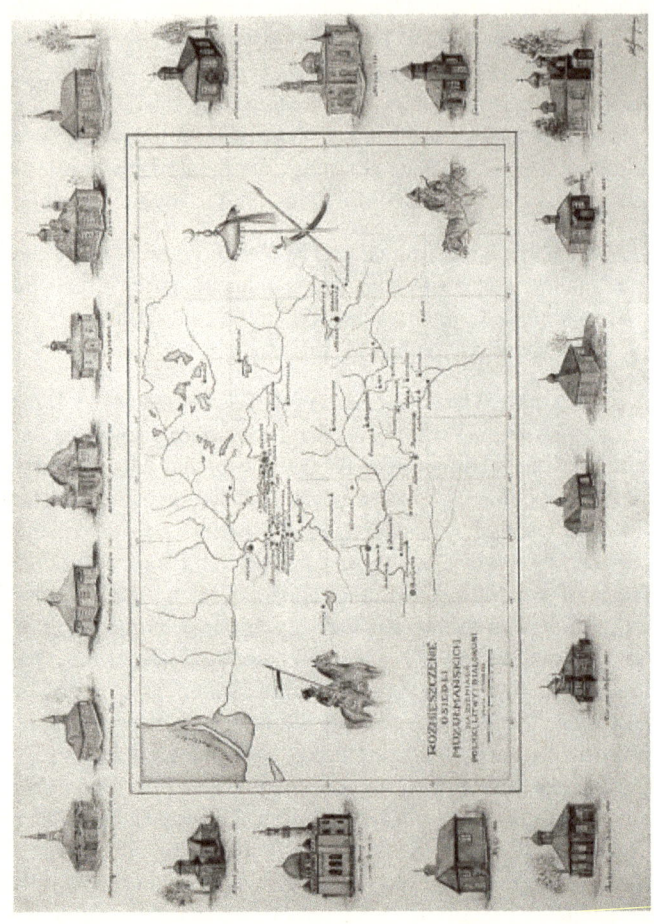

Figure 6 A reproduced map that is to be found in the Tatar collection in the Białystok Museum. It shows the distribution of Muslim settlements in the region in the early twentieth century as well as the wooden mosques and major non-wooden mosques that were located there. It was drawn by Ali Smajkiewicz of Gdańsk about 1960. Many of these mosques have been destroyed.

The toleration which was shown to the Tatars and their freedom to worship and to teach their faith to their offspring incurred the displeasure of the Vatican and spurred the missionary duty which was felt by the Catholic church, despite the centuries-old toleration of the rulers of Lithuania and Poland. According to the *Relationes Status Dioecesium in Magno Ducata Lituaniae (1. Dioceses Vilnensis et Samogitiae, Fontes Historiae Lituaniae, 1, Rome 1971*, edited by Paulus Rabikauskas, S.I., pp. 264–5:

Nec minus aemuli post conversionem et unionem factam anno Domini cercitur 1413 cum regno Poloniae, a temporibus Ladislai 1 Iagellonis, magni ducis Lituaniae et Regis Poloniae, regum qui nunc sunt progenitoris, religiosissimi, in religionae, pietate, aedificiis, templorum erectionibus, academiarum fundationibus, religiosorum hospitalium, collegiorum; in omnibus par regno Poloniae, nisi quod superstitionibus adhuc scateat et captives turmis tartarorum duce Vitoldo in Lituaniam abactis,quibus libertas ritus ethnici Machometani conceditur, ethnicorum secta et haeresi varia permixta, non nihil religionis integritatem et puritatem deformat. Nec solum licentia credenti vaga permissa, sed etiam multis in locis iuxta Alcoranum Moschee tartaris sythico ritu coluntur, passim habitantibus cum christianis bello Moschovitico captis, ex quibis prognatos filios et filias in secta Machometica, episcopis id dissimulantibus, exercent non sine magna iactura et detrimento salutis animarum.

Meczet (Polish), **Mecete** (Lithuanian) The common name applied to Tatar 'parish' mosques. These are constructed in wood, corrugated iron, or in stone and plaster. Apart from the surviving mosque in Kaunas and the recently built and architecturally splendid mosque in Gdańsk in Poland, most of these surviving mosques, and almost all of those which have vanished, could be described as 'chapels', that is, in the sense of the 'chapels', 'temples' or 'Bethesdas' of early Nonconformists in rural Britain. They are frequently isolated in remote villages in the Podlasie region of Poland east of Białystok, around Vilnius, in Lithuania, and in Belarus, usually at no great distance from graveyards and cemeteries (*mizars*, see below). The list of mosques published here is representative. It is far from complete – vanished mosques and cemeteries are unmentioned; however, it is hoped that this short list will furnish a cross-section of most of the best buildings of varied date, style and function. It is hoped that they will convey the character of these religious houses of prayer.

a **Bohoniki**. This mosque, in Poland, is located at a distance of 50kms from Białystok. It is close to the Belarus border and is amongst the most frequently photographed of Tatar mosques. It is a wooden structure, square in shape, with a stumpy false 'minaret' in the centre. An original structure dates from the seventeenth and early eighteenth centuries, and Stanislaw Kryczynski dates its foundation as a little earlier than 1795. However, it has been reconstructed, renovated and restored recently and it has lost almost all the attractive trees which once surrounded it. It has retained the design of an eighteenth-century mosque on its original site. Its cemetery is the largest Muslim cemetery in Poland. The oldest grave is that of Ismail Kardasz, dating from 1868. Its gravestones date from various periods, many of them hidden amongst the ancient trees and the thick covering of bushes.

b **Iwie/Ïvye/İvye**. This is a unique wooden mosque in Belarus. It possesses a traditional pointed minaret, with a balcony, which rises to some height above the roof of the mosque itself. It is the closest approach to the style of an 'Ottoman minaret' in any surviving Tatar wooden mosque. Iwie was once a Tatar colony. Its foundation dates back to the sixteenth century, if not earlier. The existing structure dates from the eighteenth and nineteenth centuries. It possesses an attractive pulpit (*minbar*) dating from 1884. Few graves with inscriptions survive. Those that do are noteworthy for their transcribed passages from the Arabic text of the *Qur'ān*.

c **(Kaunas (Kowno))**. This is the sole surviving mosque in Lithuania with a minaret of any height. It is a solid brick structure and is located in Rambyes Parkas, in the heart of the city. It is a twentieth-century structure, seemingly dating from 1933, and replacing an eighteenth-century wooden mosque. In style in reminds one of the 'Mamlūk type' mosques which are to be seen in Cairo, and it also bears a superficial resemblance to the destroyed mosque which was formerly in Minsk, the capital of Belarus, though photographs of the latter reveal a closer architectural kinship with the surviving Karaim *kenesa* in Vilnius. Some of the larger mosques in the Crimea are not dissimilar. After years of use for other purposes, the restoration of the mosque in Kaunas began, in 1989. It was inaugurated in June 1991, at a ceremony attended by the Lithuanian vice-president and by Muslim guests from Russia, Belarus, Poland, Estonia, Romania, Turkey, Jordan and the United Kingdom. However, its present-day pleasing appearance is largely due to the dedication of Professor Jonas Ridzvanavicius, a teacher in Kaunas University and a patron of Tatar enterprises. These have included the restoration of *Raiziai* mosque (*Rejze*, see below).

d **Keturiasdešimt (40 Totoriçe kaimas)**. In Lithuania this is one of the most historic sites of Tatar settlement. Tatars form about a quarter of its existing inhabitants. The roads and properties are laid out on the lines of a Tatar military encampment. Its history dates back to the fourteenth century and the earliest Tatar settlement by Vytautas. The original mosque on the site was built no later than 1558. After a grievous fire, it was reconstructed in 1901. It has been reconstructed on the lines of its original plan. The cemetery contains one of the oldest Tatar graves, that of a certain Allahberdi, dating from 1626, or possibly from 1621.

e **Kruszyniany**. This is situated 54 kilometers from Białystok and 10 kilometers to the south of Krynki, in Poland. In almost every respect this is the most important ancient Tatar mosque in Poland. Situated not far from Bohiniki, it is remarkably intact and it structurally dates from the late seventeenth and eighteenth centuries. A possible date for its foundation is the year 1679. Besides having a tiny central 'minaret', its western entry possesses a porch and a pair of elegant wooden towers at each corner. The entire structure is painted a light green in colour. The interior is sub-divided into a part for male worshippers and another for their womenfolk. '*Muhir(a)s*', ornamental Arabic inscriptions, chiefly passages from the *Qur'ān*, are hung on its wooden walls within. On occasions, designs which may have once been used for divining horoscopes were also kept there. As at Bohoniki, a stone outside the mosque bears an inscription which commemorates the first Tatar settlement. The garden area outside the mosque is the place where worshippers gather to celebrate Bajram-Ramaḍan and 'The Holiday of the Sacrifice' Kurban-Bajram. During this religious celebration, the faithful gather in front of the mosque, the *imām* prays, and rams and bulls are ritually slaughtered, and this is also the case in Bohoniki. The oldest grave in the nearby cemetery, on a rise above the mosque surrounded by trees, dates from the year 1790, though it has been reported that another grave dates from 1704. Tatar families from all over Poland visit the graves in large numbers during Bajram. It is not unknown for the deceased to be brought by road from western Poland in order to be buried here. The adjacent village contains many old wooden houses and farm buildings some of which date back to the nineteenth century. Its ancient street plan is retained. The Tatars are now very few in the village and the present villagers are mostly of Polish and Belarusian origin.

f **Nemėžis (Niemież)**. In Lithuania, this is almost a suburb of Vilnius. There may have been a mosque here since the fifteenth century, although Stanislaw Kryczynski has suggests the year 1684. The existing mosque is a recent structure with a substantial bulbous 'minaret' placed above and behind the porch at its west end. The oldest tomb in its adjacent cemetery is that of Anastazja Suleymanowicz, dating from 1861.

g **Nowogrodek/Novogrudok (Yenişehir)**. An important town, now in Belarus, which was once the first capital of the Duchy of Lithuania. Probably the most 'classical' design of wooden Tatar mosques in Belarus, it is sited in a locality which received a specific mention in the sixteenth century, in the document known as the *Risale-i Tatar-i Leh*. Permission for its original construction was said to have been given in 1792. Its cemetery contains a Tatar grave dating from 1774 and another dating from 1796.

h **Raiziai/Raižiai (Rejze)**. This is one of the two most historically important mosques in Lithuania. It is situated in Alytus district, the home of some five hundred Tatars and it has become an important centre for Tatar festivities throughout the whole of Lithuania. The mosque is a barn-like structure, painted red and very well maintained. The present building is a reconstruction of a predecessor which dated from 1883. The ceremonies for the inauguration took place in October 1993. There was a mosque here, to the south-west of Vilnius, as early as the seventeenth century. The mosque's oldest gravestone dates from 1752, possibly from 1742. Its most important monument is a fine Tatar mosque pulpit (*minbar*), a unique survival, formerly within a mosque in neighbouring Bazar, It is dated 1686. Attractively carved and painted, it is a very rare and valuable Lithuanian Tatar work of art.

Mizar (the form, **Mizyar**, is also known) The word indicates a Tatar cemetery which is frequently sited separately, at some distance from the precincts of the mosque itself. It is located amidst trees and is often surrounded by a stone wall enclosure which is entered through a single gate. Tatars from all parts of Poland are buried in these cemeteries. The most ancient are located near the Belarus frontier. The tombs are regularly visited and very well maintained by Tatar families. A *Zierec*, a family visit, is an important duty and the Karaims also use the word *Zeret* (from the Arabic *ziyāra*) to describe such visits. The gravestones are inscribed in Polish and in Arabic. The earliest are roughly hewn and on these the name of the deceased is usually inscribed in Cyrillic script. According to the beliefs of an older generation of Tatars, the soul of the deceased lingered near the grave for forty days prior to its journey to the world beyond to be judged and to receive the reward of Paradise. Some *Mizars* contain the tombs of saints and very holy persons, such as the herder Kuntus and important Tatar officials, *imāms* and military commanders.

Some sharing between Tatars and Karaims for burial places has occurred in past times. Dr Len Lavrin has mentioned to the author that:

I would like to highlight two situations that have happened in Harbin (China, formerly Russian Manchuria) where Karaims, Tatars and Ashkenazi Jews had large settlements. The three groups had their cemeteries, allotted to them by Russian planners, adjoining each other, the Tatar and Karaim cemeteries had a tree alley separating them, whereas the Ashkenazi one was separated by one long and rather high fence. It abounded with beautiful sculptured tombstones. At one stage the Tatar cemetery was filled and the Tatar community was waiting for a new allotment of land. Meanwhile, with the consent of Karaim elders, thirteen Tatars were buried in the Karaim cemetery. My mother's two little brothers, prior to the establishment of a Karaim cemetery, and with permission of the Rabbinical Council of Manchuria, were buried in the Ashkenazi cemetery.

Modlitewnik The term indicates written, or printed, Tatar prayer books containing prayers and supplications and information which are of value to both common worshippers and to *imāms*, principally in the performance of religious ceremonies in the mosques or in the homes of fellow believers.

Muezzin (Arabic, **mu'adhdhin**) He who calls to prayer (*adhān*) throughout the Muslim *umma*. In Tatar communities, true minarets are very rare, hence his duties, if he be found, take place within the main hall of the mosque itself, or outside in its surroundings.

Muhirs Tatar mosques have the names of the Prophet, his family, the Companions, and the early Caliphs, hung, in painted roundels, on their interior walls. Tatar mosques also normally have Qur'ānic inscriptions, passages of texts, names of patrons, and framed scenes of the Holy Places, in Arabia. Many of these pictures and tapestries are referred to as *Muhirs*. They are frequently artistic prints and paintings, with passages from Qur'ānic *sūras* which are written, as a design, in elaborate Arabic calligraphy. Other *Muhirs* are astronomical charts and a few are influenced by Ottoman Sufi art. They provide a focus for meditation in an otherwise bare and austere wooden building. The Tatars are especially interested in Biblical and Qur'ānic genealogies. The names of the patriarchs are derived from both Biblical and Islamic sources. *Muhirs* may be locally designed or imported from other Muslim lands, especially from Turkey.

Namaz This word is used for statutory prayers. It is most frequently used by the Tatars and is the equivalent of the Arabic term *Ṣalāt*, ritual and private prayer. Both words are found in Tatar documents. In the book by Niaz Maksoudoff (see above), two of the daily statutory prayers are given as both the dawn, or the morning prayer, *Salatulfajr*, or *Sabahnamaz*, and the evening *Ṣalāt al-'Ishā'* is rendered by the expression *Ishaor yasig namazi*.

Nijjet This is a most important religious term. It is to be found widely in Tatar manuscripts and publications, in homilies and it is also to be found amongst the Lithuanian Karaims in their religious vocabulary.

Niyyah This is found in canonical Prophetic *Ḥadīth*, 'works are in their intention only'. It indicates an ethical goal that is superior to that of the law. Furthermore, it maintains that whatsoever the value of the religious rite, even it be the statutory prayers and the giving of alms, it is the religious intention of the believer which is the test of his faith. If the intention is sinful then the performance of the religious act and the work of charity performed have no worth in the eyes of God.

Perkūnas Francis Dvornik, in his *The Slavs, Their Early History and Civilisation*, Boston, 1956, pp. 48–9, shows how important the influence of ancient Persian religion, deities, demonic powers and cosmology was upon the ancient Slavs. Much the same could be said in regard to the Balts including the pagan Prussians and the Lithuanians.

According to Stasys Samalavicius, in his *Outline of Lithuanian History*, Vilnius, 1995, p. 17:

One of the principal deities of the ancient Lithuanian religion was 'Perkūnas' – the god of thunder and lightning. He was considered to be the ruler of atmosphere and nature. Under his command he had water whose inexhaustible resources he kept above the stone vault of heaven. Lithuanians believed that claps of thunder were heard when 'Perkūnas' was driving in his chariot in heaven holding an axe in his hand. He was the most angry god, but at the same time he was the most just. In fact 'Perkūnas' was the guardian of man, seeing to his morals, honesty and fairness. He hated thieves and liars, struck and burnt the homes of criminals.

Qipčāq (Kipchak) A Turkic-speaking people who occupy an important position in Eastern European and Islamic history. The Qipčāq (or Cuman) steppe (Dašt-i Qipčāq) is frequently mentioned in Arabic, Persian and Turkish geographical and historical literature. In the Muslim and in the Transcaucasian sources, Qipčāq appears to correspond to the Cumans (see above), in the Greek and Latin sources.

The distinction between the two peoples is unclear. In Russian sources, the name of Polovtsi ('the pale-yellow ones') is the most commonly found. The Qipčāqs appear in the eighth-century Moyun Cher inscription and they may possibly appear in Chinese sources as the Chueh-Yueh Shih. The Qipčāqs who remained behind in Siberia are probably the ancestors of the 'Siberian Tatars' who were converted to Islam at a later date. Other Qipčāqs were driven westwards and formed a major group in the area of the south Russian steppes and in the Volga–Rural regions. The Qipčāq were absorbed within the Golden Horde but were to shape the Horde and give it a predominantly Turkic, or Turkish character, overwhelmingly Islamic in faith, though retaining many pre-Islamic features. The Lithuanian Tatars were once Qipčāq speaking; only the Karaims speak a variant of this language in Lithuania, Poland and the Ukraine, today.

Tedzwid/Ta/edjwid (y) (Arabic **tajwīd**) The correct pronunciation and vocal presentation of the Qur'ānic text. Amongst the Lithuanian Tatars it also denotes a manual for the recitation of the *Qur'ān*. Such texts are written in Arabic or in Turkish together with a commentary and translation in Byelorussian or in Polish.

Ta/efsir (y) (Arabic **tafsīr** 'explanation', or 'commentary') A full text of the *Qur'ān* either in manuscript, or in a printed, form to which is attached a gloss, or glosses, in Byelorussian, or in Polish, furnishing a detailed commentary on the content for those who are little acquainted with the Arabic language. Such works form an important contribution to Tatar literature and are of immense interest to linguists. One such *tafsīr* is to be found in the Byelorussian library, in London. Other examples are housed in libraries and Oriental collections in Vilnius and in Poland and in Russia.

Tatar The term 'Tatar' is so varied and so vague that one is at a loss to define its limits and to lay down a law as to who amongst the peoples of the world should be included. According to Professor M. Z. Zakiev (in his *Tatarstan: Past and Present, the Ethnonym of the people*, SOAS, 1992, pp. 1–2):

> The Tatars belong to the early civilised people of Eastern Europe. Their ancestors from as early as the 7th century had their own statehood known in Europe firstly as Birmland then as Volga Bulgaria and Kazan Khanate where the dominant ideology was *Tengrism* followed by Islam. The ethnonym 'Tatars' was assigned to the former Biars, Bigers, Biljars, Bulgars and Kazan people only in the early 20th century. Even now the Udmurts call the Volga Tatars the Bigers.

He adds:

> the ethnonym of the Tatars originated according to the model of other Turk ethnonyms: Ta-tar, the second part ar/ir bearing the meaning of 'people', the first part tat-dat-yet meaning foreign, not ours, tatar means 'foreign people'...
>
> The word Tatar, though known in Iran and among the Hungarians as a personal name in the past, came to Western Europe as an ethnonym during the Tatar–Mongolian invasion early in the thirteenth century. In the face of this hostile invasion, the ethnonym began to be distorted to Tartar instead of Tatar and this usage spreads throughout Western Europe associating the Tatars with the underground kingdom of the dead – Hell. In Russian history, the ethnonym Tatar also gained a negative meaning reflecting its perception of the Tatar state and its associations with the Golden Horde. All this gave the Tatars in Western Europe a reputation little better than savages.

Apart from the centre of Tatar culture in the Volga region around Bulgar and Kazan, later and more especially during the days of the Golden Horde, it was also centred around Saray and in the Crimean peninsula. The Crimean peninsula, for example, was a base for a Tatar penetration of the Dobrogea region of the northeastern Balkans. This fact was known to many in the Middle East. For example, in the year AH 700/AD 1300/1: 'Joge, son of Noqai, killed his brother Tuge. A fight took place between Joge and the governor Tonquz(?), in which Tonquz was victorious over Joge. Then Joge was victorious. Then Tonquz sought help from Toqta, and Joge could not withstand him. So he fled to the Wallach (Awlaq)(in

Romania), a people of that country, who were connected with him by marriage. The king of the Wallach betrayed him; he took Joge and confined him in the citadel of Trnovo (in Bulgaria). Then he killed him, and sent his head to the Crimea, and the kingdom of Noqai passed to Toqta' (*The Memoirs of a Syrian Prince, Abū'l-Fidā', Sultan of Hamāh (672–732/1273–1331)*, translated with an Introduction by P.M. Holt, Wiesbaden, 1983, p. 39).

The name Tatar, in fact, covers a great range of peoples who are centred in Eurasia. According to Professor Yakup Deliomeroglu (in his *Tatars and Tataristan*, Eurasia Development Association Publications, no 1, Ankara, undated, p. 27), the Tatars may be divided into five principal groups, each of which with its sub-groups: the Idyll-Ural Tatars, the Astrahan (Astrakhan) Tatars (who include the Kazan Tatars and Nogays), the Cyberian (Siberian) Tatars, the Kirim (Crimean) Tatars, who include some of the Nogays and the Tatars in Romania and Bulgaria, and lastly the Litvanian (Lithuanian) Tatars. In regard to the Lithuanian Tatars, Professor Deliomeroglu makes the following observations (pp. 16–19): 'The Litvanian Tatars were formed later as an ethnic grouping. This group was formed with the participation of the newcomers from the Great and Nogay Ordas following those coming from Altin Ordu by the end of the 14th century. The Litvanian Tatars had a trait commonly referred to as "Jagoldai", attached to the Litvania in an administration which was formed in 1438. Based upon the sources which have become known reflecting the decade between the 15th and 18th centuries, a part of the Litvanian Tatars come from the Nayman, Yalayir, Kondrat (or Kongrat) and Isin (Uysin) tribes. In addition to these, they involve the representatives of such tribes as the Bayins and Mansurs. It is clear that these did not come from Altin Ordu (the Golden Horde)'. He is here quoting *The Ethnic History of Tatars* by M.D. Isachov, Calli, 1994. The Lithuanian Tatars, like others who are Muslim in faith, look back with pride to such rulers of the Golden Horde, in Saray, as Berke (1257–67) and to Uzbek (1317–41), but especially to Toqtamish, as important examples, in many aspects of their Tatar identity and in their way of life. The small, although interesting, community of Finnish Tatars is not included in this book. It should be pointed out, however, that the reign of Vytautas was not the first occasion when Mongol/Tatars and Lithuanians had met one another. Khan Burundai, of the Golden Horde, invaded Lithuania in 1258–60, and a further incursion was faced by Duke Traidenis (1269–82). The Volga-Ural-West Siberian Tatars are surveyed in Peter Golden's

An Introduction to the History of the Turkic Peoples, Wiesbaden, 1992, pp. 393–6.

A useful definition of 'Tatar' from the point of view of the Tatarstan scholars, in particular Shihāb al-Dīn Marjānī, may be read in Uli Schamiloglu's 'The Formation of a Tatar Historical Consciousness: Sihabaddin Marcani and the Image of the Golden Horde', *Central Asian Survey*, 1990, 9(2), pp. 39–49. He noted (page 44), that:

Marcani continues that the people of the Golden Horde, including the Volga Bulgarians, first came to be known as the progeny of Berke (a mid-13th century khan of the Golden Horde). Later they came to be known as Uzbeks (Özbeks), after the name of the well-known Khan of the first half of the 14th century. According to Marcani, the Volga Bulgarians adopted both these names, but finally abandoned the name Uzbek in favour of the name Tatar. He finds it odd, though, that the descendants of Abulxayr Khān continued to use the name Uzbek in the territories of the former Chagatay Khānate which they had conquered from the north.

Schamiloglu adds later (pp. 14–15):

Another attempt to establish historical continuity can be seen in Marcani's anachronistic usage of toponyms when describing the areas which each of the Tatar khans of the Golden Horde ruled. Marcani was perfectly aware that the pre-Mongol designations for the territories of the Golden Horde were 'lands of the Saqāliba, the Kipchak steppe, and the state of the Bulgars'. He also knew that the territories of the Golden Horde included the medieval lands of Bulgar, Sibir, Burtas, Khwarezm, Kipchak, Rus, Basqurd, Lahistan, Burcan and Aflaq.

A summary of the views of the Jadidists as to the true identity of the Tatars and how they believed they differed from the progeny of Genghis Khan may be read in Ahmet Kanlidere, *Reform within Islam*, Eren, Istanbul, 1997, pp, 131–3.

A recent, very lucid, survey of this complex question of the identity of the 'Tatars' may be read in, 'Who were the "Tartars" of History?'. The enigma and paradox of the name misapplied in *Islam in Russia, The Four Seasons* by Ravel Bukharaev, Curzon, Richmond, 2000, Ch. 9, pp. 185–97.

A view by a Ukrainian scholar as to what qualifies a 'Tatar' to claim his, or her, entitlement to the epithet, time wise or space wise, may be read in Walen A. Buszakow (Askania Nowa, Ukraina), translated by Maciej Gierych into Polish, under the title of 'Etnonim "Tatar" w czasie i przestrzeni', *Rocznik Muzulmanski*, 3, 1416h (AD 1995) Warsaw, pp. 59–66.

Estimates vary as to the total number of the present-day Tatars in the Baltic region, namely those countries which formed a part of the medieval Grand Duchy of Lithuania. One figure estimates their number as 20,000: 4,000 of these in Poland, 6,000 in Lithuania and 10,000 in Belarus. The Tatars in these countries are to be distinguished from those in other Baltic States. The Estonian Tatars have only lived there since 1870 and they organised their religious bodies in the 1920s. In 1997, they numbered 3,315 souls. In Poland, the largest Tatar community lives in the province of Białystok, the second is the community of the Tri-City (a combination of Gdańsk, Gdynia and Sopot). In Poland, there are two religious organisations. The first of these is The Muslim Religious Union in the Polish Republic. This unites 90 per cent of the Muslim Tatars within six religious communes, in Gdańsk, Warsaw, Białystok, Gorzow Wielkopolski, Bohoniki and Kruszyniany. The second is The Union of Tatars in the Republic of Poland, with two branches, in Gdańsk and in Białystok. Each branch is autonomous. This Union exclusively unites members who are both Muslims and of a Tatar origin. The latter includes others who claim to be Tatars from outside Poland. The Muslim Religious Union is headed by the Supreme Muslim Council and the Union of Tatars is headed by the Central Council of that Union.

Tengri, Tenrai, Tenri   Professor Irène Mélikoff, in her *Hadji Bektach, un Mythe et ses Avatars*, Brill, Leiden, 1998, pp. 13–17, 'Tengri: le Dieu Ciel', has vividly portrayed the character and the origin of this 'God'. Like the Mongols, the Turks, including it seems the Qipchāqs, believed in a celestial deity, Tengri, who is to be identified with the invisible and blue sky of the heavens. He was also the representative of the life force, grace (*kut*) and order (*yarlik*). The ruler of the Turks, the Kaghan, in the Orkhon inscriptions, originated in the sky and was believed to resemble and to personify it in his being. It is he who is entrusted with the maintenance of the cult of Tengri on earth. In the letter sent by Mangu Khān to King Louis IX, and delivered by William of Rubruck, it is said that, 'In heaven there is but one God, who is eternal, and there is only one master on the earth, Genghis Khān, the son of Heaven.'

It is by the power of Tengri that the Shamans held their supernatural powers to heal and to punish. Tengri had no temple wherein he resided and to which one turned or journeyed, as a pilgrim. The entire Universe is his temple wherein he reigns as the supreme God of the nomadic peoples. As Genghis Khān said to the *Imām* of Bukhara who had tried to convert him, 'The entire Universe is the House of God, what good reason, therefore, is it to specify and dedicate a single locality to which one journeys in search of Him.' Besides, Tengri is a distant and passive deity and He manifests his being in cosmic signs such as thunderbolts, floods and droughts. He is also able to manifest himself, disguised, in other divinities which are more active amongst men (see *Dievas*, above).

Irène Mélikoff has drawn our notice that, amongst the Muslim Turks, the name, Tanri-Allah, appears in popular verses which seek to avoid a charge of blasphemy. The name was also far from unknown to noteworthy Sufis, amongst them men of undoubted heterodox leanings, Sufis such as Kaygusez Abdal, who lived during the fourteenth and fifteenth centuries and who died in Cairo. During the nineteenth century, Dervish 'Ali, who, in a poem (*nefes*) proclaimed that: 'Men Ali'den gayri Tanri bilmezem', I know of no God, but 'Ali'.

In the fourteenth century, Qur'ānic commentaries (*tafāsīr*) could be found which explained Allāh, by Tenrai (Tengri).

How Allāh is defined amongst Sufi thinking has occasionally led to the view that His holy name and essence should not be confused with the accepted view of 'God' as is believed and openly declared in a creed within the three Abrahamic faiths and even beyond them.

As is the case amongst the Mongols and among Altai peoples, Tengri is divided into ninety-nine tengris, the chief of them being the blue sky that is everlasting. These correspond to seventy-seven 'earth mothers'. These figures in an extended and in a multiplied form have been adopted and adapted by the Bektāshiyya Sufi order. 'Alī (b. Abī Ṭālib) who is identified with divinity, is a god of the heavenly powers, such as the noise of thunder and of lightning (compare with the Lithuanian god, **Perkūnas**, above). He is identified with Tengri.

To this day, the Muslim- and Sufi-influenced Tatars of Siberia continue to describe God as Tenri, as well as Allāh. In Belarus, Lithuania and Poland, amongst the Tatar remnant, this is not now the case, though one can suggest that in earlier centuries when the Tatars still spoke their Qipchāq language, God's name, in the form of Tienkri, may well have been uttered frequently upon their lips. Dr Selim Chazbijewicz has kindly shown the author pages of prayers in *Chamails* which were written in 1973, in Arabic and transcribed by his grandfather, 'Ali Smaikevich, who lived in Minsk (Belarus). On pages 57 and 58 of one of his documents, the prayer (*Wynosna Dua*) reads: 'Bismilahi rrechmani rrechymi, Ilahi, dzemleh iman ehlinieh bir duai ukujalum kim kylah *TIENKRI* rewa, *TIENKRI* baszdan ajaga nur ulah nur iczynde mieumur ulah, Ilahi miejite lutfi inam idasien.' Other examples of surviving Qipčāq may be read in other Polish Tatar examples of a recent date.

Tenri survives as the liturgical name of God amongst the Karaims, however. It is His name which is hallowed in their Biblical scriptures. Ananiasz Zajaczowski (see *Karaims, kenesa*, above) has furnished several examples from the Karaite scriptures.

Ta/eqvim This word is derived from the Arabic **taqwīm** (calendar), and it denotes in particular, amongst the Tatars of Lithuania and Poland, astrological tables and diagrams which facilitate the calculation of important dates in the Islamic lunar calendar.

Toqtamish (also **Tukhtamish** and **Tuqatmish**, the latter being regarded as the most correct form, by Professor E.G. Browne, see his *Persian Literature under Tartar Dominion*, Cambridge, 1920, p. 583). Toqtamish is the most important figure in early Lithuanian Tatar history. In the year of the Dragon, 1376 he went to Tīmūr (Tamerlaine) and he was received in Samarqand. The latter gave to him the towns of Otrar, Sabran and Sighnaq. After a series of setbacks and defeats he was still in favour with Tīmūr at this time. A key date in his career was the defeat of the ruler of the Golden Horde, Mamai, by the Russians on 8 September 1380. Toqtamish refused to submit to the Russians, and his aggressive response was crowned with successes. Moscow was destroyed. At that time, Toqtamish was regarded as a just ruler. However, his relations with Tīmūr were to become seriously strained until they developed into downright enmity. Later, Toqtamish sacked Tabriz, in Iran, with great savagery. Action to curb his excesses was taken by Tīmūr's son Mīranshāh (the executor of the founder of the Ḥurūfiyya, Fadlallāh al-Ḥurūfī, see *Ḥurūfī*, above). Toqtamish attacked the heart of Tīmūr's empire, in 1387, laying Bukhara waste in the process. It was at this time that he wrote to the King of Poland, Jagielo (Jagiello), from Azov, to the north of the Crimean peninsula, sending a letter to him personally, on 30 May 1393. In 1394 and 1395, Toqtamish sent ambassadors and missions to Mamlūk Egypt seeking an alliance against Tīmūr. A series of wars followed at a time when Tīmūr was heavily preoccupied in the Caucasus region. However, pressure on Toqtamish grew and, in 1395, and in the following year, Tīimūr sacked Azov, Astrakhan and

Saray. Despite this, the cionquest of the Golden Horde eluded him and Toqtamish returned to his throne. In August 1398, Tīmūr received the sworn enemy of Toqtamīsh, Tīmūr Kutlugh. It was at this time that Toqtamish fled to Vytautas, the Grand Duke of Lithuania, who became his sponsor and protector, despite the defeat of Worskala, on 12 August 1399, which proved to be a severe setback also for Vytautas. This defeat was at the hands of the ' mayor of the palace', the Tatar, Edigu/Edigey and so on. The latter had a base in the Crimean peninsula, whilst he struggled against Vytautas whose ambitions to expand to the Black Sea were thwarted. On 14 January 1405, Tīmūr promised to reinstate him, following a campaign in China. However, Toqtamish died, in unclear circumstances. He either died of natural causes, or he met his death in battle at Tumen, in Siberia, in 1406. Thus ended a turbulent life of an adventurer and an exile. Toqtamish is one of the great epic heroes of the Tatars, in general. Amongst the Tatars of Belarus, Lithuania, Poland and the Tatars of the Crimea he has become a both a legendary and a historical figure who is crucial to their current identity and who, as an ally of Vytautas, has integrated himself into the annals of Lithuanian and Polish history. Historical memories within the Crimea also survive. Outside the town of Čufut-Kalé, home to both Karaims and Tatars, is found the mausoleum of Nenkedzhan Khanim who was the favourite daughter of Toqtamish and there are today a number of Tatars in both Poland and the Crimea, who claim to be the direct blood descendants of their supreme hero, Toqtamīsh.

Vytis/Pahonia The Vytis, in Lithuania, Pahonia, in Belarus, and historically, of major significance also in Polish history from the days of the Grand Duchy, is a national symbol. The 'nation' of the Grand Duchy has no meaning in the context of contemporary Lithuania, Poland and Belarus. It should be recalled that the predominant literary language of the 'Tatars of Lehistan' was Byelorussian. However, the Vytis also has a certain religious origin and significance. The present-day Lithuanian Vytis depicts a white knight on a white horse. He holds a silver sword in his right hand and it raised above his head. He bears a blue shield on his left shoulder. The shield bears the emblem of a double yellow, or two barred, cross. It was first used as a state emblem in the Duchy of Lithuania in 1366, although it is believed to have been current in the pagan days of King Mindaugas. Jogaila's seal, in 1386, or 1387, displays this emblem in a heraldic shield. The knight was symbolic of the Duchy of Lithuania, a warrior who chased the enemy out of his native territory, vast and multiethnic that territory may have been. As time passed, the Vytis constituted a coat of arms of provinces and towns in Lithuania. Its presence above the famous Aušros Vartai (the gate of Dawn), in the defence wall of Vilnius, indicated that the city was the capital of that land. The symbol of the Vytis was of tremendous significance in the struggle of Lithuania to gain its independence.

The Vytis, in Belarus, on the contrary, is called the Pahonia (or Pahonya, or Pagonia), the sense of the word denoting the 'hunt', or the 'pursuit'. It was a symbol which originated in Navahradak, (Novogrudok/Novogrodek), which, for a time, was the first capital of the Duchy of Lithuania. For a long period it was the symbol of an independent Belarus, but now this is no longer the case. The referendum of 14 May 1995, returned Belarus to a modified Soviet-era-style flag and state seal. The Pahonia is now viewed as the symbol of those who are in opposition today in Belarus.

Some see in the Vytis/Pahonia a symbol of the ancient Indo-Iranian beliefs of the eastern and the southern Slavs and Balts, believing it to have been derived from the cult of the sun god, Jaryla/Jarillo/Jaryla: the two barred, or six-ended, golden cross, this being a symbol of that pagan Slavic deity.

The depiction of a knight, or a monarch upon a charging horse and armed with a raised sword, is a very common sight on medieval seals in northern Europe, and elsewhere. Despite the direction of the horse and the knight (in this instance a monarch), the Vytis is not dissimilar to the seal of Eirik Magnussen IV, as depicted in 1290, on seals in Bergen, the medieval seat of Norwegian royalty and independence.

According to Gitana Zujiené, on pages 21–2 of her 'The Insignia and Ceremonial of the Rulers and High-Ranking State and Church Dignitaries of the Grand Duchy of Lithuania in the Thirteenth-Eighteenth Centuries', summary of doctoral dissertation Humanities, history (05 H), Vilnius-Klaipéda, 2005:

the image of a mounted knight had been known in Europe since the latter half of the eleventh century. Holding a spear or sword in one hand and a shield in the other, he symbolised the ruler and defender of the state. Algirdas' son Jogaila, Kaributas, Lengvenis and Skirgaila had such seals. After his father's death in around 1382–1384, Vytautas began using an equestrian seal too. Similar seals were used by the Grand Duke of Lithuania Žygimantas Kęstutaitis and his son Mykolas Žygimantaitis.

Žynys and **Žynė** These are the ancient Lithuanian 'pagan' sorcerer and sorceress. Alongside these paired figures were the *vaidila* 'priest'and the *vaidilutė*, 'priestess'.

According to Stasys Samalavicius (op. cit., p. 19):

> Offerings to gods were made and other religious ceremonies were conducted by a heathen priest called ' krivis'. Krivis was an important figure in the religious and secular life of a community of ancient Lithuanians. During the religious ceremonies in his hand he would hold the symbol of the priest's power – a crooked knobbly staff, at the top of which there was a carving of an elk's head. Besides, main religious rites were also conducted by a group of women or priestesses, called 'vaidilutes' in Lithuanian. Their duty was to look after the sacred fire so that it should never be out. Before coming to serve by the sacred fire they gave an oath to remain virgins. If they broke the oath or if the fire they looked after went out the punishment was death.
>
> The sacred fire was continuously burning in certain shrines and oak-wood was used to keep it alive. Elderly priests and priestesses were appointed to watch over these shrines. The shrines were astronomically orientated.

Index

Ahmed, Brother 102–11
Akiner, S and Wexler, P. 84
Alexandrovich, Ismael 90, 135–6
Algar, Hamid 65
Algirdas 21, 29, 33
Amazonian 8–10, 13, 16–17
Amber 10, 11, 14
Applebaum, Anne 136–8
Århus 119–22
Armstrong, Karen 88
Arnold, T.W. 49, 83
Azerbaijan 64, 65, 79, 86, 97, 100
Azeri 100

Bairašauskaité, Tamara 50
Bairasewski, Mensaid 86
Bajraszewski, Aleksander 67
Bajraszewski, Stefan Mustafa 82–3
al-Bakrī, Abū 'Ubayd 'Abdallāh b.
  'Abd al-'Azīz 11–13
Batory, Stephan 67
Batu, Khān 32
Bayram 182
Belarus 2, 15, 18, 22, 28, 32–7, 52,
  55, 67, 72, 89–94, 128–30, 131,
  135, 138, 145
Bērziņš, Uldis 102–11
Białystok 24, 37, 127, 133
Biedronska-Słotowa, Beata 76
Bielawski, Jozef 123
Bielecki, Zdizław 123
Boat axe culture 14
Bohdanowicz, L. 78, 79
Borawski, Piotr 58
Browne, E.G. 62

Bulghār 39, 43, 63, 72, 134

Cabbalism 64, 69, 70
Catholicism 20, 22, 32, 37–8, 43, 49,
  54, 62, 66, 71–2, 75, 82, 83, 86,
  93–4, 98, 101, 106, 112, 122–6,
  129, 131
Chadwick, Nora and Zhirmusky,
  V. 68
Chamails 143, 182–4
Chaucer, Geoffrey 32
Chazbijewicz, Selim 46, 55–8, 65, 68,
  72, 80, 83, 123, 127, 138–9
Chelebi 57
Christianity 7, 15, 19, 22, 32, 37, 44,
  49, 66, 71, 93, 122–6, 131, 133,
  136, 144
Cišme 100
Coxe, William 76
Crimea 2, 16–17, 22–9, 32, 36, 38–9,
  44–5, 54–8, 62–71, 77–9, 86, 94,
  113, 127, 132, 138, 144–6
Cultural Society of the Lithuanian
  Tatars 85–6
Cumans 144–6, 184
Czelebi Hadji Murzicz 59
Czyzewski, Krzysztof 1–2

David IV 36–7
Davidov, Ibragim 101, 112
Denmark 9, 10, 12, 15, 118–22
Dervish 184
Dievas 184–6
al-Dīn, Jalāl 24–5, 28, 37
al-Dīn, Kamāl *see* al-Khujandī, Kamāl

216 Islam in the Baltic

Drozd, Andrzej 65, 144
Dubinski, Alexander 67
Ducène, Jean Charles 16–17

Edigey/Edigei 37, 42–4, 46, 68–9
Estonia 8, 10, 19, 94–7
European Community borders 1, 138–9
European influences 43

Faḍlallāh al-Ḥurūfī 64–5
al-Fātiḥa 186–7
Faw (fortune telling) 71, 187–8
Finland 7, 9, 11, 55, 96
Fire 33–4

Gdańsk 53, 72, 77, 80–83, 116, 124, 127, 133, 138
Gediminas, Duke 18, 20–21, 36
Georgia 36–7
Germany 10
Golden Horde 19, 22–3, 28–9, 32, 36–8, 42–3, 63, 65, 83, 95
Goths 16–17
Grand Duchy of Lithuania 2, 14, 18–30, 32–6, 55 *see also* Lithuania
Grodno/Hrodno 24, 37, 91

Hadzy 57
Ḥasan, Khwāja 63
Hasluck, F.W. 116
Hedeby 9, 12
Ḥurūfī 65, 188–9
Husnetdinov, Šakirs 112

Ibn 'Arab Shāh 39, 44
Ibn Faḍlān, Aḥmad 5–6, 13
Ibn Karbalā'ī 63
Idel 100–101, 114
al-Idrīsī 7–11, 13, 16
Imāms 58, 79, 189–91
The Islamic Review 80
Island of Men 8–11, 13, 16
Island of Women 8–11, 13, 16–17
Ita Kozakeviča's Society of the National Cultures Association of Latvia 99
Ivanovich, Dimitri 23

Jahānshāh b.'Abd al-Jabbār al-Nīzghārūti, Ḥāfiz 46–7
Jakubauskas, Adas 86
al-Jalāyirī, Shaykh Uways 64–5
Jāmī 62–3
Jogaila, King 22–3, 32
Judaism 1, 3, 21, 26, 32, 34, 48, 54, 66, 86, 88, 94, 99, 101, 105, 111, 131–2, 137, 139
Jutland 9, 10

Kadim 56–7
Kaji 59
Kaliningrad 87–8
Kanapatskaya, Zorina 51–2, 90, 94
Kanapatski, Ibragim 92, 93, 128
Karaims/Karaites 2, 15, 22, 29, 33, 36–8, 46, 131–2, 144, 191–3
Kazan 38–9, 45, 47, 51–5, 59, 64, 66, 69, 77, 86, 94, 101, 126–9, 138
Kazan Missionary Committee of Lithuania and Poland 45
Kenesa 193–4
Khaqan 194
al-Khujandī, Kamāl 62–4, 65
Kiaupa, Zigmantas 20
Kiev 21, 29, 42
Kitābs 48, 69–70, 73, 78, 143–4, 194–6
Klindt Jensen, O. 9–10
Kontus/Kuntus 66–9
Knights of the Sword *see* Teutonic Knights
Kreutzwald, F.R. 94–5
Kryczyński, Arslan 78, 80
Kryczyński, Leon Najman Mirza 79
Kryczyński, Olgierd Najman 78
Kryczyński, Stanislaw 80
Kühle, Lene 119–22
Kurpiewski, Lech 81

de Lannoy, Ghillebert 25–30
Latvia 7–8, 10, 14, 19, 33, 55, 98–115, 129
de Lébédeff, Olge 45
Lederer, Gyorgy 83, 84, 86, 90–91
Lewisohn, Leonard 63–4, 65
Lindberg, Carolus 7
Lipqa 196–9

Lithuania 2, 4, 14–15, 18–30, 32–6, 55, 72, 83–7, 131–2, 137, 144–5
Livonia 19, 22 see also Latvia; Estonia
Lowczyce 67

Macigovs, Musans 101
al-Maghribī, Ibn Saʻīd 16
Mamay, Khān 22–3
al-Marjānī, Shihāb al-Dīn 39, 43, 44
Meczet/Mecete 199–202
Melodics 71–3
Meredith-Owens, G.M. 68, 84
Mieszko I 12
Mindaugas, Duke 18–20, 34
Minsk 24, 37, 51, 52, 92, 93, 128, 133, 135–6
Miskiewicz, Tomasz 124
Mizar 202–3
Modlitewnik 203
Money and coins 9–10, 41, 42
Moscow 21, 23, 32, 39, 69, 77, 87
Mosques 15, 50–51, 57, 72, 145
 in Belarus 90–92, 128, 135–6
 in Estonia 97
 in Gdańsk 80–83
 in Kaliningrad 87–8
 in Latvia 99
 in Lithuania 85
 in Minsk 128, 135–6
 in Poland 79, 134
 in Sweden 115
Muezzin 203
Muhhamedshin, Ildar 97
Muhirs 203–4
Mutiviles 57
Murād III 66
Muslim Confederation of the Baltic Sea 127
Muslim Religious Community of the Republic of Belarus 90
Muslim Revival Movement 127
Murzich 57

Nadson, A. 68, 84
Namāz 204
Naqshabandiyya 45, 55, 73
al-Nasīmī 65
Nijjet/Niyyah 204

Norway 9
Novogrudok 35, 90, 91, 202
al Nūr al-Muḥammadī 100

Organisation for Muslim Unity 127
Otterbeck, Jonas 116–18

Paderborn, Bishop of 33
Paganism 2, 7, 9, 15, 19, 20–21, 32–7, 44, 60–62, 66, 93, 105, 126, 131, 136–8
Pečewi 48, 50
Perkūnas 204–5
Pilgrimage 4, 56–7, 59
Poland 1–2, 4, 10, 12, 22–3, 28, 32, 37, 49, 52–7, 60, 72, 75–9, 122–7, 131–2, 144–5
Potocki, Jan 59–60, 76–7
Prayers 43, 50, 70, 71, 108, 114, 134
Prussia 11–12, 14–15, 17, 19–20, 24–5, 33–4, 87, 93, 98, 138
Puzccza Bialowieska 145

Qādiriyya 45, 55, 59, 68, 73
Qipchāq 2, 15, 33, 36, 46, 60, 62, 63, 72, 139, 144–6, 205
al-Qirqisānī 32
Qurʾān 15, 44, 48, 57, 69
 translations of 51, 83, 85, 102–11, 122–3, 129

al-Ramzī, Muḥammad Murād 24–5, 38–47, 63–4
Reincarnation 33
Religious persecution 4
Reychman, Jan 77
Ridzvanavichius, Jonas 85
Rīga 10, 98–102, 111–15
Rowell, S.C. 36
Russia 10, 18, 86
 Russian missionaries 47

Salkhat (Stary Krym) 26, 28
Saltuq, Sari
Samalavičius, Stasys 15, 26
Samaletdin, Didar 117
Sapiets, Marite 103
Saray 32, 40, 63
Ščerbinskis, Valters 111, 114–15

Islam in the Baltic

Sdvizhkov, Aleksander 130
de Segur, Comte 75–6
Seifullen, Timur 95–7
Sejny 1
Seleznev, Alexander 60–61
Ševirjova, Rufija 101, 114
Shamanism 60–62, 63, 131, 136
Shawqī, Ahmad 5
Šiaučiūnaitė-Verbickienė, Jurgita 29
Sigismund III Vasa 66
Skulte, Ilva 102
Smajkiewicz-Murman, Džemila 52–3
Smolensk 18, 22
Sobieski, John 66
Sobolewski, J. 51
Soukkan, Osman 117
Šteimane, Inga 102
Stones 35–6
Sufi brotherhoods 45, 55–6, 58
Sufism 45–6, 54–74, 139
   in Århus 120
   Ottoman 65–9
Sweden 7, 10, 15, 116–18, 126
Szapszal, Seraja 48, 50, 132, 143
Szynkiewicz, Mufti Jakub 78–9

Tabriz 62–3, 64
Tabrīzī, Shamsī 6
Tafsir/Tefsir 205
Tallgren-Tuulio, G.J. and Tallgren, A.M. 11
Tallinn 10, 96, 97
Tannenberg (Žalgiris), Battle of 24
Taqvim/Teqvim 211
Tatar Cultural Association 91
Tatar Life 80
Tatars
   Crimean 38, 54, 86, 113, 144
   cross-border ties 2
   definition of 205–9
   identity of 1–2, 39, 45, 48, 51–3, 131, 138
   Islamic revival (1905–10) 45
   Kazan 45, 52, 54, 59, 86, 101
   language 12, 25, 26, 37–8, 47, 48, 118
   of Lehistan 2, 32–47, 68, 196
   literature 69–74
   Lithuanian 32–6, 54–74, 83–7
   migration 21, 47, 66
   nobility 37, 38
   princes 37, 44
   scholars and *imāms* 44, 78
   settlement in Lithuania 36–8
   social divisions 47–8
   and Vytautas 25–30
Tatarstan 43–5, 57, 64, 72, 86, 90, 95, 98, 100, 101, 127, 128, 129
Tengri 209–11
Teutonic Knights 15, 17, 19, 20, 22, 24, 33, 37, 94, 131
Timirchin, Ibrahim 29
Tīmūr Qutlugh Khān 40–43, 63, 64, 65
Toqtamish, Khān 15, 22–3, 24, 28, 37, 39–43, 46, 62–5, 211–12
Trade 7–11, 14, 23, 26
Trakai 18, 22, 25–9, 37, 66, 84–5, 132, 137
Tryjarski, Edward 16, 61
Turkey 47, 49, 54, 58, 66, 76–9, 85–6, 98, 121–2, 145
al-Ṭurṭūshī, Ibrāhīm b. Yaʻqūb al-Isrāʼīlī 9–13, 16

Urbanavičius, Agnius 21
Usmanov, Nuri 101
Uzbek, Khān 36, 44

Vernadsky, George 42
Vikings 12, 15, 17, 33
Vilnius 20–21, 24, 25, 34, 37, 53, 84, 86, 132, 133
Vitebsk 18, 91, 112
Volga region 5–6, 14, 23, 32, 36, 45, 47, 52, 57, 59, 60, 63, 134
Vytautas the Great 22, 24–30, 37, 39, 40–42, 46, 50
Vytis 212–13

Wagstyl, Stefan 1–2
Warsaw 77, 80–82, 86, 123, 133
al-Watwāt 16
Wheatcroft, Andrew 75
Witold the Great *see* Vytautas the Great

women 49, 66, 72
The World of Islam 80

Yarshater, Ehsan 65

Zakiev, M.Z. 206
Zakrzewski, Andrzej B. 47–9
Zikier/Dhikr 72–3
Žynys 214